: n

The History plays established Shakespeare's reputation as an enormously popular and dramatic storyteller, demonstrating his skill in drawing such astonishing characters as Richard III and Sir John Falstaff. Featuring detailed analyses of extracts, John Blades guides the student through four of Shakespeare's most compelling Histories.

Part I of this stimulating study:

- provides clear and engaging close readings of passages from *Richard II*, *Henry IV Parts 1 & 2* and *Richard III*
- examines major themes, characters, language and Shakespeare's dramatic techniques
- offers suggestions for further work and summarises the methods of analysis.

Part II supplies essential background material, including:

- a detailed survey of Shakespeare's literary and historical contexts
- samples of criticism from leading scholars.

With a helpful Glossary and Further Reading section, this lucid study is ideal for anyone who wishes to appreciate and explore the remarkable writing of Shakespeare's History plays for themselves.

**John Blades** has lectured in English Literature at the universities of Leeds and Durham. His publications include *Shakespeare: The Sonnets* (2007) and *Wordsworth and Coleridge: Lyrical Ballads* (2004), both also in the *Analysing Texts* series.

*Analysing Texts* is dedicated to one clear belief: that we can all enjoy, understand and analyse literature for ourselves, provided we know how to do it. Readers are guided in the skills and techniques of close textual analysis used to build an insight into a richer understanding of an author's individual style, themes and concerns. An additional section on the writer's life and work and a comparison of major critical views place them in their personal and literary context.

ANALYSING TEXTS

*General Editor: Nicholas Marsh*

*Published*

Jane Austen: The Novels   *Nicholas Marsh*
Aphra Behn: The Comedies   *Kate Aughterson*
William Blake: The Poems   *Nicholas Marsh*
Charlotte Brontë: The Novels   *Mike Edwards*
Emily Brontë: Wuthering Heights   *Nicholas Marsh*
Chaucer: The Canterbury Tales   *Gail Ashton*
Daniel Defoe: The Novels   *Nicholas Marsh*
Charles Dickens: David Copperfield/Great Expectations   *Nicolas Tredell*
John Donne: The Poems   *Joe Nutt*
George Eliot: The Novels   *Mike Edwards*
F. Scott Fitzgerald: The Great Gatsby/Tender is the Night   *Nicolas Tredell*
E. M. Forster: The Novels   *Mike Edwards*
Thomas Hardy: The Novels   *Norman Page*
Thomas Hardy: The Poems   *Gillian Steinberg*
John Keats:   *John Blades*
Philip Larkin: The Poems   *Nicholas Marsh*
D. H. Lawrence: The Novels   *Nicholas Marsh*
Marlowe: The Plays   *Stevie Simkin*
John Milton: Paradise Lost   *Mike Edwards*
Shakespeare: The Comedies   *R. P. Draper*
Shakespeare: The Histories   *John Blades*
Shakespeare: The Sonnets   *John Blades*
Shakespeare: The Tragedies   *Nicholas Marsh*
Shakespeare: Three Problem Plays   *Nicholas Marsh*
Mary Shelley: Frankenstein   *Nicholas Marsh*
Webster: The Tragedies   *Kate Aughterson*
Virginia Woolf: The Novels   *Nicholas Marsh*
Wordsworth and Coleridge: Lyrical Ballads   *John Blades*

*Further titles are in preparation*

**Analysing Texts**
**Series Standing Order ISBN 978–0–333–73260–1**
*(outside North America only)*

You can receive future titles in this series as they are published by placing a standing order. Please contact your bookseller or, in the case of difficulty, write to us at the address below with your name and address, the title of the series and the ISBN quoted above. Customer Services Department, Macmillan Distribution Ltd, Houndmills, Basingstoke, Hampshire. RG21 6XS, UK

# Shakespeare: The Histories

JOHN BLADES

First published 2013 by
PALGRAVE MACMILLAN

Palgrave Macmillan in the UK is an imprint of Macmillan Publishers Limited, registered in England, company number 785998, of Houndmills, Basingstoke, Hampshire RG21 6XS.

Palgrave Macmillan in the US is a division of St Martin's Press LLC, 175 Fifth Avenue, New York, NY 10010.

Palgrave Macmillan is the global academic imprint of the above companies and has companies and representatives throughout the world.

Palgrave® and Macmillan® are registered trademarks in the United States, the United Kingdom, Europe and other countries.

ISBN: 978–0–230–29958–0 hardback
ISBN: 978–0–230–29959–7 paperback

This book is printed on paper suitable for recycling and made from fully managed and sustained forest sources. Logging, pulping and manufacturing processes are expected to conform to the environmental regulations of the country of origin.

A catalogue record for this book is available from the British Library.

A catalog record for this book is available from the Library of Congress.

For Kyle and Orla

# Contents

# General Editor's Preface

This series is dedicated to one clear belief: that we can all enjoy, understand and analyse literature for ourselves, provided we know how to do it. How can we build on close understanding of a short passage, and develop our insight into the whole work? What features do we expect to find in a text? Why do we study style in so much detail? In demystifying the study of literature, these are only some of the questions the *Analysing Texts* series addresses and answers.

The books in this series will not do all the work for you, but will provide you with the tools, and show you how to use them. Here, you will find samples of close, detailed analysis, with an explanation of the analytical techniques utilised. At the end of each chapter there are useful suggestions for further work you can do to practise, develop and hone the skills demonstrated and build confidence in your own analytical ability.

An author's individuality shows in the way they write: every work they produce bears the hallmark of that writer's personal 'style'. In the main part of each book we concentrate therefore on analysing the particular flavour and concerns of one author's work, and explain the features of their writing in connection with major themes. In Part II there are chapters about the author's life and work, assessing their contribution to developments in literature; and a sample of critics' views are summarised and discussed in comparison with each other.

Some suggestions for further reading provide a bridge towards further critical research.

*Analysing Texts* is designed to stimulate and encourage your critical and analytic faculty, to develop your personal insight into the author's work and individual style, and to provide you with the skills and techniques to enjoy at first hand the excitement of discovering the richness of the text.

NICHOLAS MARSH

# Family Tree of the Houses of Lancaster and York, and the Early Tudors

This simplified chart shows the family relationships between principal members of the English royal families from the reign of the Plantagenet Edward III (1327–77) to Elizabeth I (1558–1603)

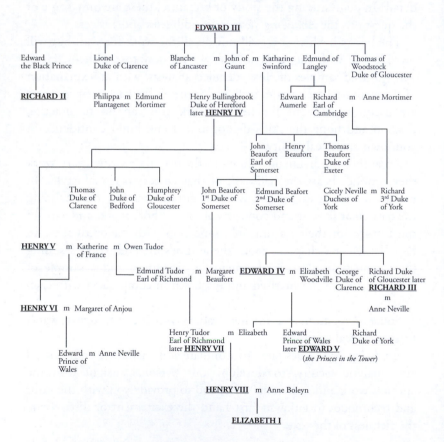

x

# Introduction

It takes a great deal of history to produce a little literature.

Henry James, *Hawthorne* (1879)

No! Shakespeare's kings are not, nor are they meant to be, great men: rather, little or quite ordinary humanity ...

Walter Pater, *Appreciations* (1889)

The closing decade of the sixteenth century witnessed the sudden rise of an amazing new phenomenon in the London theatre: the highly lucrative vogue of the English history play. The idea of a permanent theatre building was itself revolutionary, and both its subject matter and styles were rapidly developing in response to the tastes of its avid patrons. Shakespeare's theatre company, the Chamberlain's Men, ever alert to commercial trends in contemporary drama, joined their rivals in hurriedly satisfying the mounting demand for history. Shakespeare was not the first on the scene – there had previously appeared the largely amateur chronicle plays and historical pageants, and then professional writers, including Christopher Marlowe and Michael Drayton, had opened the door on a exciting new genre. However, Shakespeare's history plays, beginning with *Richard II*, represent the pinnacle of the form, its most mature expression. In their own day, his history plays were a huge commercial success, both on the stage and the page, since unusually they were printed during Shakespeare's own lifetime – *Part One of Henry IV*, for instance, was an enormous bestseller by Elizabethan standards.

1

This study examines this phenomenon of the English history play, the experimental mode that took London theatres by storm. Contemporary audiences would have already been familiar with historical drama in plays such as *Titus Andronicus* (*c.*1593) and the anonymous *Cambises: King of Persia* (*c.*1560), but among English spectators there existed a growing awareness of nationhood. England, newly regenerate, was striving to find its own way in the turmoil of the Reformation, amid the constant threat of foreign invasion, together with religious and social schism – all of these helped to foster a burgeoning curiosity in national origins. Shakespeare's history plays are both a response to and a development of these currents.

This study focuses on four of the most distinguished of Shakespeare's history plays and examines in detail the crucial debates generated in them in conjunction with their key techniques. Many of their themes are still controversial today, both in terms of their political ideas and their depiction of historical figures. But these history plays are at the same time to be considered as tragedies or comedies, or even problem plays.

As my chapter headings imply, one of the issues we discuss is that of genre and the myriad questions that this raises. What do we mean by the label, 'history play'? Is it an exclusive label? And when Shakespeare was writing these plays, did he too actually think in terms of genre? The label 'history play' was more than likely not one that Shakespeare himself used, but was possibly a useful marketing tool when it came to selling the early printed texts. The tripartite division of his plays into tragedy, comedy or history stems from his friends' publication of his collected plays in 1623, seven years after his death.

So, for example, even though *Richard III* is first described as a 'tragedy' on the play's title page, in Shakespeare's later collected edition it was included with the 'Histories' (*Richard II*, while having a better claim to the label 'tragedy', was titled simply *The Life & Death of …*). By the same token, should we think of *Julius Caesar* and *Hamlet* as history plays as well as tragedies, particularly since they are narratives of people who did once actually exist?

Because the 'history play' was itself a fairly recent phenomenon in the Elizabethan theatre, the label could be fluidly applied by editors and theatre managers. The point here is, of course, that we should not necessarily allow the label ascribed by editors to narrow our expectations of these plays or to determine the ways in which we respond to them. So while we discuss each text in terms of its interest as a history play, it is impossible not to consider too how each functions in terms of other genres.

Another interesting question is how far a history play should tell the full truth and nothing but the truth. And this raises other questions: Whose truth? Whose history? Where did Shakespeare get his facts? Is Shakespeare writing only about the lives of historical figures, or is he writing obliquely about his own period? He was certainly writing in highly dangerous and politically volatile times, and authors' work was subject to rigorous scrutiny and censorship. Thus, adopting a distant moment in history as an allegorical parallel to the present was a healthier stratagem – the merest hint of sedition could find a writer in the Tower for an indefinite sojourn, on a strictly room-only basis.

Shakespeare worked in a hard-nosed commercial environment, for a theatre whose primary drive was the staging of profitable entertainment. Yet because this market was fuelled by the audience's demand for the stirring cut and thrust of history, a writer was compelled to strike a fine balance between raw facts and rowdy fun, between chronicle and art, truth and myth. This balance provokes fascinating issues about the available sources, Shakespeare's partial use of them and what may indeed constitute a true history. These points are debated in Chapter 5.

Each of the plays in this study can of course be analysed and discussed as a single play in its own right. But each play is also part of a larger sequence which traces common lives and develops similar themes over the cycle. Consequently, the reading of any of these texts can undoubtedly be broadened and enhanced by examining how it works within the context of the other plays in its sequence. It is still not clear whether Shakespeare set out to write his Histories as a chronological series of dramas but modern critics invariably arrange them into two tetralogies: the first consists of *Henry VI, Parts 1, 2* and *3* plus *Richard III*. While the second runs from *Richard II*, through *Henry IV Parts 1* and *2*, concluding with *Henry V*. This arrangement, of course, reflects the presumed order in which they were written, rather than the sequence of historical reigns.

Having said all that, the point of departure for each chapter in this study is the analysis of each individual play, broadening into a discussion of how it interacts with and feeds off other relevant dramas by Shakespeare, as well as those of his contemporaries. The vast diversity of themes here embraces ideas of kingship, rights of ascendancy, contemporary political ideas, theories of divine or mystical validation, questions of loyalty and friendship, power and duty, political morality, public and private aspects of monarchy; the role of women in the plays; social class; intrinsic concepts of history; tragedy and comedy; the transition from the medieval chivalric to Renaissance humanist paradigms; youth and age; concepts of manhood and nationhood; carnival and, believe it or not, some practical advice on gardening techniques.

The strategy I have adopted is to concentrate each chapter on a series of important passages taken from an individual play, analysing in detail what each passage reveals of literary features such as themes, language and figures, political focus, characters and relationships, plus staging. I have used this analysis as a means of reviewing how Shakespeare builds up the whole individual drama and its relationship to other plays by Shakespeare and his contemporaries.

My aim has been to suggest a practical method of understanding, analysing and describing texts which can be applied more broadly to literary texts in general. To get the best out of this study and the texts under consideration it is important to apply this method to the whole play under the spotlight, and each chapter ends with a suggestion for further study.

For the text of the history plays under discussion I have used the New Cambridge Shakespeare, published by Cambridge University Press. Where I have referred to other Shakespeare plays I have made use of the Arden editions, published by A&C Black. Other superb editions of Shakespeare are also readily available, such as those published by Palgrave Macmillan and Oxford University Press. At the end of the book I have included a brief list of some of the most frequent literary terms and cultural themes which I have used in the discussion – please check out any which are unfamiliar (for example, it is important to understand 'metre' and especially 'blank verse'). Those whose appetite for technical vocabulary requires more comprehensive nourishment will find their cravings amply gratified in J.A. Cuddon's *A Dictionary of Literary Terms and Literary Theory* (full details in *Further Reading*).

I would like express my gratitude to the historian Dave Folkson for his inveterate friendship and trenchant wit. However, any errors or omissions which may have slipped in I claim as my own.

# PART 1

# ANALYSING SHAKESPEARE'S HISTORIES

# 1

# *Richard II*: History as Tragedy

Kings are justly called gods, for that they exercise a manner of resemblance of divine power upon earth.

> James I, 'A Speech to the Lords and
> Commons of the Parliament at Whitehall' (1610)

The exact date of Shakespeare's *Richard II* is uncertain, but by examining topical references within the play, together with its stylistic features, we can place its composition roughly in the year 1595. This is around the beginning of Shakespeare's mature phase, the period of the three plays which follow it in historical sequence, namely the two parts of *Henry IV* and *Henry V* (this cycle of plays is usually referred to as the second tetralogy). The play was written for Shakespeare's acting company, the Lord Chamberlain's Men, and probably performed for the first time in the autumn of 1595 at their theatre in Shoreditch, north London.

Because Shakespeare uses a framework of actual people and events in *Richard II* it is usually classified as a history play (for more information on Shakespeare's sources, see Chapter 5). But, as my title for this chapter suggests, we may additionally consider it a tragedy. Accordingly, my discussion sets out to trace the process by which the play builds up key tragic elements, and my conclusion to this chapter will try to assess whether we are justified in regarding *Richard II* as a tragedy and, if so, who, if anyone, is its hero.

Unusually for a Shakespeare play, the stage of *Richard II* is empty at the start, and the King's party enters upon it. Richard initiates the action by enquiring of 'Old John of Gaunt' if he has brought his son (Henry Bullingbrook, Duke of Hereford) to court to set out his specific accusations – his 'boisterous late appeal' – against Thomas Mowbray, Duke of Norfolk.

The play begins *in medias res* – in the middle of key events – which indeed it must, because as a history play it purports to take a slice out of the continuous flow of time. This tribunal, between the King and the two antagonists, has already been postponed from an earlier date and postponement and indecision are recurrent features of Richard's career. These repeated deferrals tend to challenge his authority as absolute ruler (in spite of his assertion that 'we were not born to sue but to command'; 1.1.196).

At the end of Scene 1 Richard's judgement on the dispute is again adjourned, until Scene 3, and even then, in the lists at Coventry on the very brink of combat, Richard once more postpones a decision by banishing the two adversaries. The King's propensity for dithering at crucial moments becomes even more evident when, after having chosen to exile Bullingbrook, he commutes his original sentence from ten years to six.

The action is under way. To analyse *Richard II* I have selected four passages which strike me as significant moments in the play. These passages are interesting in terms of such features as dramatic significance, language and verse, perspective, characterisation and themes. Among the important themes which these passages and the play as whole focus on are the complex question of the nature of kingship (the status of a king, the basis of his rule, plus issues concerning blood and descent), the duties of citizens and social hierarchy, the status of women, and the matter of England (its health, position and values in a changing world). In addition we will need to consider the extent to which *Richard II* may be considered a tragedy in addition to being a history play.

## Context Passage 1: 1.1.78–117

In the first passage I have selected for analysis Bullingbrook challenges Mowbray to substantiate his accusations of murder.

| | |
|---|---|
| *Mowbray*: | I take it up, and by that sword I swear |
| | Which gently laid my knighthood on my shoulder |
| | I'll answer thee in any fair degree        80 |
| | Or chivalrous design of knightly trial; |
| | And when I mount, alive may I not light |
| | If I be traitor or unjustly fight. |
| *Richard*: | What doth our cousin lay to Mowbray's charge? |
| | It must be great than can inherit us        85 |
| | So much as of a thought of ill in him. |
| *Bullingbrook*: | Look what I speak, my life shall prove it true: |
| | That Mowbray hath received eight thousand nobles |
| | In name of lendings for your highness' soldiers, |
| | The which he hath retained for lewd employments        90 |
| | Like a false traitor and injurious villain. |
| | Besides I say, and will in battle prove |
| | Or here or elsewhere to the furthest verge |
| | That ever was surveyed by English eye, |
| | That all the treasons for these eighteen years        95 |
| | Complotted and contrived in this land |
| | Fetch from false Mowbray their first head and spring. |
| | Further I say, and further will maintain |
| | Upon his bad life to make all this good, |
| | That he did plot the Duke of Gloucester's death,        100 |
| | Suggest his soon-believing adversaries, |
| | And consequently like a traitor coward |
| | Sluiced out his innocent soul through streams of blood, |
| | Which blood, like sacrificing Abel's, cries |
| | Even from the tongueless caverns of the earth        105 |
| | To me for justice and rough chastisement: |
| | And, by the glorious worth of my descent, |
| | This arm shall do it, or this life be spent. |
| *Richard*: | How high a pitch his resolution soars! |
| | Thomas of Norfolk, what sayst thou to this?        110 |
| *Mowbray*: | Oh let my sovereign turn away his face |
| | And bid his ears a little while be deaf, |
| | Till I have told this slander of his blood |
| | How God and good men hate so foul a liar. |
| *Richard*: | Mowbray, impartial are our eyes and ears.        115 |
| | Were he my brother, nay my kingdom's heir, |
| | As he is but my father's brother's son … |

Let us begin our examination of this long extract by breaking it down into more manageable sections. Since there seems to be a natural change in perspective at line 87 we can take it in two parts: lines 78–86 and then 87–117.

## (i)   Lines 78–86: *'chivalrous design of knightly trial'*

This scene is arranged around a power triangle of Bullingbrook, Mowbray and Richard, the King at the apex, arbitrating. The intense conflict here and the fact that the two antagonists look to Richard for resolution have the important effect of recognising and consolidating Richard's position as King, important because later in the play this position will be challenged in a quite profound way. Moreover, the King resembles a father presiding over two brawling sons. The king-as-father idea is also important to note here as Richard himself and his supporters will come to regard him wistfully in these terms.

In line 78, when Mowbray declares 'I take it up ...'. he is responding, of course, to Bullingbrook's provocative gesture of throwing down his gage – a gauntlet or glove. By saying this in the same process as performing it Mowbray underlines the gestural aspect of the situation. Shakespeare is eager to quickly establish the medieval setting, as one in which chivalry plays an important explicit part but also acts as a form of decorum or ritual obedience. The ritual ('chivalrous design of knightly trial') formally objectifies the aggressive relationship between the disputants, at the same time conceding their fealty to the King.

The formal business with the gages briefly allays the intense atmosphere, lightening the bitterness between these two men, and setting the matter on a rational basis. Mowbray's taking up his enemy's gage signals his acceptance of Bullingbrook's challenge. By the same token it promptly asserts his claim of innocence in the face of Bullingbrook's aggression.

Mowbray's speech directly refers to the medieval ritual of settling a dispute:

I'll answer thee in any fair degree
Or chivalrous design of knightly trial;   (80–1)

We discover too that Mowbray, as a knight, is high in the social scale – though he is not Bullingbrook's equal, since the latter is of the royal 'blood' (this will become a crucial distinction later). Significantly, Mowbray's reference to the 'sword' which 'gently laid my knighthood on my shoulder' (79) reminds Richard that he once trusted him enough to dub him.

Furthermore, the original investiture of Mowbray, involving as it does the kissing of the sword, signifies a recognition of Richard as a semi-divine figure. This idea, so crucial to later stages of the play and its tragic aspects, derives from the view that the King is appointed and anointed by God. The royal sword is a magic sword, denoting power, justice and holiness.

Richard is a figure who, like John of Gaunt, is outwardly at least attached to traditional values like honour, decorum and impartiality, a man who believes in the divine right of kings and holy trial by combat. These values derive from an ancient, now-fading period of history. Conversely, Bullingbrook demonstrates here that he is forth-right, rational and pragmatic, a man who regards the correct answer as one that achieves results.

Shakespeare is eager to fix before us this 'ancient' chivalrous paradigm because it imposes a rigorous moral and political agenda, a code that will determine outcomes later in the play (for example, 'Old' John of Gaunt believes this is what made England so 'blessed'; see 2.1.53–4). At the same time, Shakespeare seeks a broader thematic canvas here since by the sixteenth century such formal chivalry of jousts and tourneys was pretty much finished. While contemporary poets like Spenser and Malory had tried nostalgically to resurrect thoughts of chivalry in literature, these early scenes of the play would have seemed quaintly archaic to Elizabethans (compare Chaucer's satirical treatment of 'courtesy' in *The Canterbury Tales*, especially 'The Knight's Tale'). On the other hand, the existence of this chivalric code presents Shakespeare with an important moral and social framework which will also come into play in the tragic mechanism of *Richard II*.

Shakespeare's play sketches a realm which lies at a transitional moment between one colossal epoch, the medieval period, with all its religious and philosophical absolutes, and another, the Renaissance, which radically challenges and re-forms so many of its philosophical assumptions. Eventually the self-assured Bullingbrook emerges as a proto-Renaissance New Man, interrogating the old order, leading with a new sense of rationalism and humanistic justice.

Shakespeare signals this key theme in the very first words of the play, referring to '*Old* John of Gaunt, *time-honoured* Lancaster', and its nuances resonate through the first half of the play. The old order is embodied in the previous generation, the sons of Edward III: Gaunt, York and the murdered Thomas Woodstock, Duke of Gloucester, Richard II's uncles. Equally significant, the play ends with the word 'bier' (5.6.52), pointing to the demise of this old order.

Returning to the passage, Mowbray readily takes up Bullingbrook's challenge, employing three assertive verbs: 'I take ... I swear ... I'll answer'. However, in general terms his position here is weak. He is on the back foot, reactive, responding to a personal slur. And for us at this point the exact nature of the charge is uncertain. The King is curious, and his question in line 85 invites Bullingbrook to recount for the audience the causes that have brought them to this point.

All eyes turn towards Bullingbrook. In the whole of the first act he is at or near centre-stage, endorsing his function as the prime mover of the actions of the play. He is the coming man. However, note also the imagery of movement (up and down) in Mowbray's speech, a slight hint among many of the opposite courses for Richard and Bullingbrook (and see 4.1.183–8).

As Mowbray delivers his defiant challenge (the 'knightly trial'), the early part of Scene 1 reaches a momentous climax of feeling and suspense (for we still do not know the exact complaint against him). The King turns to invite Bullingbrook to respond. But note how Richard addresses him as 'our cousin' (84), reminding the audience of the family connection, a theme to which we will repeatedly return).

(ii)  Lines 87–108: '*this arm shall do it, or this life be spent*'

As the air fizzes with strong emotion and speculation, Bullingbrook cunningly pauses. He is a master of tactics both in war and in politics. He coolly takes control with a frank assuming tone:

> Look what I speak, my life shall prove it true ...

His defence is by way of attack (and remember, he is addressing his monarch here). He matches Mowbray's promise to back his claim with his very life. He takes charge, and throughout the play his speeches are typically commanding, direct and urgent. Monosyllables keep it simple, and that slight caesura (or pause – see Glossary) in mid-line creates an impression of balance, exuding composure and self-possession, at the start at least.

Until this stage in the play the charges and counter-charges have been vague. Now Bullingbrook sets out some juicy details, directly and candidly. These are three in total and he drives straight to the point.

The first indictment is that Mowbray has taken money intended as an advance on pay for the King's troops, embezzling it for 'lewd employments', that is, for his private use (line 90; 'lewd' does not in its Elizabethan sense carry our meaning of 'obscene', yet we cannot help but hear this undertone). The second is that Mowbray has instigated every treasonous act against Richard over the past 18 years (lines 95–7). However, these are relatively mild preambles to his most alarming charge: that he plotted and murdered the King's uncle, Thomas Woodstock, Duke of Gloucester.

Bullingbrook's first charge is fairly clear-cut. Put crudely, Mowbray is a fraudster. He is indicted of common theft – though it must be said that in Elizabethan armies the appropriation of soldiers' pay by generals and nobles was a common practice (Falstaff is one such swindler, evidenced in both parts of *Henry IV*). But more gravely, drawing this out into the open to public disgrace pillories Mowbray for disloyal and indecorous behaviour. These are offences against his reputation. 'Name' (89) has moral implications, touching on the theme of reputation (decorum and grace), and since it also relates to 'family' it refers to descent, and ultimately to kingship, here linking with imagery of blood. After all, 'name' is what the two are fighting about. Ironically, Richard himself will lay himself open to the same charge of embezzlement when in Act 2 he seizes the Lancaster estates from Bullingbrook.

Bullingbrook's next point is that Mowbray has been instrumental in every recent conspiracy against the King. This is probably groundless, but he throws it into the ring as a further means of turning Richard. The real Richard was not a popular monarch, and historically this scene occurs 18 years after an uprising by labourers, following his attempt to introduce a poll tax (in England in the 1980s there was a prime minister called Margaret Thatcher who vainly tried to enforce a similar tax – and, like Richard, she was ignominiously deposed).

We can note here what a highly eloquent speaker Bullingbrook is, oratory being a much-prized skill in the Elizabethan Court. In particular his deftness in the use of sound is consummate. Note, for example, his fondness for splitting and balancing his phrases, linking the halves by sounds and ideas. This is especially notable in the middle part of his long speech, where the caesura is a useful fulcrum:

> Besides I say and will in battle prove     (92)
> Or here or elsewhere     (93)
> complotted and contrived     (96)
> Further ... and further     (98)

This oscillating effect, one of many in the play, draws us towards and yet defers his momentous accusation. Likewise note the use of alliterations, which begin to increase as the emotion intensifies – in particular, the /s/ and /z/ words which hiss and sizzle through the beginning of Bullingbrook's speech (see lines 89 and 95 and then line 97, where the monosyllables punch out his indictment).

Curiously, taking into account its venom and urgency, this speech of Bullingbrook's is also characterised by quite complex sentence patterns (e.g. lines 92–7). This appears to be central to his technique of manipulating his audience (both the King and ourselves). At the same time, and given the passion and the danger of the situation, the metre of his verse is remarkably regular (see Glossary). He is quintessentially a cool man under fire.

Bullingbrook's delivery is even and controlled. It is above all premeditated, being logically organised, elaborated through winding, subordinate clauses, each clause piling on the allegations. This is not the presentation of a crazed fanatic wildly slinging mud at some helpless Aunt Sally. It is without doubt the charge sheet of a master arch-strategist, and this depth of shrewd premeditation lends credence to those readers who suspect that Bullingbrook had all along 'complotted' Richard's fall even prior to Act 1. Or perhaps Bullingbrook is actually Richard's henchman, colluding with him to rid the Court of a man who could implicate the King in Woodstock's murder.

Bullingbrook is certainly no gauche military misfit like Othello, lacking the 'soft parts of speech'. He is instead a smoothly articulate tactician. After an opening marked by the regularity of its blank verse, from line 97 the rhythm of his deposition eventually begins to break up. In lines 97–9 Bullingbrook introduces three marked caesuras, as he draws breath for the climactic allegation of complicity in Gloucester's murder. The monosyllables of line 100 help Bullingbrook to point up every word at Mowbray:

> Upon his bad life to make all this good,
> That he did plot the Duke of Gloucester's death    (99–100)

Bullingbrook is now in full vocal command, revelling in the freedom he has cleared around the stage. He adds that Mowbray has exacerbated his guilt by drawing credulous confederates ('soon-believing adversaries') into the plot. Notice here the emotive elements deployed for maximum force: 'traitor coward ... sluiced out ... innocent soul ... streams of blood'. He is in full flight and confidently slips in a sly biblical simile in line 104, of Cain slaughtering his innocent brother Abel, the archetypal murderer (Genesis 4:10; and like Cain, Mowbray will be condemned to roam the earth). The hyperbolic 'sluiced out' both suggests a copious blood-letting and implies the cynicism of the deed (and 'blood' is an important recurring motif of the play as a whole – also see line 113).

But why, we may ask, is the issue of Gloucester's murder so important? The answer is of course that this is the catalyst for the whole play. Thomas Woodstock, Duke of Gloucester, was murdered in 1397 (about a year before the events at the start of the play). Following Richard II's disastrous French campaign, Gloucester became furious at the concessions made to the French and united with two other nobles (Arundel and Warwick), who were incensed at being overlooked for honours. Rumours multiplied that these three were leaders of a plot against Richard, who swiftly despatched Mowbray to Gloucester's base in Calais. What happened next is not certain, but the best guess is that Mowbray killed Gloucester and that Bullingbrook too was in some way complicit in his uncle's elimination. Mowbray was ennobled as

Duke of Norfolk, but when he fell out of Richard's favour the King instructed Bullingbrook to accuse the former of the murder.

The blood and kinship theme is hit home by Bullingbrook when he refers explicitly to 'my descent' (107). The point is, of course, that Mowbray is not family. So when Richard (at 115–16) assures Mowbray that he will be impartial, and refuses to allow his judgement to be swayed by 'neighbour nearness to our sacred blood' (1.1.119), we recognise this to be nonsense, even cynical nonsense in the light of the following line:

> As he is but my father's brother's son ...

After all, Bullingbrook is exiled for only six years, while Mowbray suffers banishment for life.

When Gloucester's blood 'cries out' for justice, Bullingbrook claims that it cries out to him personally. In one of this act's many ironies, Bullingbrook figures himself as the seat of justice, this 'rough chastisement'. He acts out the role of king, and his validation is the 'glorious worth of my descent' (107). By using the word 'descent' Bullingbrook cunningly reminds the King that he too is descended from Edward III.

(iii)  Lines 109–17: *'this slander of the blood'*

Later in this, at 1.4.24, when Richard reflects nervously on Bullingbrook's parting words, he notes how the latter is gathering popularity among the populace. Here too, in the second part of our extract, there is uneasiness as Richard muses on his professed loyalty:

> How high a pitch his resolution soars!    (109)

The King is already aware of this young prince's easy charm with words and virile dynamism, his ambitiousness mixed in with a keen sense of justice and a readiness to act upon it.

And what says Mowbray to all this, suddenly finding himself cornered by Bullingbrook's crafty evocation of 'family'? Mowbray's reply opens with a fairly desperate emotional plea:

> Oh let my sovereign turn away his face    (111)

Where Bullingbrook commands, Mowbray merely sues. The former has adroitly set up both the agenda and the framework of the confrontation. While Bullingbrook proclaims himself as royal prince, Mowbray can only limp along as the accused, an unhappy suspect and a social inferior. As they say in sport, he is always chasing the game.

After his genteel salute to his sovereign Mowbray now turns some fierce anger on Bullingbrook. His words lucidly manifest his exasperation and fury at this fresh insult.

> ... Till I have told this slander of his blood
> How God and good men hate so foul a liar.    (113–14)

The leathery alliterations in Mowbray's outburst (based chiefly on /l/, /d/, /s/ and /t/) lucidly communicate his writhing infuriation, weaving together into a complex tangle of spit and gristle, eventually bursting out in his climactic blast of 'so foul a liar'. He hurls Bullingbrook's 'blood' trick back into his face and the final words hang in the oppressive air like a dagger.

The air has suddenly become stifling with blistering hatred and anger. The play has begun in a blaze of verbal fury.

One effect of all this is to strengthen Richard's central position as a mediator. As the guarantor of chivalric decorum (of which he is the apotheosis), he sidesteps Mowbray's provocative 'slander of his blood' – the thrust of which is that, having betrayed the royal family, Bullingbrook ought to deserve the King's contempt. Instead, Richard assures Mowbray that his eyes as well as ears remain impartial (line 115).

The ironics, hyperbole and rhetorical manoeuvring in this passage have a tendency to unsettle a newly-arrived audience from the start. Such stratagems also undermine and destabilise the text's surfaces. Richard cannot be impartial. We readers and listeners are the only impartial arbiters, since at this stage we remain unclear. Shakespeare has cunningly made us participate in this incomplete, turbulent affair.

Much of this is, of course, for the benefit of audience or readers, establishing early on the precise relationship between key players in the drama, especially that of Richard and Bullingbrook. At the same time, the clash here of the three men sets out the drama that will eventually have profound repercussions for their relationship and for the basis of the English monarchy itself.

In the meantime, the final lines of the extract, with their dramatic irony, establish that as things stand Bullingbrook is not, nor can be, heir to the throne. Yet the final line of the passage here throws out a roundabout hint that Richard knows that Bullingbrook has a viable royal claim, however indirect:

> he is but my father's brother's son ...   (117)

What, then, is the dramatic effect of this passage in terms of the rest of this opening scene? First, this scene is crucial in swiftly introducing the principal characters of the play. Bullingbrook looms statuesque and dominates, of course, even at this very early stage. His moral strength and composure, plus eloquent oratory, mark him out as a man of some moment and presence. Yet we remark too how at this point he still remains in unquestioning fealty to the monarch and is conscious of his place vis-à-vis the crown. We may also note how he is committed and driven, bullishly confrontational in his convictions.

The critical mainspring of this play (and of the tetralogy as a whole) has now been established: the protracted curse based on accusations and intrigue surrounding the earlier, off-stage murder of Gloucester. The consequences of this dispute race swiftly and momentously through the play's direct line of plot, leading to banishment, land seizure, revenge and deposition.

Several of the play's important themes are introduced and begin to develop: the nature of the King's role and the basis of his rule (as judge, guarantor of justice and root of power), in loyalty and acquiescence. We see a snapshot of Richard set up as a figure of some stature, paternalistic, a force for restraint, while upholding a semblance of order and unity. With allusions to blood and descent, the importance of the family theme is foregrounded, as well as the vital matter of royal lineage – whose ramification will become clearer in subsequent scenes.

What we see evident here already is one of the play's most presiding themes: kingship, and one which will become crucial in the play's own developing narrative. So, at this early stage it is, of course important to take firm notice of the picture of kingship that appears at this early stage. What impression do we get of the King's role here in the first scene? My own take is that the King comes across as the commander, the arbiter of the law in disputes and final court of judgement. Richard's function here is judicial: he appears not only to interpret and enforce the law but even to be the maker of it too. The King is the law.

Accordingly, the events, actions and decisions of the opening scene have rapid and vital consequences. Since each of the protagonists already knows exactly who the murderer(s) is, the scene appears (from the inside) a ground of deep political intrigue. For the outsider audience it is an elaborate and vexed riddle whose tensions and expectations draw the watchers in. After Richard fails to reconcile these two warring opponents he commands them to meet at Coventry later in the year for a trial by combat. However, on the brink of engagement, he wavers, has a change of mind, and summarily banishes the two men.

## Context Passage 2: 2.29–68

Following the long-winded fiasco of the lists at Coventry (1.3), where the two antagonists Mowbray and Bullingbrook are banished, Richard is once again unnerved by the latter's popularity among his subjects. After Bullingbrook's 'courtship to the common people' (doffing his bonnet to an oysterwench), they cheer him off into exile. The King puts an ominous, ironic spin on this significant development:

> As were our England in reversion his
> And he our subjects' next degree in hope.   (1.4.48)

These opening scenes of *Richard II* are packed with fears and expectations, driving the action forward. As the air becomes resonant with talk of exile the play's attention turns, in Act 2, to the land they are quitting, and England itself becomes the theme.

At Coventry, John of Gaunt announces that he himself would be dead before his 'bold' son's return and King Richard takes this as a cue to seize the Lancaster lands to finance a campaign against the troublesome Irish (1.4.59–61). Now, at the start of Act 2, a fast-declining Gaunt enquires of his younger brother, York, whether Richard would visit him at his home, Ely House. His dying hope is that his deathbed words may rebuke and urge 'wholesome counsel to his unstaid youth' (2.1.2). York advises him bluntly not to waste his vital breath on Richard's ear, which is receptive only of flattery and the prospect of idle pleasures. Gaunt's response has become one of the most famous passages in Shakespeare. In spite of its familiarity, its densely crowded nuances demand our close attention for analysis.

| | |
|---|---|
| *York:* | Direct not him whose way himself will choose. |
| | 'Tis breath thou lackst and that breath wilt thou lose.　　30 |
| *Gaunt:* | Methinks I am a prophet new inspired, |
| | And thus expiring do foretell of him. |
| | His rash fierce blaze of riot cannot last, |
| | For violent fires soon burn out themselves. |
| | Small showers last long but sudden storms are short.　　35 |
| | He tires betimes that spurs too fast betimes. |
| | With eager feeding food doth choke the feeder; |
| | Light vanity, insatiate cormorant, |
| | Consuming means, soon preys upon itself. |
| | This royal throne of kings, this sceptred isle,　　40 |
| | This earth of majesty, this seat of Mars, |
| | This other Eden, demi-paradise, |
| | This fortress built by Nature for herself |
| | Against infection and the hand of war, |
| | This happy breed of men, this little world,　　45 |
| | This precious stone set in the silver sea |
| | Which serves it in the office of a wall |
| | Or as a moat defensive to a house |
| | Against the envy of less happier lands, |
| | This blessed plot, this earth, this realm, this England,　　50 |
| | This nurse, this teeming womb of royal kings |
| | Feared by their breed and famous by their birth, |
| | Renowned for their deeds as far from home |
| | For Christian service and true chivalry |
| | As is the sepulchre in stubborn Jewry　　55 |
| | Of the world's ransom, blessed Mary's son, |

This land of such dear souls, this dear, dear land,
Dear for her reputation through the world,
Is now leased out, I die pronouncing it,
Like to a tenement or pelting farm.                             60
England, bound in with the triumphant sea
Whose rocky shore beats back the envious siege
Of watery Neptune, is now bound in with shame,
With inky blots and rotten parchment bonds,
That England that was wont to conquer others                   65
Hath made a shameful conquest of itself.
Ah, would the scandal vanish with my life,
How happy then were my ensuing death!

*Enter King Richard II and Queen, Duke of Aumerle, Bushy, Green, Bagot,*
*Lord Ross, and Lord Willoughby*

Gaunt's exalted meditation on England (lines 40–68) is arranged in
four clear waves: (i) lines 29–39 are a prefatory tirade against Richard;
(ii) lines 40–9 focus on the defining quality of England and on the
defences of the realm, menaced by hostile external forces; (iii) lines
50–8 concentrate on the nation's greatness, its achievements, moral
strength and healthy reputation, a land admired and respected – all of
which offer an implicit rebuke to Richard's life and career; (iv) lines
59–68 tell of how England has defiled itself by internal vice. We can
discuss each of these waves in turn.

## (i)   Lines 29–39: '*a prophet new-inspired*'

John of Gaunt's opening words are a polemic against Richard's vanity,
his unabashed hedonism and appetite for flattery. Gaunt draws our
attention to another of the play's engrossing topics, that of time (the
speech itself contains a great weight of temporal imagery: last long,
betimes, short, soon). Time, for an old man, is of course an acutely
pertinent theme but Richard only much later recognises something of
Gaunt's drift when in prison, alone, he ponders with a new sense of
clarity, 'I wasted time and now time doth waste me' (5.5.49).

Time is also a major theme in Shakespeare's *Sonnets* and the
opening nine lines of Gaunt's speech read with something of their

same compressed energy and beauty. And there is much of the same aphoristic vigour.

> His rash fierce blaze of riot cannot last,
> For violent fires soon burn out themselves.
> Small showers last long but sudden storms are short.    (33–5)

The fire that burns twice as bright burns half as long (cf. Sonnets 41 and 129).

Richard's abiding interest, according to Gaunt (and others) is in and of himself. His passion is not in the service of the state ('court-ship to the common people') but in wild, indulgent dissipation, implied in the noun 'riot'. The imagery in Gaunt's lines is indicative: rash, blaze, violent fires, burn and spurs – the heat of lechery and fop-pish dalliance. In Shakespeare the 'appetite' is almost invariably linked with lust, exploitation, or sensual desire (for example, see *Hamlet* 1.2.143–5). Richard's dissipation is furious as hellfire, engorging the appetite – the whiff of sexual deviancy is unmistakable.

In the same breath Gaunt suggests how this passionate sport is not simply an innocuous diversion from state duties but that it is a mor-bid craving ('insatiate') and self-destructive too.

> With eager feeding food doth choke the feeder;
> Light vanity, insatiate cormorant,
> Consuming means, soon preys upon itself.    (37–9)

This idea is anticipated in line 36 in the hint that the King drives himself towards an early grave. The double play there on 'betimes' has a proverbial ring to it, he wears out fast who drives himself early.

The irony of this theme of self-destruction lies in the reality that we witness a very old man fight for breath to extend his life alongside a young king hell-bent on early extinction by short-lived ecstasies.

According to an infuriated Gaunt, then, Richard is a vain self-indulgent hedonist, impetuous and decadent and imprudent with it. He is careless of his own wellbeing and thus also, of what he symbolises, namely England itself. He strikes vocally at Richard by disparaging him as a 'cormorant' (in the Elizabethan bestiary the ignoble cormorant is a proverbial over-eater, predatory as well as greedy, insatiable in appetite). The more acerbic insult however lies in theory of the Elizabethan chain of being (see Glossary for details of this).

In this idea nature consists of a series of parallel hierarchies: the king is at the summit of the human order, the lion is supreme head of the land, the eagle of the bird kingdom, and so on. With this benchmark in mind we can see that Gaunt insults the King by correlating him with an inferior creature associated with the base appetite.

Alongside Gaunt's adoption of the 'chain' concept lies another feature of Medieval and Elizabethan metaphysics: the theory of the 'elements' (see Glossary). Briefly, these are understood to be the basic ingredients of the natural world, that is air, fire water, and earth; these were believed to constitute all physical entities but in varying proportions.

This latter theory is so universally deep-seated in the contemporary psyche that Gaunt readily makes use of the elements to structure part of his speech itself: so, the air appears in his wordplay on York's 'breath' – 'inspired' meaning to fill with air (31); fire appears in 'blaze' and 'violent fires' (33–4); water, in the 'showers' and 'storms' (35); while earth itself is taken up in the major part of his speech (e.g. lines 41 and 50 plus, 'land' and 'rocky shore', etc.). There is even a hint of the fifth, the divine element in the cryptic allusion to Christ in line 56.

Why does Gaunt/Shakespeare go to this trouble? One reason is that these references infuse Gaunt's speech with a keen sense of wholeness – almost as if Richard has offended every element of creation. Shakespeare also seeks to establish Gaunt as a man of a specific era ('time-honoured'), one steeped in the lore of the medieval *Zeitgeist*. It would be natural for such a man to understand these as part of the delimiting principle of his consciousness. Furthermore, they lend an unmistakable impression of moral as well as rhetorical strength to his contempt for his flawed sovereign.

His initial ire vented, when Gaunt reaches the end of line 39 there is an almost palpable pause. It is a handy lacuna for the actor to take breath and for the new-inspired 'prophet' to change direction (as though, perhaps, despairing of the King) as his fury abates. He moves from the earlier realm of elemental physicality to the imaginative interior. No longer is the subject specifically Richard but a mythical construct named 'England'.

## (ii)  Lines 40–9: '*This royal throne of kings, this sceptred isle*'

We have already encountered feelings of exalted patriotism about England. At the heart of Mowbray's lament on his being expelled from England lies his dejection at being 'cast forth in the *common air*' (1.3.157), into 'solemn shades' (1.3.177). Bullingbrook, no less loyal, refers to England as the 'sweet soil' (1.4.305; Richard calls it his 'Dear earth') and defiantly trumpets:

> Though banished yet a true born Englishman    (1.3.308)

So, what exactly is this England-nation? The island is, first, a royal throne. In addition, the island itself partakes of a certain specialness. To describe the kings as 'royal' would be almost tautological were it not for the fact that later we have to consider if Bullingbrook himself is royal. The magical isle is somehow blessed, with lyrical echoes of Caliban's enchanted island in *The Tempest*.

First, Gaunt wishes to draw attention to the ancient longevity of the King's realm. With a queen on the English throne, this idea could strike an odd dissonance on sixteenth-century ears, but the theme will become clearer as we proceed. 'Sceptred' in line 40 hammers home the concept of England as a noble locus (sceptre being a symbol of majesty), while the word 'isle' prepares for the view of England as a discrete, self-containing entity). And even the very earth, the soil which we take to be coarse, seems blessed and shares in the glory (the land is a recurring motif of the play – and see 3.4.39).

This phrase, 'seat of Mars', reiterates the throne image yet extends it through the notion of England as the home of the god of war. The reference to this pagan deity seeks to establish Gaunt's later claim that England ruggedly asserts its identity by force of arms. Implicit in this, too, is a crack at Richard as a man wanting in discipline, wallowing in dissolute amusements. Mars, together with Jupiter, was foremost among the deities of Classical Rome, a byword for unyielding military discipline, terror and conquest. Mars was also nominated as the father of Romulus and Remus. Thus 'time-honoured' Gaunt strives to align contemporary England with Ancient Rome – a point which may have accorded with some minds in Tudor England (there was a long-held belief that Britain had been founded by Roman Brutus – and in this context, see 5.1.2).

Warming to his theme of time, Gaunt switches from pagan to biblical mythology. After identifying England with the martial Rome, he embraces England as 'This other Eden, demi-paradise'. He pushes England's pedigree even further back, to the beginning of time itself, with the paradisal Eden of Adam and Eve.

Having firmly established his glowing view of England as a transcendent idyll, Gaunt next visualises his beloved earth in geographical terms. He has become galvanised by the momentum of his own prophetic hyperbole in lines like 'This fortress built by Nature for herself' (43). After the potency of Mars and some soaring idealism, now enters the goddess Nature, who appears to validate the very existence of England. 'Nature' implies a number of positive associations here, including health, authenticity and regeneration. This personification glances back to the earlier references to 'seat' and 'throne', now enlivened with the idea of a volitional animus working through the physical environment. At the same time the feminising impulse is all one with the notion of Mother England and even of the warrior figure, Britannia (note the maternal imagery of 'nurse' plus 'womb' in line 51).

England, then, is a natural island fortress. Gaunt revisits this idea when he talks of the 'silver sea' acting as one enormous 'moat defensive', safeguarding the favoured island and its 'happy breed' from 'infection and the hand of war' (44). By 'infection' he of course refers to the reality of disease – Gaunt's fourteenth-century England had been ravaged by the imported Black Death, while Shakespeare's audience lived in unceasing horror of the plague. In addition Gaunt has in mind the moral and political contagion by which a chaste England was put in jeopardy by the menace of unwholesome foreigners.

In the time of the play the foreign enemies besieging England consisted of the powerful Catholic nations, chiefly Spain and France, while newly autonomous England prevailed almost alone following the Reformation. To be sure, Gaunt's England is itself a warlike island, insular, alone, resisting the 'hand of war' of 'less happier lands' from across the sea (note too line 62, the 'envious siege'). These foreigners are an instance of the immanent 'other' in the play – the shadowy, latent sense of challenge or antipathy that permeates the play and holds it in a constant state of friction (for example, the clash of Mowbray and Bullingbrook, Bullingbrook against Richard, Northumberland versus Aumerle and Carlisle).

Lying in constant fear at the centre of this ring of antagonism, England resembles the Holy Sepulchre (line 55), the holy of holies in Jerusalem, where it is supposedly beset by antipathetic and hateful ('stubborn') Jewry. The idea, of course, is that Gaunt identifies England with the church erected over the place of Christ's burial following his crucifixion, a beleaguered outpost of Christianity tyrannised by infidels (especially in the time of the Crusades – more on this below). Once again, Gaunt's simile invokes the assistance of the sacred in validating his beloved land.

### (iii)  Lines 50–8: '*Renowned for their deeds as far from home*'

Gaunt boasts that his England is uniquely 'this little world', 'this earth' (50). It is a microcosm of the whole order of creation, with the King at the pinnacle and the peasants at its base. Developing the 'Eden' theme, he implies that this hallowed land is self-reliant – much like a medieval city under siege, a stoical notion that politicians down the ages have perpetuated.

Accordingly, this diminutive lump of obdurate rock thrashed by the great grey Atlantic Ocean is a happy, radiant place. Amid less happy lumps of rock it is a jewel, a 'precious stone' (46; both Gaunt and his son have earlier compared it to a jewel – see 3.1.266 and 269). In this, too, it outshines others. Gaunt's pride in his country stems from its perceived pre-eminence in the world. Going further, he combines materialism and spirituality to suggest once more a feeling of wholeness: physical land but radiantly sacred, since it is a 'blessed plot' (50).

Nature authorises one form of validation, endowing health and happiness, while 'blessed' takes this further, implying the land is created and approved by God (and remember that Gaunt represents himself as a 'prophet'; line 31). But Richard and others will later remind us that he too, its sovereign, is appointed by God, for what that is worth (see Gaunt's reply to the Duchess of Gloucester at 1.2.37–8).

Gaunt's majestic oratory reaches its major climax in lines 50–1:

This blessed plot, this earth, this realm, this England,
This nurse, this teeming womb of royal kings ...

The deictic word 'This' infuses an important back-beat to the whole speech. I estimate 15 occurrences of this demonstrative pronoun, whose effect is to particularise place but also reveal to Gaunt's underlying temper, mixing pride and vexation.

Not surprisingly, the climactic lines 50 and 51 gather in many of the ideas and references which have permeated Gaunt's threnody on England: religious imagery such as 'blessed', earth (line 41 on), the realm ('royal island', 'majesty') and 'royal kings' harks back to the first line of the England section, riffing on kings again. 'Teeming womb', England's lush fertility, momentarily casts the eye back to 'breed' but introduces a new element – of vitality or vigour – to the crowded catalogue.

England is not merely precious, happy and powerful but it is a mother in the dual senses of a womb of great men and a nanny or carer ('nurse'), sustaining and protecting like the sea. Interestingly, on Richard's return to England after the Irish campaign he likewise compares himself to a mother as he greets the earth (3.2.8).

Line 51 launches the important theme of 'service' ('serve' occurs in line 47 as well) and is developed in more detail over the next few lines:

> Renowned for their deeds as far from home
> For Christian service and true chivalry    (53–4)

'Chivalry' is a word which also embraces reputation, itself an important principle for Gaunt in this speech. Crucially, it refers to the way he himself relates to Richard in the play as a whole. In essence Gaunt believes the King is scandalised by his immoral activities, polluting the throne – and by extension, the realm. Gaunt, man of old-world mores, adds one more tint in the shading of our picture of Richard that will ultimately warrant his dethroning. Lines 53–4 are important in establishing a yardstick by which to measure the King (and also Bullingbrook), but his is a small voice fading under the gathering storm.

'Christian service' here implies not only normal acts of charity to other people but making pilgrimage and/or crusades to the Holy Land to defend the Christian holy sites. This is one of many hints and references to the practice of crusade or pilgrimage – for example, in the closing lines of the play Bullingbrook as Henry IV resolves to make a pilgrimage in gratitude and atonement (see 5.6.49–50; in the *Henry IV* plays he reiterates this aim but never fulfils it; see *1Henry IV* 1.1.18–27 and *2Henry IV* 4.5. 233–4).

The true chivalry of knighthood demands selfless service – contrast Richard's egoistic indulgent 'vanity' (38) and the 'rash fierce blaze of riot' (34). Such unselfish service is epitomised by Jesus Christ, 'blessed Mary's son' (56), who as the 'world's ransom' gave his life in the salvation of others, the apotheosis of altruism. This moment marks the thematic climax of Gaunt's speech since it arrives at a *terminus ad quem* – the ultimate in possible juxtapositions, setting England on a par with Christ.

Gaunt's rhapsodic evocation of his fading England, a bygone golden place, closes with a fourfold repetition of 'dear': dear England, 'her' people and 'her' reputation. In addition the reiteration of this adjective suggests, of course, a degree of senescence and languid consciousness. Clearly pointing up his doting loyalty, the passage delivers a sort of emotional swan-song, but as a final frustration with words to articulate Gaunt's intense, quasi-religious devotion to his nation.

### (iv) Lines 59–68: *'England ... is now bound in with shame'*

After this wave of high intensity it is difficult to miss the cadence beginning at line 59. Old England, symbolised by holiness, integrity, strength and care, is rented out by King Richard like some common allotment or pelting farm (that is, a farm for the production of pelts or skins). Gaunt is humiliated by the very act of acknowledging it. After all the exalted spirituality of the middle sections of the speech he notes that the country has been reduced to a materialistic tract of real estate, mere rented earth, its happy breed sunk to bondslaves.

Now, while outwardly and in natural terms, England still resembles the same fair plot of past greatness, the kingdom has become inwardly rotten, and shamefully so. In this latter phase, England is irrevocably identified with King Richard. Thus England has now in fact conquered itself, recalling the earlier reference to the 'insatiate cormorant / Consuming means' (39). Gaunt's argument has come full circle: Richard as England is the worm that gnaws at its own body (by which, of course, Gaunt envisions civil war, historically the Wars of the Roses – as the Bishop of Carlisle will too, but more explicitly: 4.1.136–44).

Gaunt reads the 'leasing out' of England as a form of simony, the sin of selling sacred articles for profit. If we read it this way, then, as the chief salesman, Richard affronts the holy chivalric contract, an act that identifies him with the 'stubborn' heathens who menace the holy sepulchre in Jerusalem.

These final lines of Gaunt's account function as an extended sigh. But is it a sigh of despondency or of acrimony? Does he hope for consolation through his own death, or does he perhaps expect thereby to induce the nemesis of Richard (the 'scandal')? It is difficult to see how either of these can happen satisfactorily. Yet with the benefit of hindsight we, the reader, can at least recognise the heavy dramatic irony at work here (made particularly more sardonic by the imminent confiscation of the Lancastrian estate by Richard).

However, and more significantly, old Gaunt's closing lines link him with his early reflection on Christ and 'Christian service' – and the ardent desire that his death, figured as a self-sacrifice, can bring about salvation to his beloved land.

This passage represents a masterly performance of subtle and expressive oratory. A eulogy, a threnody and an apostrophe, John of Gaunt's 'England' speech is probably the most memorable of Shakespeare's set pieces, fragments of which have passed into commonplace language. For our analysis, however, we need to weigh up the implications of his speech for the wider play.

To Gaunt himself England seems on the one hand to be simply an idea, a metaphysical entity that inheres mostly in his mind. On the other hand, England resembles a living person, part maternal female, part male warrior-protector, strong, large and compassionate in the function of service. The island is in itself a monarch among nations, a precious, impregnable rock, a womb and a carer, mother and father. But as a personification and a metaphor England is more than all of these. It is a demi-god, a deity presiding over a paradisal sacred island, reified and sanctified by a Christian God.

These are of course greatly hyperbolised, highly idealised attributes. The speech refers not to England's actual historical past, since an

English golden age pre-1400 did not exist – unless we accept the Arthurian legends as literal truth (and England had hardly imposed itself overseas except for a few inconclusive mêlées in France). It is a highly flavoured romanticised vision, a kind of political wish-list or desire – what ought to be rather than a realistic account of historical facts. It injects an ideal of moral and political behaviour into the play (alongside the chivalric texture of Act 1) and talks up the prize that Richard and Bullingbrook will eventually contest, the precious object of desire.

For Shakespeare's own audience the matter of Gaunt's essay was one becoming increasingly important to a nation fighting to redefine itself in post-Reformation Europe. Renaissance England, newly sovereign, urgently struggles to assert a fresh sense of nationhood and identity as a cohesive people. No longer in fealty to distant Rome, England in the sixteenth century is beset by predatory forces. Queen Elizabeth's is only the third generation after her grandfather, Henry VIII's break with Catholicism. Her realm is yet on a perilous footing.

Thus, in political terms, Shakespeare exploits Gaunt, time-honoured figure of the past, as a mouthpiece for this Tudor desire to validate and reinforce the national status quo. The fourteenth century is made to speak for the sixteenth. None of which precludes the possibility of irony or burlesque to control an audience's response.

The past is exploited as a yardstick and a goad for the sixteenth century. To make Gaunt's words more pertinent to Shakespeare's audience, he makes some topical allusions. For instance, in Elizabethan England the new enclosure law allowed the parcelling out of the English landscape to make tenements or pelting farms of the common land. The play postulates a scenario in which a monarch ascends the throne by eliminating a troublesome rival cousin: the parallels with Elizabeth I and her cousin Mary Queen of Scots would not have been lost on Shakespeare's audience. These vivid points of contact were happily exploited by the conspirators behind the Essex plot of February 1601 who arranged for a special performance of *Richard II* on the eve of their attempted and thwarted coup against Elizabeth I.

John of Gaunt's speech has a double moment – 1398 and 1595 (treble, if we include today) – and it draws these two historical moments together in the one man. Duality is itself a recurring feature of his speech: Mars and Christ – pagan and Christian, past and present, infection and blessed, happy versus 'less happier', and ourselves against the shadowy hostile 'others'. What is more, Gaunt invokes and strives to reconcile the Platonic dualism of the material world (of rocks, plots and seas) with the spiritual aspect of England (of blessings and souls), phenomenon and noumenon.

The critic Jeremy Lopez identifies another interesting dualism: the 'vital tension between what the stage direction calls a "sick old man" and the gathering strength of his words' (Lopez, 24). Like his speech, Gaunt is a figure of contrasts. He is both a statement and an enactment of his fading England since, while we observe before us the body of a gaunt, weak and frail old man, angry, loyal and committed to deep-rooted principles, these ironically project an impression of great moral courage and strength. All of which represent implicit benchmarks for the appraisal of other key figures (a similar ethical role is played by the Gardener of 3.4, and later by the Bishop of Carlisle).

Ironically, Shakespeare presents to us visually a Gaunt that is the correlative of England frail with age, disaffected enough to rouse our sympathies and antagonism in varying degrees. This is Gaunt's indelible legacy to the play. Yet in this very mode his speech reveals a cunning mind expert in brilliantly structured political rhetoric predicated upon supple and poised oratory, not of a demagogue but a shrewd old head.

## Context Passage 3: 3.4.29–82

Gaunt's speech is the last and forlorn voice against Richard's rapine advance. Following the death of Gaunt, Richard's seizure of the Lancastrian assets provokes Bullingbrook into an early return to England in order to recoup his birthright. While the latter's allies unite in increasing strength, Richard witnesses his own supporters dissolving away, and in a climactic scene at Flint Castle (3.3) the two principals of the play come head-to-head. The King disconsolately accepts at last that his authority has been subsumed. The attention suddenly switches – in 3.4 – to the Duke of York's tranquil garden at

Langley, where an important little scene is shaped by characters absent from the main hurly-burly.


*[Langley. The Duke of York's garden]*

| | | |
|---|---|---|
| *Gardener*: | Go, bind thou up yon dangling apricocks, | |
| | Which, like unruly children, make their sire | 30 |
| | Stoop with oppression of their prodigal weight. | |
| | Give some supportance to the bending twigs. | |
| | Go thou, and like an executioner, | |
| | Cut off the heads of too-fast-growing sprays, | |
| | That look too lofty in our commonwealth. | 35 |
| | All must be even in our government. | |
| | You thus employed, I will go root away | |
| | The noisome weeds, which without profit suck | |
| | The soil's fertility from wholesome flowers. | |
| *Servant*: | Why should we in the compass of a pale | 40 |
| | Keep law and form and due proportion, | |
| | Showing, as in a model, our firm estate, | |
| | When our sea-walled garden, the whole land, | |
| | Is full of weeds, her fairest flowers choked up, | |
| | Her fruit trees all unpruned, her hedges ruined, | 45 |
| | Her knots disordered and her wholesome herbs | |
| | Swarming with caterpillars? | |
| *Gardener*: | Hold thy peace. | |
| | He that hath suffered this disordered spring | |
| | Hath now himself met with the fall of leaf. | |
| | The weeds which his broad-spreading leaves did shelter, | 50 |
| | That seemed in eating him to hold him up, | |
| | Are plucked up root and all by Bullingbrook, | |
| | I mean the Earl of Wiltshire, Bushy, Green. | |
| *Servant*: | What, are they dead? | |
| *Gardener*: | They are; and Bullingbrook | |
| | Hath seized the wasteful king. O, what pity is it | 55 |
| | That he had not so trimmed and dressed his land | |
| | As we this garden! We at time of year | |
| | Do wound the bark, the skin of our fruit-trees, | |
| | Lest being overproud in sap and blood, | |
| | With too much riches it confound itself. | 60 |

|             | Had he done so to great and growing men, |     |
|-------------|------------------------------------------|-----|
|             | They might have lived to bear and he to taste |  |
|             | Their fruits of duty. Superfluous branches |    |
|             | We lop away, that bearing boughs may live. |    |
|             | Had he done so, himself had borne the crown, | 65 |
|             | Which waste of idle hours hath quite thrown down. | |
| *Servant*:  | What, think you then the King shall be deposed? | |
| *Gardener*: | Depressed he is already, and deposed       |     |
|             | 'Tis doubt he will be. Letters came last night |  |
|             | To a dear friend of the good Duke of York's, | 70 |
|             | That tell black tidings.                    |     |
| *Queen*:    | O, I am pressed to death through want of speaking! | |
|             | Thou, old Adam's likeness, set to dress this garden, | |
|             | How dares thy harsh rude tongue sound this unpleasing news? | |
|             | What Eve, what serpent, hath suggested thee | 75 |
|             | To make a second fall of cursed man?        |     |
|             | Why dost thou say King Richard is deposed?  |     |
|             | Darest thou, thou little better thing than earth, | |
|             | Divine his downfall? Say, where, when, and how, | |
|             | Camest thou by this ill tidings? Speak, thou wretch! | 80 |
| *Gardener*: | Pardon me, madam. Little joy have I         |     |
|             | To breathe this news, yet what I say is true. |   |

The critic E.M.W. Tillyard thought little of this scene, dismissing it as 'unexceptional', and describing it's language as 'over-inflated', yet he referred to its 'intensely symbolic character'. In his study of *Richard II* Graham Holderness also brushes off this scene, as merely an 'interlude' in the action: 'it tells us little that we don't already know' (Holderness 1989, p. 11). However, he adds that it dramatises the Queen's grief and sets out a political allegory involving the Gardener. It certainly does this, yes, and it does represent a marked break in the intense dynamic and shifting complex of the Richard and Bullingbrook conflict. In one nutshell, Holderness's point is fair comment, but there are other nutshells and important ones, too, since the scene embodies some of the play's key themes viewed from new and detached perspectives.

A careful reading of this passage suggests to me that a significant theme here is that of 'care', understood in its widest, most conceptual sense. In this sense, 'care' is the principle that suffuses a wide range of conditions such as service, compassion, curiosity, loyalty, supervision and even kingship. In a subtle and profound way the focus and tone of this scene are set up by its fascinating motifs and diction, some of which informs the recurring imagery of the play as a whole (custody, excess, foresight, justice). At the same time the allegory or parable of the scene is weightier and in many ways more complex than Holderness gives credit.

With its dramatic lull in tempo and mood, this scene is the first in which we see the action from anything other than the converging lines of the two main power groups. Consequentially, the scene is not concerned with naturalistic details of military or factional manoeuvrings, but takes stock of them through intricate metaphors which enact the play's thematic issues.

At the start of this relatively quiet scene, which functions as a kind of entr'acte, the doleful Queen is oblivious of recent political developments. Her sorrowful mood has extended here from 2.2 when last she appeared. With each rejection of her ladies' suggestions her melancholy deepens, and the sound of the approaching gardener prompts her to take cover in the gloomy shade of nearby trees.

For the purposes of our discussion the extract I have chosen can be managed fairly naturally in four sections, with their underlying topics forming a kind of dialectic: (i) lines 29–39, the gardener giving instructions for rehabilitating the garden; (ii) lines 40–7, the servant developing these instructions into an allegory, forging a parallel between garden care and state governance; (iii) lines 47–71, the Gardener rebuking the servant's seditious talk, while also acknowledging the King's carelessness; (iv) lines 72–82, the Queen scolding the Gardener for his impertinence and defeatism.

(i)   Lines 29–39: *'All must be even in our government'*

The anonymous Gardener enters with a terse imperative, directing subordinates to their day's tasks. His first line both underlines his authority and introduces the theme of care:

Go, bind thou up yon dangling apricocks,

This is typical of his discourse with his underlings, adopting short, brisk instructions: 'Go ... Give ...Go ... Cut off ... Hold thy peace'.

His role and identity as lord over the garden is immediately established, while 'apricocks' promptly discloses his rustic labouring-class
stock. He labours with his hands, a man of the soil, and a man of
some experience. He is well versed in the ways of 'noisome' weeds,
especially their readiness to run ragged and choke up vulnerable cul-
tivars. The noun 'apricocks' is obviously dialect for 'apricots', but not
being a native of England it is a difficult fruit to cultivate out of
doors, requiring careful attention.

His simile matching apricot branches to 'unruly children' (30)
focuses exactly on his diligent manner. The phrase implies both the
need for discipline yet a sensitive care of young growths that challenge their 'sire' (father or lord), threatening to wreck the main brac-
ing stem. His particular choice of lexis here, 'unruly children' and
'sire', carries some strong dramatic irony in the light of the servant's
explicit allusions in line 40 onwards.

Is the Gardener himself conscious from the outset of the ironic
allegory that develops, of the garden as a microcosm or synecdoche
for the political state? His role can be played either way, and he may
of course be directing his meaningful words at the hidden Queen,
especially with his reference to 'prodigal', making a glance in terms
of the 'wasteful king' (l.55). And yet it is barely conceivable, given
the political situation, that he is unaware of the heavy import of his
words.

'Supportance', in line 32, points to one aspect of care, of nurtur-
ing, while in the next line 'executioner' suggests the obverse side of
his job, ruthless clinical eradication. Those ambitious growths that
grow too fast or reach above their given rank should be ruthlessly cut
down to size.

All the same, within the developing garden/commonwealth allegory, who exactly are these over-reachers, the 'too-fast-growing
sprays' (34)? The gardener is referring obliquely to those courtiers
allegorised in line 59 as 'over-proud in sap and blood'. In other
words, the Gardener is cryptically referring to Richard's failure to
curtail the debilitating influence of flatterers like Bushy, Bagot and
Green, those

noisome weeds, which without profit suck
The soil's fertility from wholesome flowers. (38–9)

According to the Gardener, the maxims of good kingship are not only care, management and discipline but judicious vigilance too. A diplomatic overseer, his language is carefully guarded lest he himself seem 'too lofty' or 'over proud'.

Having laid the ground for the play's celebrated parable, the Gardener turns away to get on with his own tasks. His assistants will tie up and prune the disordered branches, twigs and sprays while he gives his personal attention to the noisome harmful weeds, parasites which, like Bushy, Bagot and Green, suck at the vigour of the commonwealth. His method is hands-on, of total gardening, a top-to-bottom, root-and-branch elimination of seditious nature.

Although the idea of gardening as a parable for state government has many precedents in medieval literature (and see Matthew 20), this particular scene is Shakespeare's own invention: there is no parallel in Holinshed. The role of the Gardener itself is unusual in Shakespeare, too, since characters below the rank of knight enter his plays chiefly as murderers, thieves, disruptive comics or useful dramatic devices. Our Gardener here is a device, for sure, but there is much of the rounded character about him.

Unusually, too, for a figure of his social class the Gardener speaks in regular blank verse with a fine poetic beauty. Commonly in Shakespeare, peasants and labourers are identified by prose speech (for example, contrast the speech patterns of the tavern hostess in *1Henry IV* 2.4, or the 'hempen homespuns' of *A Midsummer Night's Dream*). Consequently the gardeners here are not quite as authentic-sounding as, say, the gravediggers in Act 5 of *Hamlet*.

That said, the Gardener's opening line is slightly irregular in metre in order to accommodate his commanding first word 'Go', and Shakespeare makes line 38 uneven in order to get across the point about parasites. Even so, everyone in *Richard II* does speak in verse, and consequently these humble labourers have their status elevated by speaking in the same mode as the King.

And what are we to make of the character of the physical garden itself? For an accurate idea of an English medieval or Elizabethan garden we must first dismiss modern images of bird feeders, barbecues, sunloungers and even a velvety sward of fescued lawn. The contemporary meaning of 'garden' was of something more akin to what we might think of as an orchard or maybe a *parterre*, a highly formalised plot laid out in a pattern of criss-crossing pathways containing flowers or herbs. It is a place of profit as well as of recreation (as demonstrated in the important garden scene of *1Henry VI*).

During Elizabeth's reign the formal laid garden was beginning to come into its own during a period of growing ease in which elegant manor houses gradually replaced the brawny castle. Writing in 1589, the Tudor commentator George Puttenham offered practical gardening tips, pointing out how the gardener, like the doctor, can restore human health and improve on nature:

> the Physician and the Gardener [may] be called good and cunning artificers ... the Gardener by his arte will not only make an herbe, or flower or fruit come forth without impediment, but will also embellish the same ... any of which things nature could not do without mans help and art.
>
> (*The Arte of English Poesie*)

A cunning artificer, curbing and improving on the landscape, a gardener may possibly be regarded as a pioneer in the humanist enterprise, akin even to the necromancer in his apparent mastery of nature.

Seen in this context, the Gardener of *Richard II* is, in practice, the monarch of his blessed plot. Even the Servant understands their garden as a 'model' of the 'whole land' (42–3), a microcosm with the Gardener as their leader-king. The Gardener's utterances are short practical directions and his reply to the servant of 'Hold thy peace' (47) is brusquely executive. He is a direct pragmatic ruler of this patch, a forthright, proactive leader of his team, dutiful in regard of his responsibilities. They in turn respect his wisdom as well as his ascribed status, truly a man born rather to command than to sue, and more akin to Bullingbrook than to the rightful King.

The Gardener is a man of discretion, we understand. By the same token he is acutely aware of his fixed place in the chain of society, submissive to the nobles. So when the Servant makes the central allegory too plain (line 40 on), perilously exposing the crew to severe penalty, he swiftly distances himself from its subject matter, plunging back into the refuge of his verdurous metaphors, 'fall of leaf' ... 'broad-spreading leaves' (49–50).

The Queen later reminds us that the Gardener has been 'set to dress this garden' (73). This description is precisely what defines

him as a man in this society. Care or 'dressing' signifies management or stewardship, involving the double role I mentioned above:
of nurture (bringing on) and control (cutting back) of the Duke's
plants and trees. In general terms the Gardener's task, like the
King's, is to nurture nature: to encourage natural growth while
imposing a human discipline upon it. The Gardener's view thus
contrasts with that of John of Gaunt, who describes the land as
'This other Eden', and 'built by Nature for herself'. Nature itself is
'This nurse'. Where Medieval Gaunt understands it as a wild teeming place with nature as a self-regulating force for good, the practical, realistic Gardener envisages the land as a wild, riotous plot
whose virile energy would eventually strangle England's culture if
left to itself, untended.

Where Gaunt's is a prelapsarian, Edenic garden in which nature is
freedom and stability, our pragmatic Gardener here knows it to be a
parcel of choking ambition permeated by sin out of which freedom
emerges only through ruthless domination. The return of the
dynamic, rigorous Bullingbrook brings about the systematic elimination of the realm's choking weeds.

(ii)  Lines 40–7: '*Keep law and form and due proportion*'

While the Servant has only nine lines in total they (and he) make a
vital contribution to the colour of the scene. His resounding 'Why',
opening his challenge to the Gardener, brings about a sudden switch
in the direction and tone of the scene. He represents as the principal
agent of 'desire' here, probing and unsettling the Gardener and his
beliefs. His quizzicality lights on key words in his supervisor's opening speech – 'unruly', 'commonwealth' and 'government' – to spell
out the political nuances in the horticultural allegory.

Although lower in the social hierarchy than even the Gardener, the
outspoken Servant also speaks in verse. Unlike his superior's, however,
his own verse is most irregular. This could indicate his lowly standing,
by making his verse resemble prose, yet its irregularity is equally in
tune with his radical candour. In historical terms, the Servant vocalises a contemporary mood of dissent in England, arising from the
deep and widespread economic crisis during the 1590s resulting in
part from a prolonged state of military mobilisation (likewise, many

readers have noted the parallel between the rebellions of *Coriolanus* and the corn riots in the English Midlands in 1607).

He is articulate both in his complex sentence structure and in his felicity with the passive voice ('choked up', 'unpruned', 'ruined' ...), which allows him to avoid specific accusations. In this scene as a whole the Servant's speech consists, in total, of three questions: 'Why ... What ... think you ...?' His naive quizzing functions as a catalyst to their chitchat, prodding and fomenting the tension of the dialogue until the Gardener is pressed into an uncomfortable political corner:

> Why should we in the compass of a pale
> Keep law and form and due proportion ... (40–1)

The hendiadys in the latter of these two lines (each term repeating more or less the same idea – 'law', 'form', 'proportion') matches the Servant's own laxity or clumsiness in speech. Is he simply puzzled at the apparent hypocrisy of the ruling classes, or is he actually truly seditious? He is blithely successful, however, in sustaining the uncomfortable tension for his boss.

The Servant's acute sensitivity for even-handedness and balance makes him one more spokesman for the play's theme of justice. He makes common cause with Mowbray and Bullingbrook in Act 1, with Carlisle later, and with the Duke of York:

> How long shall I be patient? Ah, how long
> Shall tender duty make me suffer wrong?
>
> (2.1.163–4)

The play has scores of such references to justice, judging (e.g. 4.1.123) and trials (in 1.1, 3.1 and 4.1). Bullingbrook confronts Bushy and Green over their 'foul wrongs' (3.1.15) and the same strain of justice sits behind York's reprimand of his 'traitorous' son Aumerle. York prizes integrity over familial loyalty and his contempt for Bullingbrook: 'All must be even in our government.'

The Servant too has an important view of the garden in quasi-symbolic terms. Curiously, his rich verse envisages his garden/England as female, '*her* fairest flowers', '*Her* fruit trees', and so on, and sees her as passive, supine, a victim who has been raped. This view is evident in his diction of 'choked' and 'ruined', and the Gardener speaks of her 'fall of leaf', the victim 'swarming' with phallic caterpillars. As any gardener will testify, caterpillars are brutal ravagers of beauty (the Queen too refers to the 'serpent' of the garden; line 75).

The idea here becomes more explicit when we revisit Bullingbrook's earlier depiction of these voracious larvae:

> Bushy, Bagot and their complices,
> The caterpillars of the commonwealth
> Which I have sworn to pluck and weed away.   (2.3.163–5)

Where formerly the garden was 'whole' (43) and 'wholesome' (46) she has now been sacked and sucked. For a clearer picture of Shakespeare's connection of caterpillars and rapine lust, take a glance at his long poem *Venus and Adonis* (1593), where Adonis strives to distinguish lust, the 'hot tyrant', from love:

> [the] fresh beauty, blotting it with blame,
> Which the hot tyrant stains, and soon bereaves,
> As caterpillars do the tender leaves.   (796–7)

In the spirit of the play's many crusades, the knightly Gardener goes forth to rescue the maiden England, former Eden – which indeed is also Bullingbrook's objective. The Gardener's cause is to recover her from this abuse and make her whole and fruitful again. Her fruitfulness thus contrasts with the Queen, who has similarly been 'uncared for'. In point of fact, until Richard is en route to imprisonment, we can discern little affection between himself and his wife. She has borne no fruit – being childless – and her own gardener, Richard, is a 'wasteful king' (line 55; at 5.5.49 he confesses how 'I have wasted time ...'). As a fecund garden the Queen, though devoted to Richard, has been abandoned by him, a man who more generally prefers the companionship of his male courtiers.

(iii)   Lines 47–71: *'the wasteful king. O, what a pity is it'*

Perhaps taken aback by the Servant's unexpected dissension (and possibly conscious of the Queen's proximity), the Gardener's response is swift, trenchant and monosyllabic, 'Hold thy peace' bringing the flow to an abrupt halt.

The directness of the Gardener's rebuff, in keeping with his firm leadership, is of course an ironic contrast with the King's hesitancy. Conversely, it does share some of Bullingbrook's dogmatic attitude to things bushy and green:

> The weeds which his broad-spreading leaves did shelter ...
> Are plucked up root and all by Bullingbrook,    (50, 52)

I mentioned at the outset to this discussion of passage (iii) that the focus and tone are set up by the imagery and diction. For me, three words in particular stand out as most indicative: 'waste', 'blood' and 'land'. All three refer to the King and England and are elements central to the play as a whole.

In the passage as a whole, 'waste' and its cognate 'prodigal' occur three times (in lines 31, 55 and 66). I have already referred to the word's autoerotic connotations, but there are more literal, political meanings at work here too. In addition to its sense of 'to devastate', which applies to the Servant's description of the garden, 'waste' suggests squandering and exhausting potential and virility – in a word, it has described what has gone wrong in the King's reign. 'Prodigal' in line 31 has unmistakable biblical overtones, while the two other references divide into two further emphases: 'wasteful' in line 55 implies that Richard has exhausted resources self-indulgently, without profit, while 'waste of hours' in line 66 points to a sense of opportunities missed and lapsed, implying indolence.

The term 'waste' occurs at least five times in the play, each time with a tinge of immorality. All of these ideas linked with 'waste' gather to a head in Act 5 and Richard's epiphany in his celebrated refrain of 'I wasted time and now time doth waste me.' It would be difficult not to recognise the contrast between the profligate, dissolute Richard and the virile, striking Bullingbrook. But we should also observe the contrast between the King and the busy labouring gardeners whose *present* arduous industry is directed towards the prospect of *future* 'fruits of duty'.

'Waste' may also signify 'neglect of duty', and in this regard *The Tempest* offers an interesting comparison. Like Richard, Prospero complains that his kingdom has been usurped by a scheming ambitious relative. However, where Prospero is the victim of treachery by a perfidious brother who exploited his trust, in *Richard II* we are more likely to feel that the King becomes the victim of his own greed and ineffectiveness.

As a king, Richard has acted out of bad faith. He has wasted the holy body, the land, and the blood of England, the total body-politic. At line 56 the Gardener bemoans the fact that the King has not 'so trimmed and dressed his land'. 'Land, 'earth' and 'ground' are among the most commonly recurring images of the play – in Gaunt's island speech it is this 'earth of majesty' (2.1.41) and a 'dear, dear land' (line 57). It is Gaunt's land of Eden. The Servant describes it as this 'whole land' (43), implying ironically that it is or should be a united kingdom. The Queen seems to regard the land in terms of Eden, too. However, among the play's multifarious descriptions, the land is qualified as 'waste' (2.1.103), 'declining' (2.1.240), 'woeful' (2.2.99), 'fearful' (3.2.110), 'fresh, green' (3.3.47), 'revolting' (3.3.163), 'blessed' (4.1.18), and so on.

Allusions to the land are a key factor in the persistent materialism of the play. Critic Andrew Gurr offers a valuable insight when he notes that 'most of the images in the play are organised in relation to the four elements: earth, air fire and water' (Gurr, p. 23). In a manner specific to the early modern period the earth/land also represents wealth (and therefore power). Richard's seizure of the Lancaster estates is of course a major driving force in the play's theme of justice, since his sequestration is a species of sin (and in Act 2 York complains that Richard had wantonly surrendered important lands to the French).

To the Servant the land is a woman, snatched and ravished like Helen of Troy, and to be redeemed by knightly Bullingbrook. Richard himself recognises that the virgin land is sacred:

> For that our kingdom's earth should not be soiled
> With that dear blood which it hath fostered ...

> (1.3.125–6)

On his return from Ireland he salutes his 'Dear earth' (3.2.6), his 'gentle earth' which is so hallowed that he actually believes 'This earth shall have feeling' (24).

If the whole earth is their hospital, their temple or shrine, then the blood is its balm, humectant and living essence. The imagery of blood in the text is every bit as luminous as that of the land. In Act 1 blood is identified with the passionate rivalry and hatred between Bullingbrook and Mowbray, and we have already noted (in context 1) how blood stands for vitality, elite kinship and nobility of action (see especially 1.2.1, 1.2.10). At 1.1.119 Richard links 'our sacred blood' to kinship and to God, the 'best blood' (line 149). In widening the connotations of the sign, 'blood' therefore likewise encompasses Christ's self-sacrifice so much so that at the end of this play (and the start of *1Henry IV*) Bullingbrook's intended pilgrimage to the Holy Land of Palestine aspires to

... wash this blood off from my guilty hand    (5.6.50)

There is good blood and there is blood gone bad. Here the Gardener conceives of blood in medico-horticultural terms – chiefly the release of superfluous or bad blood from the body in order to restore the balance of the humours (see Glossary) and thus good health. In the above passage, the Gardener's scrupulousness serves as a foil to Richard's ineffectualness. The Gardener draws superfluous 'sap and blood' (line 59) to extract the 'overproud men who threaten the body politic'. By contrast, in Act 1 imprudent Richard misjudges the time and the need for the same operation with the 'overproud' Mowbray and Bullingbrook:

Wrath-kindled gentlemen, be ruled by me
Let's purge this choler without letting blood

(1.1.153–4)

What makes this passage one of the most fascinating in the play derives from two major features in particular. The first is the cogent and creative allegory of government which the Servant draws from a germ of the idea in the Gardener's instructions. The other is the cross-current of conflict and unresolved desire or aspiration which it ignites. The most evident tension in the extract is that between the two principal characters and their desire for good and stable government of the land.

The Gardener's instructions are advice in action. The King ought to have been more direct and ruthless to those who either sought to parasitise or challenge his right ('Had he done so ...', 61). And he ought to have cared for this sacred land to nurture a healthy and virtuous commonwealth.

### (iv) Lines 72–82: *'yet what I say is true'*

'When Adam delved and Eve span, who was then the gentleman?' Did Shakespeare, when he was writing *Richard II*, recall these words of John Ball's? This couplet, the opening words of a sermon by Ball, was directed at farm labourers at the start of the movement that developed into the Peasants' Revolt of 1381 in the fourth year of Richard's reign. Along with Wat Tyler, Ball was a principal mover in the rising that became a pivotal and inspiring moment in England's social history, a radical outburst against the entrenched injustice in the English social order. His sermon closed with the rousing entreaty: 'I exhort you to consider that now the time has come, appointed to us by God, in which ye may (if ye will) cast off the yoke of bondage, and recover liberty.'

Whether or not Shakespeare knew these momentous words, their spirit matches that of the Servant's misgivings, and they are rekindled in the Queen's seething ripostes to 'old Adam's likeness', 'What Eve, what serpent', 'thou little better thing than earth'. Her response to the labourer's mutinous hubris reveals how much of their conversation she has gathered:

> O, I am pressed to death through want of speaking!    (72)

Her impatient 'O' seizes their attention with the abrupt shock of discovery. 'Pressed to death' refers to one Elizabethan method of torturing Catholics who chose to remain silent under interrogation (by loading heavy rocks on the victim's chest). Then, as she emerges swiftly from the shadowy verdure of her hiding place she scolds the workers:

> Thou, old Adam's likeness, set to dress this garden,
> How dares thy harsh rude tongue sound this unpleasing news?    (73–4)

The great majority of scenes in *Richard II* open with a command or stabbing question. People here are accustomed to barking out questions and commands (with the exception of the servants, all of them feel *they* were born to command rather than to sue). These, along with the turbulent action, work to generate the almost palpable feeling of stress and hypertension in the play; everyone seems to be under a constant strain.

The Queen furiously blasts the Gardener for his rude impertinence and then lambasts him with four withering questions. Yet we suspect that her dudgeon stems less from his insolence than from his enunciation of her worst fear, Richard's overthrow.

Unlike her vacillating, inattentive husband, the Queen comes over as more focused, more resolutely single-minded. Yet, seen in the context of the play as a whole, she is without genuine political power, a consort rather than an effectual queen. Her authority derives vicariously through relationship with her husband, whose power, the Gardener recognises, comes from value, status and respect, which in turn is predicated on power, force and fear.

Like the rest of the women in the play, she is removed from the main important action, based as it is on the politics of men – literally so here, removed to York's garden. The Duchess of Gloucester tries in 1.2 to incite ancient Gaunt to avenge her husband's murder and, later, the Duchess of York pleads with Bullingbrook for her son's life. Typically then, in a play about power and politics, the women are presented as essentially marginalised, powerless figures restricted to influence at one or more stages removed and to actions that must issue through intermediaries. In practice the Queen's power is limited to bossing around a few ineffective attendants and servants.

Having said that, what is the function of the Queen in *Richard II*? Her presence comes across as more like a role than a character. In this scene she is the hidden but ubiquitous power of subjugation, given a tender façade. Does this mean she is merely a type, a stage device? To answer this, try to imagine what would have been lost had she been entirely omitted from the play. She is a useful escort to the King in 2.1, when he visits Gaunt at Ely House, but in all the scenes in which she appears her input is chiefly emotional. Her outburst here gives her a clearer outline, while more substantial speeches in 5.1 have fine feeling and touching poetry. And still, after 2.1 her lot is that of grief, the heavy thought of care.

In her expression of genuine and selfless devotion to Richard, the Queen is a counter-presence to the King's fawning caterpillars. The grief that she feels here and in 2.1 is mostly in response to her husband's disaster – and if, as many readers believe, Richard is homosexual, then her unswerving loyalty to an unresponsive spouse is perhaps even more commendable. She responds to desperate news less as a queen than as a woman, a wife, and this is what, above all, she brings to the play.

It is no surprise to discover that the Queen's incensed verse has an irregular metre here. Her sentences are direct and hostile, typically made up of insistent and harassing questions and imperatives (five questions in her short volley in the above extract). She underlines her aggression and hauteur by demeaning the Gardener by using 'thou', 'thee' and 'thy', which in Shakespeare are the characteristic forms of address to a servant or child by a social superior or adult (see lines 19 and 23). Commonly, servants and children address individuals of higher class as 'you' and 'your' – as in line 90 (though Shakespeare is by no means consistent in this).

Accordingly, the Gardener directs *his* underlings as 'thou' (29, 33) and 'thy' (47) and the Servant defers to him as 'you' (67). On the other hand why, after the Queen has exited, does the Gardener speak of her as 'thy' (see lines 102–3)? The reason may simply be that understanding her downfall, he patronises her somewhat sentimentally, as a protective father would a child.

This pronoun pattern has highly interesting implications for some other key exchanges in *Richard II* and it is worth noting some of these here. For instance, in the opening scene of the play Bullingbrook insults Mowbray by speaking to him as 'thou', for example at 1.1.35; and Mowbray throws the insult back at him at 1.1.124. Richard, as we may expect, treats them both equally below him as 'thou'. On the other hand, despite his ordeal of exile and then triumphant deposition, Bullingbrook persists in deferring to Richard as 'you' (there are many examples in Act 4). But we can never be sure whether this is genuine fealty or simply a symbolic gesture (this is more important than it may at first appear, since if the former is true then this could imply that Richard's murder was not perhaps directed by Bullingbrook).

## Context Passage 4: 4.1.162–214

Following his surrender at Flint Castle in Act 3, Richard is escorted to London for the formal resignation of his kingship (foreseen by the gardener in 3.4). Act 4 consists of only one, long climactic scene, and contains the famous 'deposition' section which, on account of its seditious potential, was excised from the early printed Folios (and perhaps performances) of the play. It is an Act of fierce emotions and decisive confrontations enacted in the Westminster Hall.

The scene begins with opposing factions hurling barbed accusations at each other over the still-unresolved question of Gloucester's murderer, the very issue which had kick-started the play. It presents a number of dramatic and formal echoes of 1.1, creating some interesting ironies. Now we witness Bullingbrook conducting himself as if he were already king, centre stage, sitting in judgement on competing allegations of treason. After York announces that Richard resigns his crown to Bullingbrook (111), the Bishop of Carlisle recoils in horror at a sin 'heinous, black, obscene' (131), and prophesies disastrous civil wars as a direct result (140). Bullingbrook now commands that Richard be brought before them for a public show of surrender, to keep the business 'Without suspicion' (157) and that Richard's abdication be seen as voluntary.

I have selected a passage for discussion from the central section of the scene. Richard, now effectively deposed, looks dejectedly back on those seemingly faithful supporters who deceived and betrayed him:

*Re-enter York, with Richard, and Officers bearing the regalia*

| | | |
|---|---|---|
| *Richard*: | Alack, why am I sent for to a king | |
| | Before I have shook off the regal thoughts | |
| | Wherewith I reigned? I hardly yet have learned | |
| | To insinuate, flatter, bow, and bend my knee. | 165 |
| | Give sorrow leave awhile to tutor me | |
| | To this submission. Yet I well remember | |
| | The favours of these men. Were they not mine? | |
| | Did they not sometime cry 'All hail!' to me? | |
| | So Judas did to Christ, but he, in twelve | 170 |

Found truth in all but one, I in twelve thousand none.
God save the King! Will no man say Amen?
Am I both priest and clerk? well then, Amen.
God save the King, although I be not he,
And yet Amen if heaven do think him me.                          175
To do what service am I sent for hither?

*York*:          To do that office of thine own good will
Which tired majesty did make thee offer,
The resignation of thy state and crown
To Henry Bullingbrook.                                          180

*Richard*:       Give me the crown. Here, cousin, seize the crown,
On this side my hand and on that side thine.
Now is this golden crown like a deep well
That owes two buckets, filling one another,
The emptier ever dancing in the air,                            185
The other down, unseen and full of water.
That bucket down and full of tears am I,
Drinking my griefs whilst you mount up on high.

*Bullingbrook*:  I thought you had been willing to resign.
*Richard*:       My crown I am, but still my griefs are mine.         190
You may my glories and my state depose,
But not my griefs. Still am I king of those.

*Bullingbrook*:  Part of your cares you give me with your crown.
*Richard*:       Your cares set up do not pluck my cares down.
My care is loss of care, by old care done.                      195
Your care is gain of care, by new care won.
The cares I give I have, though given away.
They 'tend the crown, yet still with me they stay.

*Bullingbrook*:  Are you contented to resign the crown?
*Richard*:       Aye – no. No – aye, for I must nothing be,           200
Therefore no 'no', for I resign to thee.
Now, mark me how I will undo myself.
I give this heavy weight from off my head
And this unwieldy sceptre from my hand,
The pride of kingly sway from out my heart.                     205
With mine own tears I wash away my balm;
With mine own hands I give away my crown;
With mine own tongue deny my sacred state;
With mine own breath release all duteous oaths.

All pomp and majesty I do forswear;                    210
My manors, rents, revenues I forgo;
My acts, decrees, and statutes I deny.
God pardon all oaths that are broke to me;
God keep all vows unbroke are made to thee!

I have chosen this passage because it represents a key watershed in the action, the strategic and thematic climax to the play, which draws together important elements of theme and character. The scene has gone by many names – depending on the observer's point of view – including the deposition, abdication, resignation, Westminster or Parliament scene. As an ironic mirror of 1.1 it marks a new, if most troubled and untidy beginning, and conversely a ragged ending to the medieval order, a significant moment in England's history.

This important passage seems to me to move through three fairly clear stages from (i) Richard's entry and complaints of disloyalty (lines 162–76) through (ii) York's and Bullingbrook's promptings to him (lines 177–99), ending with (iii) Richard's formal submission (lines 200–14).

### (i)   Lines 162–76: 'So Judas did to Christ'

How can we describe Richard's mood and state of mind here? Accustomed to giving commands rather than suing, his first words consist of a weary question. The summons from Bullingbrook seems premature – though Bullingbrook is anxious to proceed. 'Before I have shook off ...' refers to the regal office but also, and with grave irony, to life itself – implying his conviction of personal doom. The question points directly to his loss of power, being now at Bullingbrook's beck and call, and he appears passive, without the direction of his former 'regal thoughts'.

All the same, in the next sentence, his imagery of sycophancy (insinuate, flatter, etc.) casts ironically back to his prime as king. In this regard, the presence of Bagot here is significant, and perhaps Richard's remarks are aimed at him, recalling 'these men' on whom his favours (gifts and advancements) were once conferred. This also indicates just how much political negotiation has been carried out since his surrender at Flint Castle. Crestfallen, he finds the transition too hurried and *begs* for time to grieve and get accustomed to his new lowliness (yet another postponement!).

He enquires if these nobles were 'mine'. As a monarch, indeed, he possessed them in a feudal sense, as they owed him their life and fortunes, but in a more general sense he had mistakenly assumed their loyalty to him, counted in the lists as his own. But he focuses on memory, 'before', 'remember', 'sometime' – he is yesterday's man. While he does not have the ferocious defiance of Coriolanus, he will not go gently, and he warms to the attention that now locates him once again centre stage.

At first Richard sounds as if he is talking to himself, as though he is slightly psychotic. Feeling alone in mind, he may actually be muttering to himself. With its many rhetorical questions, much of Richard's opening section comes to resemble interior monologue, the inner voice, distracted until York and Bullingbrook snap him into the reality of the moment.

Yet he *is* centre stage, for the nonce, with stage presence and some spirit yet, even in defeat. He conceals his dejection for now with a lambent stoicism. This is the God-shielded King who once called on angels to hurl back the Bullingbrook's troops (3.2.60–2), only to discover that either they cannot or that the angels too have deserted him. Centre stage again, he is conscious of himself as the sacral King, ordained by God, now brought low.

Shakespeare's kings are seldom magnificent men – almost all the kings and dukes in early modern drama are either weak or wicked or both (there are numerous instances, such as Marlowe's *Edward II*, or the duke in Tourneur's *The Revenger's Tragedy*). However Shakespeare does presents to us an idea of what a good king would be. A king is but ordinary humanity thrust unto greatness by dint of power or default. With Richard we become progressively aware of the man underneath as we peer increasingly deeper into his consciousness – from here on we see more of what Richard *is* than what he *does*.

Richard's opening speech here begins and ends with a question – 'why am I sent for'? This seems to imply that negotiations had been going on off stage and he believed the transfer of kingship and power was complete, hence 'to a king'. He wonders why he has been summoned hither. Perhaps it is to torment and humiliate ('bow and bend') in a formal 'submission' (167). As a result he is testy, and rather than acknowledge his own large part in his demise he seeks some object on which to externalise his frustrations.

This scene is one of several points on the long downward cadence of Richard's unremitting decline, beginning at 2.4.19 (if not earlier). Behind this fall lies the characteristic situation of Richard facing a crucially decisive moment, but vacillating as the opportunity fizzles away, usually in bathos (for example, in 1.3). Here he is acutely acquiescent. It is the sad slow waste of time, dissipating Richard like a sickness that has a brief remission before drawing on inexorably to its fatal conclusion.

The profusion of religious imagery in this, linked with Richard, has some crucial reverberations. As well as identifying himself with Christ, it reminds the audience of the religious theme of kingship. For the third time it stigmatises his betrayers, and Bullingbrook in particular, as not merely renegade impostors but simoniacs too (John of Gaunt insinuated that Richard too was guilty of this in 'leasing out' the 'dear land' of England; see Context Passage 2 above).

Christ, too, was God's appointed 'captain', but few are less Christlike in the play than Richard. Christ loved his fellow man but Richard loves himself. The 'Judas' reference may also be simply a gestural flourish, a feeble twitch to grab the high moral or political ground. To reach this Richard strives for a narrative by which to frame his dire predicament and thus strike a blow at Bullingbrook. On the other hand, it can be argued that Richard has a tendency to live at one remove from the present, living out a role rather than 'being' in any vigorous, engaged sense, in contrast with the spirited Bullingbrook. Now he plays the role of Christ before Pilate on his own *via dolorosa*. This role-play is an extension of his fondness to take refuge in narratives about himself (the play teems with references to story-telling):

> For God's sake let us sit upon the ground
> And tell sad stories of the death of kings ...
>
> (3.2.155–6)

(ii)  Lines 177–99: '*Part of your cares you give me with your crown*'

York judiciously reminds Richard to keep to their prior agreement, that he resign his 'state and crown' (cf. line 189). So many important events and negotiations occur in this play which are out of sight, off-stage. For example, the key trigger of the play, the murder of Thomas Woodstock, happens before the first scene and we never find out for certain who committed it or why. How is Bagot suddenly in attendance in the current scene? Likewise, who if anyone gives the order for the murder of Richard at Pomfret? Via these and other unanswered questions Shakespeare sustains the ambivalence, maintains suspense, and keeps us at arm's length.

Returning to the passage, notice how York is equally judicious in his choice of words about the exact nature of Richard's quitting – is it a deposition or an abdication? In applying a firm but careful pressure York treads a most tricky line, one replete with irony: 'of thine own good *will*', 'make thee *offer*', '*resignation*'. In reality Richard is, of course, forced to resign, to abdicate, and it is a *de facto* deposition. Yet in his attempts at diplomacy York succeeds only in drawing attention to the very question of why the King is resigning.

York cunningly refers to Bullingbrook as 'tired majesty', that is 'attired', clothed in the garments of king. York is old-school, medievalist, essentially a loyal supporter of the Establishment and of the rightful monarch, but he is also a pragmatist, a man of Realpolitik, and knows the transition from Richard to Bullingbrook has to be managed, coaxing Richard towards his displacement before the new order.

York is an adept mediator. As an interface he tries to palliate the tension between the true King and the pretender. Moreover, by referring to Bullingbrook as 'attired majesty' he drops in an affront to Bullingbrook, implying that the upstart is nothing more than military power dignified by royal costume. Bullingbrook wears the garments of a king and he has the stronger force but he is not the heir by right and certainly not while the true King is alive. York's final obeisant insult is to refer to the deposer simply as 'Henry Bullingbrook', not even as the Duke of Hereford.

For this reason, Bullingbrook is content to stand back and see if York can swing it, no doubt by prior agreement. The critic John Russell Brown has made the interesting point that 'The audience is continually aware of Bullingbrook's presence but he seems to stand further back from them than Richard does' (Brooke, p. 88). In fact, and ironically, Richard effectively manages to dominate the scene.

Poignantly Richard asks them to 'give' him the crown, actually his own crown. Aware of his central position he becomes playfully expansive, indulging the attention, goading his cousin to a game of tug-of-war with the golden crown as plaything. Following two or three relatively quiet, verbal scenes the stage suddenly comes alive with visual drama and fun, albeit a kind of gallows humour.

Richard could well become highly animated here, taking his cue from items like 'seize, 'dancing', 'in the air', 'mount up on high', 'bucket down'. Certainly his conceit about the movement of two buckets is a brilliant piece of figurative dexterity.

Bullingbrook had intended the scene to be a set piece to publicly authorise the transfer of power, but Richard awkwardly jacks up the tension, exploiting it as a *coup de théâtre*. By taunting Bullingbrook with the crown, precious object of desire, Richard contrives to satirise it, deflating its iconic power (at 3.2.160 it is visualised by Richard himself as the 'hollow crown'). In the process, Richard's game succeeds with clear irony in robbing back some of Bullingbrook's new power.

Richard's dexterous performance is skilfully structured and his metaphor of the reciprocating buckets is apt and of good credit. For any readers not accustomed to drawing their water at the well, the idea is that the two buckets are roped around the winding axle in such a way that as the full one is wound up, the empty descends to the water below.

The implication in Richard's metaphor is that their relationship is mutually causal – the action of one intimately driving the other. The movement of the two buckets matches the antithetical careers of the two protagonists. The water of the well and of Richard's tears echo and extend the play's aquatic and lustral imagery. At the same time there is something menacingly perverse about the sportive movement of the two buckets, a cruel joke played on their relationship, almost like two convicts shackled to each other by their mutual disaffection.

Not surprisingly, Richard's choice of the phrase 'mount up' (line 188) is trenchant since it implies that Bullingbrook was the author and mover of the rebellion. Moreover, in Elizabethan lore 'mount' has symbolic negative connotations because it is linked with single-minded political ambition, as in Shakespeare's *King John*, where the

Bastard is a 'mounting spirit' (1.1.206), and in *Titus Andronicus* Aaron steels himself to revenge with

> Then Aaron, army thy heart, and fit thy thoughts,
> To mount aloft with thy imperial mistress
>
> (2.1.12–13)

For once Richard's mind is energised, and like a sparkling dynamo his thoughts are nearing full power. He grasps the audience's full attention in his fist, as he did in Act 1. But under this high-pitch bravura we may infer that the driving force is really only pure emotion, bordering on hysteria. It is his final turn of the meagre screw. He waspishly stings Bullingbrook by linking him with the 'empty bucket', lacking substance, a parvenu bereft of hereditary right to the throne.

Moving to Bullingbrook, his short, highly disciplined direct statements contrast with Richard's more prolix expansive poetry. The latter's utterances are consciously looser, winding and mauve, making the most of his obdurate fifteen minutes in the limelight. In due course, Bullingbrook's short pithy rejoinders abruptly bring Richard's flight to a stop, holding him to the subject. It is a backhanded rebuke.

Bullingbrook's three sharp bullet points can be summed up as something like:

– Are you backsliding?   (189);
– I'll relieve you of any anxieties about   (193);
– I want everyone to know that he does this freely   (199).

Clearly Bullingbrook's patience approaches the tipping point, and these three curt utterances show the pressure that is building inside Bullingbrook, his outward words holding back the inward impatience with this procrastinator.

Yet why is this even happening? Why does Bullingbrook endure this mocking performance? And why hasn't he already despatched this troublesome itch away to Pomfret? We have already noted that Bullingbrook wished the transition to be 'Without suspicion' (157).

It is not difficult to imagine that Bullingbrook himself desires the whole intricate transaction. Manipulating this Richard's play-acting has a strong eroticising effect, as power often does. A *coup d'état* being such a blunt instrument, Bullingbrook desires respectability, which is why he also insists on the spectacle. For the man who originally sought merely the restitution of his Lancastrian property, the golden crown looms up as powerfully seductive bonus. It has become a bold assertion of his masculinity as he emasculates the withering monarch.

Richard's reply to Bullingbrook's invitation to resign is crucial in its dramatic weight

My crown I am, but still my griefs are mine.   (190)

In this single line Richard points directly to the dual aspect of kingship: the King and the man (the semi-divine and the mortal). He may formally surrender the crown but there yet remains the man, characterised by his 'griefs', the pains, a sea of troubles, which all mortals are heir to. Does this then mean he is an ordinary man, one who just happens to have held the job of king for a time? Not in Richard's eyes.

(iii)   Lines 200–14: '*All pomp and majesty I do forswear*'

Bullingbrook's third terse challenge at line 199, cool and direct, renders Richard highly confused, a mind distracted and confined, struggling desperately to reassert a kingly demeanour.

*Bullingbrook*: Are you contented to resign the crown?   (199)

Richard seems entirely wrong-footed by Bullingbrook's brusque confrontation, which suddenly compels him back to a reality somehow detached from words. His immediate response may be delivered as either garbled – or indeed exquisitely adroit:

Aye – no. No – aye, for I must nothing be ...

To a reader this can look like incertitude, or even impotence: 'Yes, er, no. No, er, yes.' But to a listener it is a sound pun, designating a deeper malaise; so his words can sound like: 'I? no. Not I, because

I must become nothing.' And there can be complex permutations of the two positions (this complexity may itself be a symptom of a mind in free-fall).

Richard's next line extends this notion of the sound pun: 'Therefore no "no"' – punning on 'no/know'. Or, more likely, he intends to mean: 'no, I do not deny you, for here I resign'. Bullingbrook's persistence at last hits home.

The cadence in line 201 operates like an enormous sigh of capitulation, 'for I resign to thee'. In some ways it marks the semantic climax of the entire play. After the pause, however, at the end of this line Richard once more wrests centre stage from Bullingbrook in a final, defiant grand remonstrance. It is a ritualistic performance, literally the dismantling of power, ('Now, mark me ...') 'now, everybody, take notice of *me*'. Accordingly his diction switches from repetition of punning wordplay to repetition of high sacrament.

What follows is a litany that reverses the usual rite of coronation. The chanting spell of anaphora (opening each of a series of lines with the same phrase) echoes the rhetorical force of true religious litany, and this has the effect of stressing the finality of Richard's action. In addition, the repeated intoning of 'mine' together with 'I' (nine times) and 'my' (eight times) stresses the egocentricity and the pride (the 'pride of kingly sway') which have characterised his career since the outset. It is of course one more of Richard's 'sad stories' with himself its centre.

Lopez finds all this ceremonious undoing very much pre-scripted by Richard (Lopez, p. 59) and A.D. Nuttall believes that when Richard undoes himself he is actually 'half-able to enjoy the process of his own unmaking' (Nuttall, p. 305). This contrasts markedly with King Lear, mad on the heath, ripping away his clothes in an tumult of anguish. Richard, ever able to stand aside from himself, seems to me to be assuaged by this final act of his kingship, gratified to be rid of its 'cares'. It is this knack of becoming detached (and see line 173) that makes possible his satirical bravura – at least at this point.

If we spool back momentarily to Gaunt's 'sceptred isle' speech we can see how the old man's words reverberate through the play to cast their judgement on the current scene. His idealism of the 'royal throne' and 'teeming womb of royal kings' imparts a sense of justice to Richard's unmaking here, casting the current scene in a quite scabrous light. However, it almost goes without saying that in the moral scales, Richard's reckoning nowhere redeems Bullingbrook of his usurpation.

For better or worse, it is a different kind of Richard we witness here compared to the opening act of the play. In many ways this is a rounder, fuller man, at last seasoned. The alarming prospect of his uncrowning has focused his mind consummately. He is not quite at the point of full self-realisation – that will come in Act 5. His language in this extract maps an arc in close affinity with his metamorphosis. His mind phases here via interior confusion, vacillation, lucidity, public candour. Utterances toggle between questions, obscure statement and flippant satire, through to bold if despondent proclamation at just about the point where he resigns his identity to Bullingbrook ('I must nothing be').

In a seminal study of 1957, the critic E.H. Kantorowicz explored the concept of the 'king's two bodies', a concept holding that in the medieval bitmap, a king is thought to comprise two integral selves or 'bodies'. The divine self is derived from God, and the human or legal self is mortal and so shared with all mankind. Kantorowicz describes *Richard II* as the 'tragedy of the King's Two Bodies' since, in the end, 'kingship itself comes to mean Death, and nothing but Death' (Brooke, pp. 171–3).

In the above passage we see a clearer view of Richard the man, uncoupling from Richard the King, paring away what we know to be the mask of kingship, his royal identity.

Now, mark me how I will undo myself   (202)

Richard declares what to a medieval listener would have been unthinkable, that it is possible to separate the dual aspects of a king, the divine office and the mortal being, the pair being in fact being facets of an indivisible one.

In an earlier scene York calls Richard a 'sacred king' (3.3.9), a being composed of the essence of 'kingliness'. When Richard attempts to resist Bullingbrook's coercion, he proclaims, 'My crown I am' (190), in other words, that Richard as King is an indissoluble entity of man and divine. Likewise, when he asks, 'Am I both priest and clerk?' this is a rhetorical question since, as King, he combines within himself both godly and secular elements. In contrast Bullingbrook ushers in the modern view, King as purely the office, his duties, and 'tired majesty', man made king.

For many people *Richard II* represents above all a discourse on the nature and powers of kingship. For sure, a multiplicity of references, actions, discussions on the theme surge to a dramatic and thematic peak here in 4.1. More exactly, symbolically and dramatically the play climaxes at the point when in line 287 Richard smashes his glass/mirror, following which comes the epiphany:

> How soon my sorrow hath destroyed my face.    (4.1.290)

William C. Carroll identifies two ideas on kingship prevalent in the early modern period: the 'providential' view in which the King is understood to be ruling as God's own vice-regent, and the 'contractual' view, where validation of the divine right of a monarch lies in the consensus of their subjects. Carroll goes on to describe two further themes which dominated the discussion of kingship in this period – one, the matter of whether it was ever right to kill a king or rebel against his rule and, two, the question of the principles of royal succession (in practice, the patrilinear model tended to prevail, that is, eldest son of the eldest son – see Dutton and Howard, pp. 127–39)

Clearly Shakespeare taps into these topical themes, not solely in the English histories but also in *Hamlet* and *Macbeth*; for instance:

> *Hamlet*: A bloody deed. Almost as bad, good mother,
>      As kill a king and marry with his brother.
> *Queen*:  As kill a king?
>
>                        (*Hamlet* 3.4.28–30)

To murder a king would not simply be to commit a crime and a sin but would also be to threaten the universal order itself. Given the Tudor view of a hierarchical cosmos, the assassination of the King by any member of the lower orders would amount to a devastating act of hubris, an act of disruption against the whole of the human sphere.

Given both the above strictures on kingship, Bullingbrook has no natural right to the throne. Clearly he is not appointed by God and he is not even next in line of descent (the rightful heirs to Richard are the Mortimers, descended from Lionel, Duke of Clarence – see *1Henry VI* 2.5.64–78 and *1Henry IV* 1.3.142–55, and the family tree above, p. x). Furthermore, Richard is manifestly still alive.

As we have already noted, York refers to Bullingbrook as 'tired majesty', stressing that Bullingbrook's claim really only rests on his might. For York, a man of the medieval school, Bullingbrook's kingship would be solely as a persona. Taking away from Richard all the robes and crown, throne, palaces, etc., would amount to merely stripping away the appurtenances, the badge of the office, not the essence of king-ness. Likewise, Carlisle, in one of the most powerful speeches of the play, recoils at Bullingbrook's threat to 'ascend the regal throne' (4.1.113):

> What subject can give sentence on his king,
> And who sits here that is not Richard's subject?
>
> (4.1.121–2)

He speaks out against Bullingbrook, warning that such an outrageous offence against the present order will bring down tumultuous civil wars on generations to come: 'Disorder, horror, fear and mutiny' (l.142).

The idea of a ruler as a god or demi-god can be traced back to pre-Christian times. Before the Reformation the assumption of Divine Right of kings is a commonplace. Shakespeare himself refers to the idea of a king being sacred in *Macbeth*, where Malcolm describes how a king possesses miraculous healing powers derived from God (4.3.147–59). And after the Reformation the new Protestant rulers seized on this ideology as a source of their own authority, in order to bypass Rome. And in 1597, about the same time as the first staging of *Richard II*, James VI of Scotland published a book in which he declared that kings are by God himself addressed as 'god'.

## Conclusions

As a means of a concluding our discussion we can consider one of the most vital questions for audiences of *Richard II*: to what extent is this history play also a tragedy? When the editors of the first collected edition of Shakespeare's plays, namely Hemminge and Condell, were splitting up his oeuvre into three distinct genres, COMEDIES, HISTORIES, TRAGEDIES, they naturally enough placed this play with the other English histories. But supposing Shakespeare had written no other English histories, how would you have classified it? The obvious answer is in the TRAGEDIES, and indeed the printer of the first Quarto (1597), one Valentine Simmes, titled it 'THE Tragedie of King Richard the second' – though there are no grounds for supposing that Shakespeare himself had any hand in this. Yet if we do pronounce it a tragedy there must be some positive and internal reasons for this choice. These reasons begin with a consideration of the interaction of Richard's identity and fate.

From 4.1 onwards we become increasingly conscious of Richard's psychological complexity. His anxieties (or 'cares' again) grow and draw to a crisis in his grasp of his own character, of what and who he is. If the play had ended at the close of 3.3 we may have been less inclined to see Richard himself as a tragic figure. But it does not, and what follows is central to understanding Richard as a tragic figure:

> My crown I am ...
> Aye – no. No – aye, for I must nothing be ...
> Now, mark me how I undo myself.
>
> (3.3.190–202)

First Richard identifies himself with the crown, metonymy of kingship. But then he becomes uncertain, *I? ... no. No 'I', for I must be or become no thing. Watch me undo myself.* Without kingship he feels he is nothing, bereft of identity, especially as this was everything, all that defined him as a man as well. Richard talks of removing the 'pride of kingly sway from out my heart' (205): from out my *heart*. And there's the rub. Line 205 protests how integral kingship is to Richard's personality; it is his very heart (and consequently a deposed Richard will later tell his wife to think of him as dead; 5.2.38).

Is *Richard II*, then, a tragedy? Is Richard, therefore, a tragic hero? Is Richard a victim of others' machinations, or is he chiefly the author of his own demise? The usual starting point for a discussion of tragedy is the work of the ancient Greek philosopher, Aristotle, and in particular his book on the theory of poetry and drama, *The Poetics*. Written in the early fourth century BC, this treatise has had an enormous influence on literature, especially on the dramatists of the early modern period, and accordingly it will be helpful to examine some of its key points both for our current discussion and for other history plays in this study.

First, Aristotle's comments are less prescriptive than descriptive. His typical approach in all his philosophy is to observe characteristics in the status quo; in other words, he asks what are the characteristics of the most successful tragedies. He finds that these usually contain a single plot that imitates real life, with a serious theme that has 'magnitude'. Usually the plot is complete in itself, with a unity of time, place and action (i.e. over a short period, with one or very few locations), since Aristotle believed that these constraints intensified the action and feelings. The incidents in the drama should arouse pity and terror in order to bring about catharsis, a purging of feelings, for the audience. He cited *Oedipus Rex* by Sophocles as embodying the best of these tragic features.

On the tragic hero, Aristotle observed that he or she would be of a high reputation and status (usually aristocratic), but not someone who was 'pre-eminently virtuous or just'. The hero's fortunes change from happiness to misery, a fall in fortunes caused not by 'depravity' but by some great error on his own part. It is important for the tragedy that the plot and hero should have universality, to enable the audience to identify with the central figure and thereby purge their emotions. Aristotle adds that usually there occurs a reversal in plot or situation (*peripeteia*) which would enable the hero to have insight on himself, a realisation (*anagnorisis*) just before their inevitable catastrophe comes about.

This is a simple plan, but it is important to distinguish the literary use of the term 'tragedy' from that of the media. The tabloids and the BBC often refer to stories such as 'Tragic Fire in Warehouse' or 'Tragedy of Man Killed in M-way Crash'. In these cases, what they usually mean is something like 'a serious', 'horrifying' or 'lethal incident'. They are not necessarily tragic, according to Aristotle's criteria.

Which is not say that these criteria are hard and fast. A great many modern playwrights have manipulated and expanded this classical view of tragic drama. Samuel Beckett, Bertholt Brecht, Henrik Ibsen, Federico García Lorca and Arthur Miller are among many writers who have created tragic heroes, often out of everyday men and women and commonplace situations.

Equally, the action of *Richard II* is not of a single plot, and Shakespeare's plays seldom are (*King Lear* is a good example of a tragedy with multiple but interlocking threads of action, over diverse locations). As the 'buckets' metaphor demonstrates, while Richard and Bullingbrook experience different careers they are nevertheless reciprocally connected, and this reciprocity is a crucial factor in the tragic outcome. The figure also graphically illustrates Aristotle's notion of *peripeteia,* that the hero suffers a reversal of his fate which brings insight:

> That bucket down and full of tears am I,
> Drinking my griefs whilst you mount up on high.   (187–8)

Their are other characteristics of tragedy that also apply to *Richard II.* For instance, some ancient Greek theorists believed that the hero could only be a semi-divine figure – the depiction of Richard as a king ordained by God aptly fits this requirement.

Aristotle stressed that good tragedy was generally framed in a heightened form of language – and *Richard II* perfectly meets this condition in that every character speaks in verse, including the gardeners, as we have noted above. But what about universality? in other words, can we relate to or identify with Richard?

The answer is something of a paradox. Few of us are card-carrying monarchs, so the extent to which we can empathise with Richard will depend instead on the degree of his shared humanity, his errors and suffering as a person. Nevertheless this facet of the tragedy is necessarily compounded with his role as king, his flaws and vulnerability, and the elevated position from which he falls. The extent of the tragedy would depend on the extent of our seeing the king as a person, which Richard himself denies. Important signs of mortality include his venality and his gradual recognition of time's dominion over him. But above all these is Richard's vanity, entailing as it does his egocentricity, arrogance and folly. Vanity (with its twin source in the man as the king) is ironically both the origin of his tragedy and the measure of his catastrophe. We come to the conclusion that kingship, but especially Richard's own strain of it, is indeed his tragedy.

## Suggested Work

To help develop your critical skills, examine another passage from
the play. For example, read again Richard's monologue in Pomfret
Castle at the start of 5.5, lines 1–66, and compare this speech with
that at 1.3.125 on. Try to describe how Richard the King differs
from Richard the man. (A useful starting point is to contrast
Richard's use of personal pronouns in each passage.)

# 2

# *Henry IV Part 1*: History as Comedy

Comedy is the imitation of men worse than the average
Aristotle, *The Poetics* (1449)

Of all Shakespeare's plays printed during his lifetime, *The First Part of Henry the Fourth* sold by far the most copies. By any contemporary standards the play was a huge best-seller. The first two printings, in 1598, sold out immediately, to be followed by four further printings over the next 14 years – an exceptional record for the period.

My title for this chapter describes *1HenryIV* as a comedy as well as a history. To some extent each of Shakespeare's history plays is also a comedy, and my approach throughout this study is to challenge the notion that any play is only of one genre. Here, in *1HenryIV*, there is, of course, plenty of evidence of what we may term conventional comedy, including verbal jokes, knockabout, and the sardonic humour of Sir John Falstaff.

However, there are other important strands of comedy to explore, especially of a structural or dramatic nature. My argument will be that this kind of comedy arises from the perception that the play lacks any central or unifying figure in the way that the other histories do not. This amounts to a vacuum or evasiveness that continually threatens to undermine the equilibrium of power – in the same way that comedy in everyday life can itself be subversive. It is a vacuum that Prince Hal will fill most spectacularly in *2HenryIV*.

64

Because *Henry IV Part 1* is a sequel to *Richard II*, it is no surprise to find some continuity of themes and characters, as well as new directions of the narrative line begun in the latter play. Even so, *1 Henry IV* readily stands on its own many feet, aesthetically autonomous of its prequel, and there are some compelling new characters, such as Falstaff and the tavern hostess, plus Hotspur and Prince Hal now thrust forward to centre stage.

*1 Henry IV* extends the discussion of the kingship theme and the character of King Henry comes under fresh scrutiny, his attention more explicitly embroiled in the anxieties of fatherhood. Consequently the father–son theme (intensified by questions of loyalty and duty) is foregrounded, and this is interconnected with a discussion of state versus private loyalties, duties and ambition. The subject of honour is a major interest of *1 Henry IV* and is examined in the context of themes of friendship and commitment, egotism, honesty and war.

In historical terms *1 Henry IV* opens two years on from Henry's closing avowal (in *Richard II*) to make pious atonement in the Holy Land for the ousting of Richard. His objective has been thwarted by the intervening years of 'civil butchery', and the current play opens with a reaffirmation of his intention.

Henry IV, formerly Henry Bullingbrook, activates the drama with overtures of regret at the turmoil that has befallen himself and his realm since his ousting of Richard:

So shaken as we are, so wan with care ... (1.1.1)

His opening speech carries strong intimations not only of weariness but also of illness ('wan'), as well as churnings of guilt at the domestic war ('civil butchery') that has broken out in the wake of his coronation (he has been king now for about three years). His fearful words bear heavy witness to Carlisle's grim warning of 'disaster, horror, fear and mutiny' if Henry succeeded to the throne (*Richard II* 4.1.142). His prediction appears to have come to pass (and the strife will resonate through the reigns of the Plantagenets until Richard III is killed on Bosworth Field).

I have selected the first passage for analysis from Act 1 Scene 1, which takes place in London at the King's palace. Like *Richard II*,

Part 1 of Henry IV opens with its title character, perhaps indicating that, like Richard, he is soon to be overtaken by more threatening or dynamic people. Even the extract below talks in detail about other men, reporting other protagonists and distant events, making the King a passive spectator on the touchline of history.

## Context Passage 1: 1.1.52–89

The Earl of Westmoreland has already described how the King's general, 'the noble Mortimer', previously despatched to quell a Welsh insurrection, has been captured and his troops butchered by the legendary Welsh general Owen Glendower. Better news is to follow, or so at first it seems:

| | | |
|---|---|---|
| *Westmoreland*: | On Holy-rood day, the gallant Hotspur there, | |
| | Young Harry Percy, and brave Archibald, | |
| | That ever-valiant and approved Scot, | |
| | At Holmedon met, where they did spend | 55 |
| | A sad and bloody hour; | |
| | As by discharge of their artillery, | |
| | And shape of likelihood, the news was told; | |
| | For he that brought them, in the very heat | |
| | And pride of their contention did take horse, | 60 |
| | Uncertain of the issue any way. | |
| *King*: | Here is a dear, and true industrious friend, | |
| | Sir Walter Blunt, new lighted from his horse, | |
| | Stained with the variation of each soil | |
| | Betwixt that Holmedon and this seat of ours; | 65 |
| | And he hath brought us smooth and welcome news. | |
| | The Earl of Douglas is discomfited. | |
| | Ten thousand bold Scots, two-and-twenty knights, | |
| | Balked in their own blood, did Sir Walter see | |
| | On Holmedon's plains. Of prisoners Hotspur took | 70 |
| | Mordake, Earl of Fife and eldest son | |
| | To beaten Douglas, and the Earl of Atholl, | |
| | Of Murray, Angus, and Menteith. | |
| | And is not this an honourable spoil? | |
| | A gallant prize? Ha, cousin, is it not? | 75 |

| | |
|---|---|
| *Westmoreland*: | In faith, it is a conquest for a prince to boast of. |
| *King*: | Yea, there thou makest me sad, and makest me sin |
| | In envy that my Lord Northumberland |
| | Should be the father to so blest a son - |
| | A son who is the theme of honour's tongue,      80 |
| | Amongst a grove the very straightest plant, |
| | Who is sweet Fortune's minion and her pride - |
| | Whilst I by looking on the praise of him |
| | See riot and dishonour stain the brow |
| | Of my young Harry. O that it could be proved      85 |
| | That some night-tripping fairy had exchanged |
| | In cradle-clothes our children where they lay, |
| | And called mine Percy, his Plantagenet! |
| | Then would I have his Harry, and he mine. |

To help our analysis we can readily divide this extract into three parts: in the first, lines 52–61, Westmoreland gives news of the Battle of Holmedon, although he does not yet know the outcome; next, in lines 62–76, the King has received an updated report from Sir Walter Blunt giving details of Hotspur's bloody victory over Archibald, Earl of Douglas; and finally, in lines 77–89, the King's joyous admiration of Hotspur is toned down by chagrin at his own son, Harry Prince of Wales.

(i) Lines 52–61: *'uncertain of the issue'*

The first point I notice about this passage is its detailed particulars, mostly names. Westmoreland refers to 'Holy-rood day' (52), a specific date, 14 September, and an important date in the Christian calendar which commemorates Christ's crucifixion, 'rood' being a traditional synonym for the 'cross'. The Battle of Holmedon, in Northumberland, took place on this day in 1402, when the English, under Lord Percy, Northumberland, routed Archibald's Scottish army.

So we begin with particulars, an exact time and place. And then Westmoreland follows this up with more detailed information: gallant Hotspur, young Harry Percy and brave Archibald, with 'artillery' and 'horse'. His copious adjectives are pressed in to glorify these particulars of the battle – gallant, young, brave, ever-valiant, sad and bloody – (though his account comes second-hand). Conspicuous is the praise of his ally Hotspur, fighting for the English king, and of his foe, the 'approved' Archibald (that is, 'put to the test and acclaimed').

It is almost as though he were commentating on a sports match. Yet Westmoreland acknowledges the savagery of the civil war while at the same time honouring the bravery of a worthy opponent. Such a report for a valiant adversary is a fading reminder of the chivalric ethos that was almost moribund by the close of *Richard II* – and there is more to come on the theme of 'honour' in our discussion of *1Henry IV*.

The play is very much about allegiances, taking sides and loyalty, and also the awareness that loyalties can be altered (another aspect of the play's broader theme of 'honour'). Westmoreland's description, then, has a strong feel of partisan exaggeration about it, and one of its key dramatic objects is to set up in the audience's mind both the courage and the constancy of the young Harry Hotspur.

The ferocity of the battle is measured by the volume of the 'artillery' deployed (57). At first, this word may seem an anachronism, but in reality in the fifteenth century it referred to arrows and other manually powered missiles, rather than to cannon and musketry. It was a 'sad and a bloody hour', as Westmoreland's hendiadys reports, and this is backed up by Blunt's account of the horrific Scottish casualties.

However, the suspense is heightened by the fact that the messenger had quit the scene while the battle's outcome, its 'likelihood', was still in the balance. The suspense is also increased for us by the strong possibility that the messenger was not actually present at the conflict, so we too remain briefly 'uncertain of the issue'.

This brief account has some striking ironies within it, not least of which is that word 'issue' in line 61. In addition to its sense of 'outcome' of the battle, this can mean 'child', here specifically 'son', and we will return to this point shortly. Another irony is that Westmoreland draws attention to the day of the battle: Holy Rood – Christ's crucifixion is concerned with love of humanity, and here we have humanity hell-bent on slaughter. A further irony is that Westmoreland speaks of the two antagonists as though he and the King were equally intimate with the two, as though perhaps he were describing to his head-teacher a brawl in the playground. At the same time, his speech is crucial in setting up some important terms by which the King will judge Hotspur and his own son, ironically his own 'issue', in both senses of the word (lines 77–89).

At the start of this section the unmistakable impression is of reports hurriedly pouring in to the King's headquarters from the distant Holmedon battlefield, mixing rumour and confused facts. The military situation is in a dangerous balance, with risk of grave consequences. Westmoreland was not present at the battle, and his informant may not have been either, and so his is a report of a report, possibly from another source.

Another important effect is to raise Hotspur's heroic stature so much that at this distance he soon becomes heroicised. He is the 'gallant', 'young' conqueror, capturing valuable prisoners, while the King describes him as 'blest' (79) and 'Fortune's minion' (82). Long before we meet him in the flesh, Hotspur has achieved mythic stature, and is marvelled at and respected. In its references to gallantry, duty and loyalty, the passage draws attention to the noble theme of honour, which Hotspur himself epitomises. His youth is stressed, and this makes all these achievements appear the more astonishing – though at this point, in real life, he was aged 39.

These points are fleshed out later in the extract when young Hotspur emerges as the apotheosis of honour. Also, in his decorous conduct and his fealty to the King, he demonstrates the essence of the medieval knight, a ideal whose ominous shadow has lingered over Henry Bullingbrook since the opening to *Richard II*, gradually deepening his sense of guilt.

Stressing Hotspur's youth (in lines 53, 85 and 87) has the additional advantage of functioning as a handy rod to beat Prince Hal's back, propounding a yardstick of the correct action. This is important, for the play is, amongst many things, a *Bildungsroman* – a coming-of-age story, the passage from youth to adulthood – and this element begins to emerge more explicitly in the next section of the above extract.

(ii)  Lines 62–76: '*an honourable spoil*'

From its troubled opening line to its unsettled ending, the play teems with anxiety – fear of military threats, stress about a recalcitrant son, insecurity and uneasiness concerning robberies, riot, threats to rule, plus worry over malign influences and loss of control. 'Care' is now understood as angst. All of these uncertainties intensify during the play and will eventually converge on the battlefield at Shrewsbury. For now, the turmoil simmers away under Westmoreland's report, gradually climaxing in his suspenseful confession:

Uncertain of the issue any     (61)

Yet a new report brings promise of relief:

Here is a dear and true industrious friend ...    (62)

Here the word 'industrious' means 'devoted', and the King seems relieved to have at least one friend he can rely on, trusting his version to be authentic. The realm is under great threat and Henry needs to know who his true and trusty allies are. Clearly Blunt is one such and Hotspur another, for now at least.

The King describes Blunt as 'stained with the variation of each soil' between Holmedon and London. 'Variation' is a curious word here. Henry is emphasising the distance the man has travelled, the many variations in landscape, the word 'soil' being used as a synecdoche ('stained', too, is interesting, and hints at the political dangers at work in the land). Ominously he could equally be pointing to the great variety of political allegiances fracturing the land, since his kingdom is in no way united, the political landscape by no means homogeneous.

But if the land is variable in loyalty, at least Blunt has returned with 'smooth and welcome news' (66), which extends and resolves the uncertainty in Westmoreland's first bulletin. Two important points arise from this news. The first is that the King's allies, the Percys, have vanquished Archibald, killing 10,000 Scots, 'balked' or piled up at the battle. When the King describes the Scots as 'bold' he is not praising their valour (as Westmoreland talked of the 'brave Archibald') but referring to their brazen insubordination (compare the use of the same word at 1.3.16 and 4.1.36). To a large extent Henry regards these attacks as assaults on his own person, his own body standing as a symbol for his realm.

Secondly, Hotspur has captured some notable hostages, seizing Scottish aristocrats such as Mordake and Atholl, as well as Archibald/

Douglas. It is interesting to note too that Hotspur has captured Douglas's 'eldest son', since this phrase anticipates the prickly theme of eldest sons, pointing the discussion in a new and uncomfortable direction after line 76.

So Blunt brings not just news of victory but a catalogue of valuable prisoners, valuable in the sense that these can be ransomed as well as humiliated. The significance of this lies in the fact that Hotspur will later deploy these as leverage in his attempt to free Mortimer, who has been captured by the Welsh. Kinship is a highly important element in the play's complex mechanisms of loyalty and motive (note the King's tag of 'cousin' in referring to Westmoreland, to whom he is related by marriage; line 75).

Edmund Mortimer is Hotspur's brother-in-law and for him, the Scottish prisoners represent a handy bargaining tool for the release of a man who is regarded by the Percy faction as the lawful king of England. We hear this from them later:

> ... [the King] trembling even at the name of Mortimer.
> *Worcester*: I cannot blame him. Was not he proclaimed
>     By Richard that dead is, the next of blood?
> *Northumberland*: He was, I heard the proclamation,
>     And then it was ... the unhappy king
>
> (1.3.142–6)

So with some irony these hostages, a source of welcome news to the King, will become a poisoned chalice in a vortex of intrigue. When Hotspur refuses to release them (they rightfully belong to the 'King'), Henry himself will become a kind of hostage to the Percys.

But this is terrific news to cheer a King 'wan with care', and his exclamation, 'Ha', points to his great relief and the depth of anxiety momentarily lessened. Describing capture as an 'honourable spoil' and a 'gallant prize' draws attention again to the honour theme and Hotspur as its quintessence. It is difficult, however, not to see the oxymoronic effect in 'honourable spoil' which hints at the problem which these prisoners will bring. The sound of the word 'spoil' coalesces with 'stained' (64) and 'stain' (84) to help expand the dualism at work here. It forges a contrast with the discourse of 'honour', and at the same time hesitates the new mood of exaltation.

This sense of ambivalences is brought out into the open by Westmoreland's reply in line 76:

In faith, it is a conquest for a prince to boast of.

Is Westmoreland here making an ingenuous affirmation, or does he intend to direct a loaded remark towards the King's own eldest son? Either way, the result is the same, for the line is a crucial turning-point in the tone of the passage. Hotspur is not a 'prince', so the King interprets this reply as directly pointed at his own 'eldest son'. It is a niggling distraction.

(iii)  Lines 77–89: '*a son who is the theme of honour's tongue*'

When the King speaks of Hotspur's hostages he uses modifiers like 'honourable' and 'gallant', implying that honour demands he should venerate the captor. Not merely has Hotspur won a great battle, but victory has boosted his reputation. And, of course, we should not forget that it attests his loyalty to his king.

Westmoreland's agreement, while ostensibly a positive avowal, produces the effect of suddenly puncturing the King's euphoria. Talk of the exemplary Hotspur reminds him painfully that his own son, Harry the Prince of Wales, was absent from the battle, detained by hedonistic diversions.

The next five lines return to the subject of Hotspur and the father/son theme. Note the irony in the King's citation of '*my* Lord Northumberland': Northumberland had been Henry's principal agent in helping him attain the crown (for example, see *Richard II* 4.1.150 on), and there is a strong idea here that it is actually the Percys who are the backbone, guarantor and true safeguard of the Plantagenet kingship.

To Elizabethan Christians, envy is of course one of the deadly sins. But King Henry has a knack of translating sin into virtue – in *Richard II* he transformed the sin of deposing a rightful king into a virtue by redefining kingship in terms of deserving and pragmatics. He is little if not deft in deployment of words (as Falstaff famously is – and the best of Shakespeare's villains). Thus pride and boasting (not to mention slaughter) can with ease become virtues and part of the drama of honour.

What a magnificent testimonial he confers on Hotspur, the perfect son-warrior. He is 'blest', 'honour's tongue', quintessence of honour and Fortune's favourite. Within his nature and career are combined the best of both Christian and pagan energies, being blessed as well as favoured by the goddess of Fortune. It addition to serving as Fortune's minion, Hotspur is clearly Henry's too, and the King keenly feels the paternal pride of Northumberland, even as he recalls his own pain.

The King adopts the plural or impersonal form of the first-person, 'us' (and 'ours') in line 66 and then switches to the personal form at 85 for his private space, in 'my young Harry'. The pain of what he sees as dishonour is acutely personal. At this moment we do not yet know the details of the 'riot and dishonour' that stain the brow of Prince Hal, although he does make a brief appearance in *Richard II*. There the Prince's proclivities are likewise a source of humiliating irritation to his father, newly crowned as *Henry IV*:

> Can no man tell me of my unthrifty son?
> 'Tis full three months since I did see him last;
> If any plague hang over us, 'tis he.
> I would to God, my lords, he might be found:
> Inquire at London, 'mongst the taverns there,
> For there, they say, he daily doth frequent,
> With unrestrained loose companions,
> Even such, they say, as stand in narrow lanes,
> And beat our watch, and rob our passengers;
> Which he, young wanton and effeminate boy,
> Takes on the point of honour to support
> So dissolute a crew.
>
> (*Richard II* 5.3.1–12)

His repugnance at his son, heir to the Plantagenet crown, is deep and long-lived (there is in real time a three-year gap between the two moments). If to riot and dishonour we also consider his words 'unthrifty', 'wanton' and 'effeminate', we get a good idea of why the King admires so much the virile, manly Hotspur.

Returning to our current extract, in line 85, the King sighs once again, perhaps with exasperation, 'O that it could be proved ...'. 'Night-tripping fairy' is, like 'sweet Fortune', a personification of fate. Then the image of the two cradles side by side subtly establishes the idea that Hotspur and Hal are coeval and therefore apt for comparison in their natures and experiences (in reality Hotspur was actually three years older even than the King!). The King's speech in this section contains a number of alliterative pairs that allow him to spit out his irritation: 'makest me', 'tongue amongst a grove', 'cradle-clothes'.

His comparison climaxes in another alliterative pair:

And called mine Percy, his Plantagenet!

a line which deftly brings together these two parties that will form the major struggle of the play. Henry's intense irritation with his son, combined with the almost religious veneration of Hotspur, sets the stage for the bathos of Hal's appearance in the following scene and for the ironies of allegiance in Scene 3 – both of which have significant ramifications for our appraisal of the King.

What impression, then, emerges of the King from this passage? After Henry's thrilling struggles in *Richard II*, he now comes over as relatively inert and frustrated. He is static, receiving second-hand reports of other men performing great deeds on his behalf. Poring over maps and waiting on news of battle, Henry has become an armchair soldier, transfixed behind the metaphorical desk. He comes across as passive, a victim of age and circumstances. His stage image is poignantly congruous with his own casual allusions to fate in lines 82 and 86.

In reality, fifteenth-century kings did engage in combat, and eventually Henry himself will do so. But for now his power has lapsed. He fights the battle vicariously through his champion, the mighty strutting Hotspur. In line 85, when he gasps with 'O', he demonstrates succinctly his sense of exasperated helplessness. Contrasting with the Henry of the prequel, King Henry's desire is thwarted: he cannot reform his own son and will soon learn that Hotspur thwarts his injunction to surrender the hostages.

The description of Hotspur's achievements points up the gap between himself and Prince Hal. Yet the King is more than proud that his surrogate son, Hotspur, has achieved his knightly *'devoir'*, that is, fulfilled his obligation to his sovereign in terms of courage, dignity, selfless restraint and loyalty. Compare the Henry Bullingbrook of Scene 1 of *Richard II*, whom in many ways Hotspur here resembles: history repeating itself with a difference.

Shakespeare aims to set up in our minds the idea that Hotspur and Prince Hal are coeval (even though in reality Hotspur was by 21 years the elder). This, like the 'cradle' image (87) and the common forename, helps to set them side by side for the purpose of judging. Without doubt this speech is the starting point for the tacit rivalry of the two Henrys that will gather pace and reach its decisive peak in their single combat in Act 5.

This speech is equally significant in demonstrating important strands of the medieval kingship theme which we first encountered in Chapter 1: the idea of the King's different bodies. This theory takes many forms, based on the notion that the King has many 'bodies'. One strand of the concept that holds that a king's identity comprises two integral 'bodies' or selves: the divine derived from God and the mortal or biological shared with all mankind.

A sovereign thus has two 'bodies', almost two separate beings contained within a single entity. Another, more complex, strand holds that the King's mortal self consists of two subdivisions. On the one hand there is the physical, his/her own 'body private', and on the other, the metaphysical, representing the 'body politic' of the political state of which he is the ruler (the King is both himself and the state).

This passage begins by focusing on threats to the body politic – since an attack on England is automatically an attack on its sovereign – and Westmoreland's input then turns the focus onto the body private, with Henry's anxiety over his own son.

King Henry is striving to establish his realm and reign in terms of the heroic mode as a means of asserting a legitimate sovereignty (thereby palliating his troubled conscience). It is thus within this framework that he appraises his own son, having a view to the future and the new line of the Plantagenet dynasty (hence that reference in line 88). Critic James Knowles makes the interesting point that following his triumphant victories and the deposing of Richard, Henry's reign has become an anti-climax of disillusionment: 'It is as if the hopes embodied in Richard II ... have dissipated, to be replaced by militarism and a regime devoted to political control' (Dutton and Howard, p. 429).

The heroic mode foregrounds the ideals of honour, stoicism and selfless dedication to Fortune. These are juxtaposed against and utterly undermined by the comic mode deriving from Falstaff and his domestic milieu. The bathos, as the centre of attention moves from one to the other in the next scene, is almost palpable.

We are only some eighty-plus lines into the play and already we have many of its major interests. It exposes a great deal of the King's identity, and his present status. It obliquely introduces, discusses and compares the characters of Hotspur and Prince Hal and presents the seeds of the King's gathering dispute with the Percys. All of these key elements will impart to the play much of its structure and the major terms of its thematic discussions. It presents a snapshot of a kingdom in turmoil, together with some crucial issues: honour, duty (including filial obligations), loyalty and friendship.

Further, and crucial for the sardonic humour of the play, this opening scene sets up the heroic ideals that will be so shamelessly and riotously subverted by Falstaff's dissolute self-indulgence.

## Context Passage 2: 2.4.298–346

The immense popularity of both parts of *Henry IV* has always been due in large degree to the enormous appeal of its most engrossing character: Sir John Falstaff – thief, jester, corpulent wit, father-figure, satirist, and so on. He instantly engages the audience through his outrageous insouciance and seduces it into the heart of the play's impudent humanity. He is everything that King Henry is not – or almost anyone else, come to that.

Originally, Falstaff was to be 'Sir John Oldcastle' (one of the stage directions in *2Henry IV* contains a residual reference to this), but tradition has it that Shakespeare's acting company, the Chamberlain's Men, was constrained to restyle him after protests from that actual knight's influential descendants.

The original Oldcastle in question was a religious fanatic, dynamic warrior, and a youthful 39 at his death, thus utterly unrecognisable from Shakespeare's comic libertine. The same Falstaff appears also in *The Merry Wives of Windsor*, where he is merely a buffoon, a mere shadow, metaphorically speaking, of the sparkling wag in *Henry IV*.

We first encounter Falstaff and Prince Hal in the second scene of the play, amid the roistering banter of the Boar's Head tavern, where they plan a highway robbery on Gad's Hill. At the end of that scene the Prince utters an important soliloquy that casts doubt on his own commitment to Falstaff's company and which we will consider below.

Meanwhile the civil crisis intensifies after King Henry refuses to ransom 'foolish' Edmund Mortimer. The Percys, affronted by a man whom they had raised to the throne, determine on a rebellion to supplant the ungracious Henry with Mortimer, the man they now regard as the true heir.

The second extract I have selected for analysis appears in Act 2 Scene 4, set in the Boar's Head tavern. Falstaff's disconsolate crew return empty-handed and roundly smarting from the Gad's Hill caper, where they are double-crossed by Hal and Poins. Amid some pungent repartee, Falstaff first fumes at the recent swindle, brags of his valour, then bullies the tavern staff, while Hal demonstrates that despite the constant reminders of his royal position, he is on surprisingly affable terms with the tavern's tapsters, drawers and underskinkers.

Shakespeare alternates scenes of a gravely worsening political crisis with scenes of what the King earlier calls 'riot and dishonour'. After a striking report of virile northern rebels, Shakespeare slots in a picture of wanton dissipation where the taverners seem rapturously oblivious of the national emergency, until Sir John Bracy brings 'villainous news' of the 'mad fellow of the north' (276):

| | | |
|---|---|---|
| *Prince*: | Why, then, it is like if there come a hot June, and this civil buffeting hold, we shall buy maidenheads as they buy hob-nails, by the hundreds. | 300 |
| *Falstaff*: | By the mass, lad, thou sayest true, it is like we shall have good trading that way. But tell me, Hal, art not thou horrible afeard? Thou being heir apparent, could the world pick thee out three such enemies again, as that fiend Douglas, that spirit Percy, and that devil Glendower? Art thou not horribly afraid? Doth not thy blood thrill at it? | 305 |
| *Prince*: | Not a whit, i' faith, I lack some of thy instinct. | |

| | |
|---|---|
| *Falstaff:* | Well, thou wert be horribly chid tomorrow when thou |
| | comest to thy father. If thou love me, practise an answer. |
| *Prince:* | Do thou stand for my father and examine me upon the particulars 310 |
| | of my life. |
| *Falstaff:* | Shall I? Content! This chair shall be my state, this dagger my |
| | sceptre, and this cushion my crown. |
| *Prince:* | Thy state is taken for a joint-stool, thy golden sceptre for a |
| | leaden dagger, and thy precious rich crown for a pitiful bald crown. 315 |
| *Falstaff:* | Well, an the fire of grace be not quite out of thee, now shalt |
| | thou be moved. Give me a cup of sack to make my eyes look red, |
| | that it may be thought I have wept, for I must speak in passion, and |
| | I will do it in King Cambyses' vein. |
| *Prince:* | Well, here is my leg. 320 |
| *Falstaff:* | And here is my speech. Stand aside, nobility. |
| *Hostess:* | O Jesu, this is excellent sport, i' faith. |
| *Falstaff:* | Weep not, sweet Queen, for trickling tears are vain. |
| *Hostess:* | O the Father, how he holds his countenance! |
| *Falstaff:* | For God's sake, lords, convey my tristful Queen; 325 |
| | For tears do stop the floodgates of her eyes. |
| *Hostess:* | O Jesu, he doth it as like one of these harlotry players as ever |
| | I see! |
| *Falstaff:* | Peace, good pint-pot, peace, good tickle-brain. Harry, I do |
| | not only marvel where thou spendest thy time, but also how thou 330 |
| | art accompanied. For though the camomile, the more it is trodden |
| | on the faster it grows, yet youth, the more it is wasted the sooner it |
| | wears. That thou art my son I have partly thy mother's word, partly |
| | my own opinion, but chiefly a villainous trick of thine eye, and a |
| | foolish hanging of thy nether lip, that doth warrant me. If then thou 335 |
| | be son to me – here lies the point – why, being son to me, art thou |
| | so pointed at? Shall the blessed sun of heaven prove a micher, and |
| | eat blackberries? A question not to be asked. Shall the son of England |
| | prove a thief, and take purses? a question to be asked. There |
| | is a thing, Harry, which thou hast often heard of, and it is known to 340 |
| | many in our land by the name of pitch. This pitch – as ancient |
| | writers do report – doth defile, so doth the company thou keepest. |
| | For, Harry, now I do not speak to thee in drink, but in tears; not in |
| | pleasure, but in passion; not in words only, but in woes also. And |
| | yet there is a virtuous man whom I have often noted in thy company, 345 |
| | but I know not his name. |

The action here follows the Gad's Hill muggings and, like the other scenes of the Falstaff's pot-wallopers, is played out at night. This makes an obvious contrast with the day setting of the 'political/ state' scenes (the association of Falstaff with the night and the moon marks a symbolic contrast with the King's repeated 'sun' leitmotif). Although the text is unspecific, the setting is customarily taken to be the Boar's Head tavern in Eastcheap, close to London Bridge (by tradition, Shakespeare's own watering hole was the Mermaid near St Paul's, a tavern popular with Jonson and other penmen).

To help in our analysis I would like to divide this passage into three sections: (i) lines 298–311, which refer to the threat from the 'rebels'; (ii) lines 312–28, Falstaff preparing his part as the 'king'; and (iii) lines 329–6, Falstaff's 'pint-pot' speech.

## (i)  Lines 298–311: '*could the world pick thee out three such enemies*'

Among the many points we are likely to notice about this passage in contrast to the first, the most apparent is that almost all of it is in prose. This is one of the many ways Shakespeare signals a change of tone, personnel or scene. Yet the scene itself, like all of those through which the hefty figure of Sir John Falstaff shambles, is anything but prosaic.

As commonly in these scenes, Prince Hal goads him into a corpulent response, and the Prince's opening lines reveal the profound influence of Falstaff on his impressionable mind. Prompted by 'barebone Jack', Hal translates a situation of urgent national danger into a mercenary opportunity for a sexual binge. The heat of June is not simply a meteorological reference but a pointedly lustful one too (his offhand proposal reveals just how deeply the Prince of Wales has become engrossed in the hedonistic life and lingo of Falstaff's tavern world).

Falstaff concurs, licking his lips – 'By the mass lad', maidenheads by the hundreds. He extends the commodity idea by speaking of 'trading that way'. Addressing the heir-apparent as 'lad' and with the diminutive 'Hal' points, of course, to the warm familiarity between the old jester and his young protégé. Prince Hal is but a lad, a teenager – in historical reality aged about 15 or 16.

However, when Falstaff asks Hal if he is 'horribly afeard', what is his tone of voice? – is he himself 'horribly afeard' (he uses the epithet three times over the next few lines) or does he lampoon such talk of distant civil war? Hal as heir apparent, however, would be the target and potential loser of the conflict – and Falstaff cautions that the world has picked him out (303).

Throughout the play Falstaff continually reminds Hal that he is heir apparent. Why does he do this? Perhaps it is a calculated deference, aimed at maintaining his standing with the future power and wealth. At times he does feel anxious over this prospect. Or maybe Shakespeare wishes to keep before us the problems of royal lineage, embarked upon in *Richard II* but still to be resolved. However, it would be prudent for both their causes if the Prince eventually faced up to his father.

The repartee begins to warm up when Falstaff reminds Hal of his father's summons. If the distant 'rebels' cannot make him 'horribly afeard', the likelihood of being 'horribly chid' by his father may wipe the smile of his face. His tone changes, and Falstaff reassures his friend with an offer of rehearsal:

If thou love me, practise an answer.    (309)

And perhaps it is Falstaff himself who is afeard the King will 'chid' or rebuke Prince Hal, because this would threaten their special friendship. 'Love' is a highly charged word to employ here – not 'like', or 'have a care for', but 'love'. Many readers have seen a homosexual partnership of varying intensities between these two seemingly devoted men, some a more platonic relationship, and still others something of a father–son bond – very possibly all three at different times.

The father–son idea finds even more credence in Hal's Freudian acceptance:

Do thou stand for my father and examine me upon the particulars of my life.    (310)

The pun in the phrase 'stand for', as well as meaning 'substitute', contains the idea that Falstaff would have to 'rise for' or defer to

Hal's father, the King. Many critics would argue that he is already a surrogate, and this is indicative of the King's neglect of his son, bent upon matters of state as he is. Also, Falstaff's entreaty that he heed his father's solicitude is itself a sort of fatherly injunction.

## (ii)  Lines 312–28: '*a great actor prepares*'

Falstaff's chosen word 'practise' (309) can of course imply 'fabricate' as well as 'rehearse'. The situation resembles that of a lawyer coaching a defendant with prepared excuses, mitigations and alibis. When Falstaff muses 'Shall I?' (312) his fervid imagination quickens at the prospect.

First, this cameo performance demands a setting, a local habitation, with metonymy to work upon our imaginary forces. On the Elizabethan stage a throne could represent a whole state, one man could stand for an army, a tree for a forest. In the theatre, standing-in-for is a customary practice, and Falstaff is a great 'stander-in-for', a deceiver, a con-man (witness how he hacked his sword to mimic battle damage at 2.4.252).

His agile mind swiftly turns a dagger into a royal sceptre and then, for dramatic bathos, he plops a cushion onto his head as 'my crown'. He resembles an actor preparing a role by first fitting a framework of props. Then further bathos ensues when the Prince punctures his fantasy:

> Thy state is taken for a joint-stool, thy golden sceptre for a
> leaden dagger, and thy precious rich crown for a pitiful bald
> crown.   (315)

The play has many such instances of the dualism of ideal alongside the real, notably manifested in the polarity of values such as honour versus pragmatism, and duty versus opportunism, honesty and duplicity.

Theatrical Falstaff too is a dreamer, the stuff that dreams are made on. Yet there is an edge of irony in the Prince's words. In dreaming up his fake kingship Falstaff momentarily and symbolically shows the usurping of the crown – something which Henry himself has done and Hal himself will do in dumb show in *Henry IV*, Part 2. His shadow kingship is shown by Hal as 'leaden' and a 'pitiful bald crown'. With heavy and unintended irony he insinuates his own father's illicit kingship.

Falstaff may of course actually be bald or balding but Hal's point about the 'pitiful bald crown' (line 315) is that it diminishes both Falstaff's authority and the English crown itself. This is grist to Falstaff's merry mill and he waves aside the pseudo-political dig by focusing on his coming performance. His metaphorical phrase, the 'power of grace' (316), is interesting because while on the one hand it censures the Prince for his chastening gibe, on the other it foregrounds the play's imagery of nobility (referred to in line 321) which he likes to scoff at.

Falstaff prepares for his quixotic role with tongue lodged firmly in his cheek, mixing gravitas with gravy. He seeks to move the Prince by sympathy, which demands a draught of sack, so he may fake a doleful countenance – but he naturally savours the sack for its own dear taste. He hopes to move his 'son' by emotion, speaking in passion, emulating the hero of Thomas Preston's hugely popular tragedy *The Life of Cambises, King of Persia* (another anachronism, since it was not written until after 1560).

Play-acting is part and parcel of the sport of the tavern crew. It is not confined to this section of the play. Falstaff's predisposition to braggadocio and duplicity, plus his swaggering faux-knight, is typical of this role-play. Earlier in this scene, too, Hal proposes playing the part of Hotspur while Falstaff 'shall play Dame Mortimer his wife' (2.4.94–5).

Falstaff the fat fraudster, dissembler, impostor, man of many parts (all in reality himself), is a connoisseur of pantomime and disguise. Instance: earlier in the current scene's banter, when Falstaff's craven masquerade at Gad's Hill is exposed, his response is to have 'a play extempore' (2.4.231). This readiness to partake in an alternative fantasy is consistent with the play's ludic inclination for storytelling, creating alternative versions of reality (for example, descriptions of the Battle of Holmedon, reports of the rebels' disposition, tales of the Gad's Hill robberies, rumours, gossip and plain lies).

Stephen Greenblatt notes that 'Hal's characteristic activity is playing or, more precisely, theoretical improvisation – his parts include his father, Hotspur, Hotspur's wife, a thief in buckram, himself as prodigal and himself as penitent' (in Dollimore and Sinfield, p. 33).

While Falstaff pretends to be his father, Prince Hal is readily complicit in his share of this knockabout charade. Play-acting (or duplicity, if you prefer) is likewise a significant facet of the Prince's general performance among the taverners, drawers and underskinkers. More so if we take at face value his 'I know you all ...' soliloquy at 1.2.155, with its imagery of play-acting and illusion: 'uphold', 'imitate', 'playing', 'falsify', 'show' ...:

> I know you all, and will a while uphold
> The unyoked humour of your idleness.
> Yet herein will I imitate the sun ...

                                                            (1.2.190–2)

In this striking speech, appearing after plans for the Gad's Hill robbery have been finalised, the Prince appears to confide in us how his loyal affiliation with the tavern idlers is merely a subterfuge. His statement that 'I shall hereafter be more myself' (3.2.92–3) implies that all along he has been play-acting. Some critics even go as far as to regard Hal's presence in the tavern as akin to an insider gathering local intelligence for the King or for himself in order to increase his later royal power.

The significance of that soliloquy lies in the stage convention that the speaker is revealing the truth about him/herself, like an interior monologue – in spite of what they may say elsewhere in public. Employing ideas such as 'imitate' and 'falsify', Hal seems to confess that he abuses his friends for amusement, or idle 'holidays', simply as a means of beguiling the time until he ascends the throne.

(iii)  Lines 329–46: '*a question not to be asked*'

Adopting the role of the father-king, Falstaff begins imperiously – as he does so often as lord over his own tavern-dominion. He calls for 'Peace', but his own reign resembles one of chaos. 'Peace good pint-pot' and 'good tickle-brain' – it is at ourselves too that he is roaring.

When he launches into his fatherly address to the Prince, Falstaff's speech becomes progressively more stylised and patronising. He adopts an over-genteel mode, for instance in 'marvel' and 'accompanied', thus satirising the King as well as himself. His use of fanciful maxims in his homily is a pastiche of another Tudor dramatist, John Lyly, whose character Euphues is much given to these overcooked flourishes:

> For though the camomile, the more it is trodden on the faster it grows, yet youth, the more it is wasted the sooner it wears.

Although this sounds at first like a clever analogy, it is in fact a whimsical simile, there being no obvious connection between trodden camomile and 'wasted' youth.

Also typical of the euphuistic style is the balancing of contrasting clauses, as though the speaker were involved in a drawn-out internal dialogue, the overall effect being to preposterously cancel each other out in a quagmire of farcical nonsense. Typically the style uses mazy sentences of extended, suspended and embedded clauses to beguile its captive listeners.

The shrewdly comic Falstaff, practised in the wily arts of oratory, makes full use of euphuistic style to brilliant comic effect. First he parodies the King-as-father, using the familiar form 'Harry'. The fact that Shakespeare also presents us with the actual confrontation of father and son in 3.2 increases the comedy here by back-projection.

The play's running paternity theme surfaces again in line 333: 'That thou art my son ...'. This is, of course, Falstaff's leg-pull, since none of the three grounds given for supposing Hal to be the King's true son (and therefore heir) are very conclusive. In other words, paternity may always remain tentative – and so may inheritance or birthright. Thus Falstaff's next statement begins with a conditional 'If then thou be son to me ...'. This idea seems to hint at the constant sense of uncertainty running through the play, whether about legitimacy or birth or Henry's right of ascendancy.

How, then, does this passage contribute to the play as a whole? First, its tone of wit and conviviality stands as an important dramatic counterpoint to the gravity of the civil emergency seething away in the political distance. The passage treats of some of the play's major themes from a new angle, including those of paternity and the relationship of father and son, the notion of Falstaff's alternative values and the topics of justice and honour. It is Falstaff's supreme moment as acting father-figure.

In dramatic terms this section brings to the fore the increasing tension between Hal and his father, the King, regarding the previous charge of idleness ('riot and dishonour'; 1.1.84). The extract gives a good flavour of the carnival lifestyle indulged at the Boar's Head, the 'idleness' and game-playing that the King suspects his son to be caught up in. Falstaff parodies this, bringing it out into full view. The allure of hedonism for Hal lies in a desire for the very inverse of duty and especially ambition, the will to power that has energised King Henry and which he in turn craves to discover in his son.

This passage spotlights the interplay of the characters of Prince Hal and Falstaff as the play develops its two principal and rival spheres of influences or values: the tavern and the Court. It casts clear light on the easy nature of the companionship and offers audiences a key point at which to experience this and the character of Falstaff, the major comic and political personality in Hal's consciousness. Although he dwells at some remove from its political and military machinations, his commanding presence in the play succeeds in questioning and satirising them.

Sometimes Falstaff's scenes appear to exist outside the play's normal time scale. This feature is so compelling that, secluded within the grand duchy of the Boar's Head, that 'plump Jack' convenes his alternative Court, safely inured from the oppressive shifts of the Plantagenets. 'Father ruffian' is a debunking dissembler, idle hedonist, coward and bully. A boaster and a bester, a man of great contrasts and contradictions – Falstaff is a man both of swelling ego and a riotous sense of self-deprecation. His weapon of choice is language, as he is an inveterate and voluble sweet-talker.

Chief among the many strands that animate *1 Henry IV* is the vitality of Falstaff's speech. It is a sparkling cache of rhetorical figures–metaphors, puns, euphuism, chiasmus, proverbs, biblical snatches, personification and zeugma, together with a fertile assortment of imagery. As a Rabelaisian figure, oaths, insults, abusive epithets and luxuriant curses come readily to his lips as leaves to a tree, and these are both sporting and ingenious. At the same time, and crucially, they have a political as well as dramatic significance. On the one hand

Falstaff's language exists as a vividly plastic entity extending even beyond the plane of action. On the other, his polyphonic utterances precisely epitomise those anarchic values and behaviour that the authoritarian king abhors.

In the monologue above, with delicious irony, Falstaff coyly models himself as a 'virtuous man'. Then immediately following the above passage he catalogues himself as portly, corpulent, cheerful, of pleasing eye and noble carriage, with 'virtue in his looks'. Of years, he is

> some fifty, or by'r lady, inclining to three score
>
> (2.4.350)

The Prince then rejoins with a famous description of his comrade as

> that huge bombard of sack, that stuffed cloak-bag of guts, that roasted Manningtree ox with the pudding in his belly, that reverend Vice, that grey Iniquity, that father Ruffian, that Vanity in years? ... wherein cunning, but in craft?
>
> (2.4.374–9)

stressing his large size and appetite, his cunning, iniquity and vanity. One of the play's great attractions is the wealth of insults playfully traded, and this scene is well stocked with these ('clay-brained guts', 'knotty-pated fool', greasy tallow catcher', and so on).

In reality, Falstaff's many narratives invariably position himself at their centres. His vanity is proverbial and readily feeds both his bragging and his self-deprecation. His larger-than-life self-overstatement is equally the source of his comedy and a hedge (in contrast to the King) against taking himself and life in general too solemnly.

Many readers regard Falstaff as the antithesis of Henry IV's regimen of order and duty. Certainly his outrageous usurping of the 'monarchy' (as well as his paternity) in the above passage symbolically satirises that of Henry himself in *Richard II*, and thus Falstaff's mockery devalues the prize (via a stool, a dagger and a cushion). The idea that a king is merely the most powerful hoodlum extends one of the themes of the passage in Context Passage

1 and revisits a claim made in *Richard II* that Henry is a king only in name and appearance.

Falstaff enjoys and indulges his time to the full in holiday idleness. It is a timeless time, a kind of drifting with no firm or political goal, except that of gratifying amusement, to which he is a bondsman ('I live out of all order'; 3.3.15). Hal describes the situation as the 'unyoked humour of your idleness'. Some will see Falstaff as an idle Jack, and he himself would not be at odds with that description.

But a coward? He is somewhat irked by this accusation. True, he does take part in the original Gad's Hill robbery, though he cunningly absents himself from the subsequent 'attack' by Hal, on the grounds of 'instinct', that is impulsive self-preservation. Elsewhere Falstaff playfully figures himself as a Hercules (2.4.224) and a 'valiant lion' (2.4.227). For all his insouciant bonhomie he is uncommonly touchy about the charge of cowardice.

This sensitivity is more curious in the light of his famous rejection of 'honour' (5.1.129 on). His susceptibility about cowardice springs not from some external code of honour, nor even from some odd notion of bravery. But the charge does offend his self-image.

In Shakespeare's depiction of Falstaff can be traced a variety of theatrical antecedents. From classical Latin plays comes the figure of the *miles gloriosus*, which later became reincarnated as 'Il Capitano', the boasting, cowardly soldier of the Italian *commedia dell'arte* theatre, popular in the sixteenth century. Another interesting type feeding into Falstaff's character is 'the Vice' of English medieval morality plays – an allegorical figure of wicked influence. In this mould Falstaff is a corrupter of youth, anti-establishment, and a disrupter of the peace (see again the passage above referring to 'that reverend Vice'; 2.4.375). At the close of the original morality play, the Vice would typically be seen lumbering on stage with the devil on his back (compare Falstaff bearing off Hotspur's body on his back in 5.4). Yet one more source for Falstaff is the popular Christmas mumming play performed in rural areas, which the young Shakespeare must have witnessed in Stratford. These starred a Lord of Misrule, a figure of chaos, and the one who initiated the holiday merriment, for instance at Christmas time.

## Context Passage 3: 4.1.42–85

Hereford United v. Warkworth Hotspur

In Act 3 the attention shifts to Wales, where Glendower, Mortimer and Hotspur convene to settle on their 'indentures tripartite' (3.1.76), the carve-up of Britain, Gaunt's 'sceptred isle', following their insurrection. As the first stage in the plan of installing Mortimer as king, their 'lawful heir', they decide to muster troops near Shrewsbury.

Meanwhile, after King Henry's stern rebuke of his son for shameful conduct, the Prince undertakes to amend his life. Back at the tavern, Falstaff is astonished by the transformation in his 'mad wag' (who has also repaid the Gad's Hill booty). He is equally stunned by news that he is to command a troop of infantry against the insurgents. And then, at the start of Act 4, the outlook opens wide on to fields and sky, on to Hotspur's battle encampment near Shrewsbury.

The passage I have chosen for detailed analysis is taken from near the beginning of Act 4, a decisive moment in the Northumberland fortunes. A spirited Hotspur receives news that because of sickness, Lord Percy cannot now rendezvous with them. He is thus faced with the dilemma of either engaging the King's army with depleted forces or pulling back to safety. Where Worcester is understandably discouraged by this bulletin, Hotspur appears strangely enervated by it:

| | |
|---|---|
| *Worcester*: | Your father's sickness is a maim to us. |
| *Hotspur*: | A perilous gash, a very limb lopped off– |
| | And yet, in faith, it is not! His present want |
| | Seems more than we shall find it. Were it good      45 |
| | To set the exact wealth of all our states |
| | All at one cast? to set so rich a main |
| | On the nice hazard of one doubtful hour? |
| | It were not good, for therein should we read |
| | The very bottom and the soul of hope,      50 |
| | The very list, the very utmost bound |
| | Of all our fortunes. |
| *Douglas*: | Faith, and so we should. Where now remains |
| | A sweet reversion – we may boldly spend |
| | Upon the hope of what is to come in.      55 |

|              | A comfort of retirement lives in this. |     |
|--------------|----------------------------------------|-----|
| *Hotspur:*   | A rendezvous, a home to fly unto,      |     |
|              | If that the devil and mischance look big |   |
|              | Upon the maidenhead of our affairs.    |     |
| *Worcester:* | But yet I would your father had been here. | 60 |
|              | The quality and hair of our attempt    |     |
|              | Brooks no division. It will be thought, |    |
|              | By some that know not why he is away,  |     |
|              | That wisdom, loyalty, and mere dislike |     |
|              | Of our proceedings kept the Earl from hence. | 65 |
|              | And think how such an apprehension     |     |
|              | May turn the tide of fearful faction,  |     |
|              | And breed a kind of question in our cause. | |
|              | For well you know we of the off'ring side | |
|              | Must keep aloof from strict arbitrement, | 70 |
|              | And stop all sight-holes, every loop from whence | |
|              | The eye of reason may pry in upon us.  |     |
|              | This absence of your father's draws a curtain | |
|              | That shows the ignorant a kind of fear |     |
|              | Before not dreamt of.                  |     |
| *Hotspur:*   | You strain too far.                    | 75 |
|              | I rather of his absence make this use. |     |
|              | It lends a lustre and more great opinion, | |
|              | A larger dare to our great enterprise, |     |
|              | Than if the Earl were here. For men must think, | |
|              | If we without his help can make a head | 80 |
|              | To push against a kingdom, with his help | |
|              | We shall o'erturn it topsy-turvy down. |     |
|              | Yet all goes well, yet all our joints are whole. | |
| *Douglas:*   | As heart can think. There is not such a word | |
|              | Spoke of in Scotland as this term of fear. | 85 |

*Enter Sir Richard Vernon*

One of the many things to emerge from Hotspur's lines here is a clear emphasis on gambling and risk-taking, which is perhaps what we have come to expect. Conversely, Worcester's diction is concerned with flagging up caution alongside references to concealment (confirming impressions about his character as a shrewd and prudent strategist).

I would like to tackle this important passage in two sections: first, lines 42–59, where Hotspur puts his argument for engaging in battle, and second, lines 60–85, in which Worcester offers a counter-argument and then Hotspur replies. For me, three words loom larger here than others: 'hazard' (line 48), 'division' (line 62) and 'reason' (line 72), the latter being given a slight twist by Douglas in his words, 'heart can think' (line 84). We can exploit these words as useful trig points by which to orient our discussion.

(i)   Lines 42–59: *'On the nice hazard of one doubtful hour'*

Having quelled the rebellion in his son, King Henry has now turned to do the same with the Percys and to bring Hotspur to heel. The play has many ironies, particularly connected with 'turning', and it is interesting to recall how in our first extract the King was so full of praise for young Hotspur's loyal heroism: 'so blest a son', 'sweet Fortune's minion ...' (1.1.79–82).

Yet here, close to Shrewsbury, a different mood prevails. Lord Percy, nominal commander of the rebels, is absent and news arrives later that Glendower is not yet ready to join them. Even worse, Vernon reports that the King's army will number thirty thousand in total.

In the high adrenalin crisis of battle preparation, amid excitement and alarum, Worcester's opening words sound eerily ominous;

Your father's sickness is a maim to us.

Notice how he personalises this news for Hotspur – he could have phrased it as 'My brother's sickness ...'. Perhaps this now acknowledges Hotspur as their military chief, moving him centre stage. Or perhaps he phrases this to fix on his nephew the gravity of its cold truth, the 'perilous gash'. Note too the word 'sickness', which squats on the line, implying a moral stain at the heart of their cause. This is a typical Shakespearean metaphor: illness usually implies a moral as well as medical infection, and thus functions as a bad omen.

Worcester seems stunned and so too Hotspur ... at first, anyway. The blow is dangerous, a gash and then an amputation of the body. 'Lopped' implies finality, decisive and irreversible. Revealingly, no one has a thought for Lord Percy himself, father and uncle. Are they indifferent, immersed in their own dilemma, or simply in shock, perhaps?

When Hotspur introduces the keynote word 'hazard' (line 48), he appears to accept that perhaps it would be reckless to gamble the whole of their forces on one uncertain and decisive battle. 'Cast' (of the dice), 'main' (a stake) and 'hazard' all, of course, refer to gambling in one form or another, and give a good insight into the general complexion of Hotspur's thinking. Yet this is ironic. The great appeal to Hotspur of this situation and of war in general is the immense risk involved – to risk not merely an army, or even a dynasty, but to cast life itself on the table gives him an enormous frisson. The argument he puts forward to dismiss Worcester's reservations is actually the principle that motivates him: namely, 'hazard'.

Hotspur goes on to expand his argument. A battle deploying all of their total forces could subsequently obliterate all of their power as well as undo the wider prospects for their enterprise, 'the very utmost bound / Of all our fortunes' (51–2). He snatches at the idea that it would be wiser to engage now with a limited army and regard the rest as a back-up reserve of troops. He really is thinking on the pulse here, fired up with emotion as he is, and this is evidenced in his language, particularly his repetition of 'very' and the hyperbole in 'very utmost', a double superlative (Hotspur's exhilaration is also echoed in the metre of his verse, which is far more irregular than either Worcester's or Douglas's).

In line 50 the signifier 'hope' speaks of their true predicament. In fact there is more of despair than hope in Hotspur's attitude. At the end of his first utterance, line 52 is a catalectic line, that is, not the full ten syllables of regular blank verse (see Glossary). There could be many reasons for this, but one effect is that there arises a pregnant pause at that point, the expectant air resonating with Hotspur's startling proposal. Out of the nettle despair he plucks a strange misshapen rose of wild optimism.

And yet one good reason for his optimism may lie in the fact that the King has previously been repelled three times by Glendower's army (the Archbishop of York confidently describes Percy's army as 'in the first proportion'; 4.4.15). The odds based on previous form look quite favourable.

Now Douglas offers timely support when he complaisantly chips in with

> we may boldly spend
> Upon the hope of what is to come in.    (54–5)

Using a financial metaphor, he suggests that if we invest effort and blood now we can reap the profits later. While a reticent Worcester is still pondering alternatives, the Scotsman follows up by claiming that this offers both a comforting promise of victory while still keeping open the option of retreat ('retirement').

Hotspur himself seizes gratefully on this: we should think of Percy's absence as a reserve army, 'a rendezvous, a home to fly unto' (57). However, this is only a provisional fall-back position in case of the unexpected, which he thus expects,

> If that the devil and mischance look big
> Upon the maidenhead of our affairs.    (58–9)

This can be glossed as: 'if, because of malevolent intervention or just plain bad luck, we fail in this, the outset of our great enterprise'. Yet even these contingencies exude a relish of perverse stimulation.

'Maidenhead' is an unexpected word here. It can be translated as the 'beginning' of our affairs but it inevitably carries with it too the halo of 'virtue', or morally right, as a contrast with the reference to 'sickness' that opened this extract.

(ii)  Lines 60–75: '*The eye of reason may pry in upon us*'

After the early optimism of the two combatants, Worcester now turns the tone swiftly back to cool reserve:

> But yet I would your father had been here.    (60)

His two opening words, opening a plain, direct statement, act as a sharp brake on the swelling boldness of Hotspur and Douglas, returning them to the reality of the situation: namely their depleted forces.

After arresting their galloping fervour he states the predicament baldly: their project ('attempt') to topple the King is so enormous in its possible consequences (for themselves if they fail and the kingdom if they succeed) that it permits or 'brooks' no possibility of division in their forces. Again, he delivers this in a plain, direct statement of fact. In other words, he regards even a slight reduction in their army, their 'enterprise', as undermining the whole operation.

'Division' is a key word here, and ironically. his statement itself underscores that very division he has discovered; the division between himself and Hotspur regarding strategy. Then, from line 62, he expands on his analysis in order to bring home to Hotspur the true implications of Lord Percy's absence There will be rumours among the ignorant that his absence is due to their weakened circumstances ('wisdom'); some will believe his loyalty has reverted to the King; and others may believe Lord Percy has lost conviction in the success of the approaching battle.

Worcester is clearly a very shrewd judge of their danger. A cool intellectual and a cunning Machiavellian politician (see Chapter 4 for a more extensive discussion of Machiavelli), he is quietly acute to their circumstances, where Hotspur is too immersed, too full-on, to see the broader implications of actions.

In dramatic terms, too, the word 'division' is important because it generates such a lot of the high tension in this crucial scene. The concept of division is linked here with imagery of loss and separation: 'maim', 'lopped off', 'faction', 'absence' (as well as its antithesis, 'whole'; 83). Unsurprisingly, Worcester is expertly apprised of the danger here – Lord Percy's absence already divides them, but rumours will create 'apprehension' leading to further division, plus doubt and vacillation ('question') within their ranks. He has the perspicacity to realise that their coalition is even now a fragile, contingent entity.

Having said all this, we can note too that Worcester's response marks an almost imperceptible shift towards his decisive adoption of Hotspur's position:

For well you know we of the off'ring side
Must keep aloof from strict arbitrement ...

(69–70)

The first stage is to bring these rumours under strict control: in other words, censorship. As the aggressor (the 'off'ring side'), they must prevent close analysis of their operational status by either enemy spies or their own infantry.

Consequently his reflex impulse here is a blanket suppression of truth. He actually sidesteps Hotspur's demand to stand firm, by arguing along the lines of 'even before we get to that question we have to stem the haemorrhaging of information or we are undone'. From the theme of 'division' he moves on to that of 'reason':

> ... stop all sight-holes, every loop from whence
> The eye of reason may pry in upon us.
>
> (71–2)

His military metaphor cogently addresses Hotspur's febrile mind-set, while the word 'reason' relates more to Worcester's own province. With some irony here, 'reason' can of course mean 'common sense', so in a backhanded way he hints that in order to pursue Hotspur's line we must first abandon sound reasoning.

Following his own precepts of counter-espionage, Worcester closes by reiterating his earlier claim: ignorance will create rumour, speculation and consequently cowardice.

What do these early exchanges tell us of these characters? Where Hotspur is a man of direct action and danger, one who would seek to shun the serene hypocrisy of courts and dissembling princes, liars and flatterers, Worcester finds himself readily at ease in the soft furnishings of power-brokerage. Remember that it was Worcester who first suggested retaining the hostages, especially Douglas's son, to curb the Scots and irritate the King. As Westmoreland observes:

> This is his uncle's teaching, this is Worcester,
> Malevolent to you in all aspects.
>
> (1.1.95–6)

Worcester is a much shrewder, more pre-emptive tactician than his impetuous nephew. If Hotspur in different moments demonstrates the sanguine and choleric dispositions, Worcester's dominating humour is the phlegmatic (for more details of the humours see Glossary). His suave archness later strikes the King himself, after the failed summit in 1.3, sensing the uncle's input:

> Worcester, get thee gone, for I do see
> Danger and disobedience in thine eye
>
> (1.3.14–15)

But as Worcester himself has earlier argued (1.3.11–13), it was the Percys who installed him on the throne in the first place, and in *Richard II* Worcester had surrendered a very senior post in Richard's Court in order to support him.

## (iii)  Lines 75–85: '*Like the Roman*'

I mentioned at the outset of the discussion of this passage that one of the key words here is 'reason'. Worcester's tenor is one suffused with the theme as well as the method of reason. As we have previously noted, Hotspur's is of a more emotional hue. In line 85 the conciliatory Douglas synthesises the two temperaments with his pithy observation: 'As heart can think'.

In a strong sense Douglas also encapsulates within his epigram a hint about the structure of this passage. Because of the figure here, of one voice answering another, the conversation has a dialectical structure: first, Hotspur proposes taking a risk, then Worcester challenges this by saying the news about Percy undermines our strength, finishing with Hotspur arguing that, though weakened, if they could win this battle they could overwhelm the King altogether.

Worcester, the apotheosis of reason itself, compels his nephew to reflect rationally on their precarious situation. And yet, does Hotspur's reply (from line 75 on) constitute sound reasoning? We need to delve deeper.

'Young' Hotspur's first response shrugs off Worcester's solicitude: 'You strain too far' (75). He suggests that older Worcester is too nervous, exaggerating the danger. However, is he really accusing his uncle of cowardice? The fact that his four words complete Worcester's line implies that he cuts across his words with some impulsiveness. But at least he continues to employ reason to articulate his case:

I rather of his absence make this use.

What he is actually admitting here is that he prefers to twist ('use') the argument round to make a virtue of necessity. The loss of his father's force can make the achievements of their outnumbered army appear all the greater and more daring – if they win.

When Hotspur compares their audacious endeavour to a 'great enterprise' he is using the state-of-the-art imagery of the Elizabethan era, likening themselves to the merchant adventurers setting off across the oceans and against all odds in search of new lands and treasure. Such mercantile enterprises were highly risky (see Shakespeare's salutary *The Merchant of Venice*). Predictably Hotspur identifies himself wholly with the prizewinners: they who dare win (see *2Henry IV* 1.1.181, where this idea is made more explicit).

With his thoughts spiralling blithely towards an imaginary glorious victory, there suddenly arrives the pivot of his whole argument. Amidst all the fervent energy it is almost imperceptible:

If we without his help can make a head ...   (80)

What a massive burden is borne by that one word 'If'. It represents the whole turning point of his argument and of his fortunes. The gravity of the word is intensified by the irony that the Percys are not even fully aware of the huge enemy forces, advancing towards them like a juggernaut.

Hotspur becomes so pepped up by excitement at their slim chances that it is easy to imagine that he actually relishes this colossally unequal trial. So much so that it has blurred his logic. *If* their outnumbered force can overcome a mighty army then it bodes well. With unintended irony he closes by adding that everything is still going well, and all their ranks are cohesive and fit.

And then comes that paradoxical comment from Douglas:

As heart can think.   (84)

We would not normally regard the heart as the thinking organ, so what is he getting at here? 'Heart' can mean 'love' or maybe 'loyalty', so Douglas could be arguing that Hotspur is speaking truthfully, sincerely. Or 'heart' may signify 'courage' or 'spirit' (cf. 4.3.7), that reason may be *felt* through sheer determination. On the other hand, the statement can mean that feelings, instincts ('heart'), can be as reliable as a source of truth or advice as intellect ('think'). The line tugs in opposing directions.

In general terms, Douglas aligns himself with Hotspur's standpoint. As if to make this clearer – and perhaps to irk Hotspur – he adds that the plucky Scots have no use for the word 'fear'. (Douglas reiterates this spirited defiance at the very end of this scene.)

I mentioned earlier that the figure of Falstaff, through the comic subtext, functions as a counterpoint to the King's values vis-à-vis Prince Hal. By the same token he is a counterpoint to Hotspur's character and values, especially his commitment to martial prowess and the concept of honour. Both of these elements come to the fore in this passage. Where Falstaff is the *miles gloriosus*, full of insubstantial bluster, Hotspur is the real deal, gushing with courage, honour and a fierce sense of duty.

Glory, what the Elizabethans would call 'fame', was one of the principal drivers of the Renaissance enterprise. Fame was regarded as a double-edged quality, with good fame and bad fame. What Hotspur craves is of course good fame, fame that is guided by honour, which both curbs and expresses the ego. It offers a kind of earthly immortality and a baulk against malicious rumour.

While Glendower is convinced that Hotspur is uncouth and uncultured, Hotspur is somewhat articulate and his verse is rich in diction and figure. But because his thinking is powered by feeling and pugnacity, his argument sometimes reads like a Möbius strip.

In 3.2 the King describes Hotspur as 'Mars in swaddling clothes / This infant warrior' (lines 112–13). And he does occasionally remind us of some of Shakespeare's Roman generals – Coriolanus, Mark Antony and Marcus Brutus – single-minded, audaciously brave, driven by pride and loyalty to a selfless cause, dedicated to the god of war. He battles first for the King and then against him. The crucial cause for the martial Hotspur is of course the battle itself, the fetish of combat:

> They come like sacrifices in their trim,
> And to the fire-eyed maid of smoky war
> All hot and bleeding will we offer them.
> The mailed Mars shall on his altar sit ...

(4.1.113–16)

Whether or not we agree with the sentiment, the verse, as usual, is magnificent.

That said, there is little evidence to suggest he would make anything of a decent general in battle. An incurable risk-taker, an impetuous and unflagging optimist ... his own uncle describes him as 'hare-brained' while his wife dubs him a 'mad-headed ape' (H.B. Charlton considers him so unsystematic that he is 'unable to control or even organise himself'; in Hunter, 1970; p. 86). Clearly, however, in all such descriptions of him, Hotspur is understood to be fixed in his nature, a nature which no amount of name-calling (and this play is full of name-calling) is going to alter. Unlike the Prince, he has a form that cannot be changed. Put plainly, he is hard-wired for war.

What does this passage contribute to the play as a whole? First, in terms of plot this passage presents to us the causes of and the arguments for and against the Percys' decision to engage in the crucial battle at Shrewsbury. Tension and suspense are also generated by the conflict in the two points of view, Hotspur's and Worcester's, as well as by the contrast of Hotspur's impetuous energy with Worcester's studied reserve, emotion and reason. Further, the extract explores the important themes of military action, such as strategic planning, risk-taking, the balance of drive and caution, and the broader political repercussions of hostilities. Above all, the passage offers us revealing insights on the characters and motivations of Worcester and Hotspur. It reminds us of what each brings to the play, particularly Hotspur, whose magnetism buzzes and fizzes throughout – his presence is felt from the beginning right through to the play's end. He impels it forward with his drive, commitment and sense of proud honour.

One way in which Hotspur's dramatic importance is evidenced lies in all the diverse nicknames by which he is abused (Falstaff, on the other hand, is a name-coiner). We care about him, his danger, because he excites our interest. He and Falstaff are the twin turbines of the play, bringing it fiercely alive, each obeying the impulse of the moment in his different way.

Crucially, many commentators understand Hotspur as motivated principally by a code of honour. James C. Bulman is fairly typical in arguing that, 'impulsive and valiant, young Harry Percy embodies all that is glorious about feudal chivalry — its code of honour, its passion for heroic achievement in arms' (Hattaway, p. 159). Many readers, too, have gone so far as to hold him up as a vestige of the medieval knight, the epitome of the ideal of chivalry, that he makes a valid choice out of good faith and is wiped out, as the Middle Ages too become wiped out by a new mercantile pragmatism of the Renaissance. There is little evidence here of the code of honour. But in Context Passage 4 Falstaff has a few sharp words about it.

## Context Passage 4: 5.1.118–38

Following Hotspur's bold decision for combat, Vernon delivers a grim report of the strength of the King's army. The play's attention then switches briefly to Falstaff, leading his ragged troops north. Back at Hotspur's camp, Blunt brings the King's offer of a pardon and a promise to hear the Percys' grievances. Meanwhile, at York Archbishop Scroop makes plans for the aftermath to Hotspur's anticipated routing.

Act 5 opens with sunrise on the King's encampment. It is the morning of the decisive battle. The King's repeated offer of terms is met by Worcester's claim that Henry has reneged on previous promises. The Prince of Wales steps forward with his own proposal for Hotspur: that the two of them should meet together to decide the conflict in single combat, and 'save the blood on either side', though he doubts the challenge will ever be taken up.

*King Henry's encampment near Shrewsbury*

*King*:      Hence, therefore, every leader to his charge,
             For on their answer will we set on them,
             And God befriend us as our cause is just!                           120

                                    *Exeunt. The Prince and Falstaff remain*

*Falstaff*:  Hal, if thou see me down in the battle and bestride me so, 'tis
             a point of friendship.

*Prince*:    Nothing but a Colossus can do thee that friendship.
             Say thy prayers, and farewell.

*Falstaff*:  I would 'twere bed-time, Hal, and all well.                         125

*Prince*:    Why, thou owest God a death.                                    *[Exit]*

*Falstaff*:  'Tis not due yet – I would be loath to pay him before his day.
             What need I be so forward with him that calls not on me? Well, 'tis
             no matter, honour pricks me on. Yea, but how if honour prick me
             off when I come on, how then? Can honour set to a leg? No. Or an     130
             arm? No. Or take away the grief of a wound? No. Honour hath no
             skill in surgery then? No. What is honour? A word. What is in that
             word honour? What is that honour? Air. A trim reckoning! Who
             hath it? He that died a' Wednesday. Doth he feel it? No. Doth he
             hear it? No. 'Tis insensible, then? Yea, to the dead. But will it not   135
             live with the willing? No. Why? Detraction will not suffer it. There-
             fore I'll none of it. Honour is a mere scutcheon – and so ends my
             catechism.                                                          *[Exit]*

After the high tension in the early part of this scene, during Worcester's impassioned negotiations with the King, there is now a slight cadence. Uncertainty over terms is not yet resolved, but the King now seizes the initiative.

A first reading of this passage yields some clear ideas of mood and tone. With a rising optimism, the King's forceful rhetoric energises his captains for the anticipated battle. The Prince comes across as fully focused, steeled for action, while by comic contrast, Falstaff appears in nervous disarray, highly alarmed. The passage exudes a great sense of urgency which is intensely visible and dramatic. Likewise, there arises a marked tension between the King's eagerness and Falstaff's diffidence.

A rich variety of tropes is equally apparent: puns on 'cause' and 'prick'; metaphors in 'Colossus' and 'scutcheon', imagery of death, incision and injury. We will take each of these in turn, and to give the analysis a sense of form I have chosen three important items of diction that will help us to navigate the thematic currents of the extract: 'just' (l.120), 'friendship' (123) and 'honour' (129).

### (i)   Line 120: *'our cause is just!'*

Speaking in regular verse, the King's speech is decisive, direct, inspiring. His verbs, directed at 'every' officer, are forceful or imperative (for instance 'Hence' and 'will we'); even his prayer to God resembles a command to the Almighty: 'befriend us as our cause is just!' In line 119 his determination to 'set on them', the enemy, that is, when they return with a reply, has prompted some debate amongst critics.

Does the King mean 'we will pounce upon them regardless of their answer', possibly implying an ambush? Many readers have seen this as a sign of treachery in the King, further evidence of the infamy that was shown in *Richard II* (in the coming Battle of Shrewsbury he employs doubles of himself to deceive the enemy, which some regard as unchivalrous).

Other readers understand the word 'set' to mean 'plan accordingly' (see 1.2.106) or 'measure their strength', while elsewhere in Shakespeare the word 'set' usually means 'resolve', or 'harden against'.

His words actually draw attention to the slow and deliberate fashion in which the battle lines have been drawn up. After all the sabre-rattling and colloquy, we still do not yet know if there will even be a battle. Moreover, the mounting tension holds back and whets the appetite of those members of the audience eager for lusty swordplay.

Briefly, we can contrast the King Henry of Act 1 with the same King here in Act 5. In the first extract we observed an executive style of kingship, his pugnacity against the Scots working vicariously via Hotspur. Now we have a proactive, hands-on, fully engaged commander-in-chief.

He declares triumphantly, 'our cause is just!'(120). Since a king is supposedly appointed by God, this would seem to sanctify any of the King's wars: *'la causa e santa'* was the cry of the Crusaders – our cause is blessed. But one problem here is that it is not at all clear that Henry is appointed by God in the first place, since in *Richard II* he ousted the rightful king and installed himself. If, however, we accept Mortimer as the legitimate heir (as the Percys do), then Hotspur would have a better right to claim his cause as the 'just' one. In the next scene, immediately before battle, Hotspur does exactly this (if slightly more volubly than the King):

> Now, for our consciences, the arms are fair
> When the intent to bear them is just.
>
> (5.2.87–8)

On the other hand, here, in an otherwise quite godless play, Henry IV's attempt to invoke the support of God in a 'just cause' looks like a shameless piece of opportunism. The vacuous rhetoric of the King's cry is lampooned by Falstaff's observation that honour is merely a 'word', it simply sounds good. The whole concept is muddled and in reality the phrase clearly operates as a blast of political rhetoric, a blatant attempt to claim a spurious moral superiority.

## (ii)  Lines 121–2: "*'tis a point of friendship*'

After the King's rousing flourish in lines 118–20, the dramatic tension on stage noticeably subsides. The pathos in Falstaff's plea for Hal to shield him in battle is transmuted by his friend into bathos since his great size makes shielding impossible except to someone of colossal size. This joke turns on the pun in 'bestride', meaning to protect or, in the case of the legendary Colossus of Rhodes, to loom over the battlefield like a giant.

The pronoun 'nothing' which opens Hal's lines intimates an absolute, sombre rejection of his old friend, and this is followed in the next line by a breezily chill 'Farewell'. His tone of voice now is offhand, dismissive, evincing a gallows kind of humour that serves only to deepen Falstaff's terror. Notice how brusque and cold is Hal's demeanour in contrast with the hearty cordiality of their dialogues in the two tavern scenes. This curtness can be accounted for in part by the imminence of battle, but it more nearly marks the shift in their relationship since Act 3 Scene 2. Hal is on the path to redeeming his ties with his father – a goal that he eventually achieves with his rescue of the King from Douglas:

> Thou hast redeemed thy lost opinion [i.e. reputation]
>
> (5.4.47)

Hal now takes it that proximity to father presupposes detachment from Falstaff.

The Prince's parting shot (and his final word here) refers to Falstaff's death. The word 'death' resonates in the air behind him (Falstaff has preferred the euphemistic 'down in battle'). In pressing Falstaff to 'say thy prayers', he first of all urges him to hope for the best in the encroaching battle. But the Prince also warns that he should make his soul ready for death. This is the new reality of Hal – imperatives and intimations of death.

Falstaff's whimpering wish for bedtime is a cry for 'safety', where formerly 'bed' was invariably linked with fornication. His sob is met by an equally grave retort:

> ... thou owest God a death.   (126)

This sets a cavernous (and hilarious) gulf between the timid Falstaff we observe here and the once-strutting, cheery braggadocio of the character in the tavern episodes. For example, in the safety of the tavern he crowed:

> ... yet a coward is worse than a cup of sack with lime in it. A
> villainous coward. Go thy ways, old Jack, die when thou wilt.
>
> (2.4.106–7)

In the Prince's short exchange here, three words ring loudest: 'nothing', 'farewell' and 'death'. All three of them jokingly play upon and bait his friend's alarm. They may even seem somewhat callous, in the light of their past amity, and are especially painful when we recall that a major reason for Falstaff's attendance here is the presence of his comrade.

Falstaff might 'owest a death' in two senses, turning on a pun in 'owest'. One is that since Christ died for him as for others, his life is in debt to Christ, and the other that he has led such a disreputable life he is now due to pay for his debauchery (with an aural play on debt/death). The actor's tone of voice is crucial here: should it be played as a hearty joke, baiting the old man, or as a dire censure, a snub? (cf. *2 Henry IV* 3.2.192).

This is all the more poignant because of the Prince's allusion to 'friendship' in line 123. The whole of the Falstaff–Hal sequence of the play seems gathered into this one iridescent word. Each of Falstaff's utterances are addressed familiarly to 'Hal', making this a genuine cry from the heart, a cry that is equally a test of their friendship.

The theme of friendship *per se* was one of increasing intellectual interest in the Early Modern period. In his seminal handbook *The Book of the Courtier* (1528) Baldesar Castiglione maintained that 'the supreme degree of friendship ... contains the best of life' (p. 138), and Francis Bacon devoted a whole essay to the topic, holding that true friendship 'completes a man, making him whole' (*Essays*, 1612, no. 27). Chief among theorists on the theme, Michel de Montaigne, in his highly influential *Essays* (1580), held that friendship was to be prized above all human activity, Court politics and public office, family ties, material wealth and carnal love; unlike marriage, friendship does not, ultimately, depend on obligation:

> A unique and particular friendship dissolves all other obligations whatsoever ...

For Montaigne, friendship between two men is not contingent and never instrumental but always autonomous, unconditional (*Essays*, Ch. XXVII, 'On Friendship'). Since the play has devoted a considerable weight to the mores of hospitality, it would be fair to say, that by Montaigne's litmus test at least, Prince Hal offends the sacred norms of friendship. His brusque 'Farewell' and nod towards 'death' are muffled anticipations of Hal's final renunciation of Falstaff in Part 2 and so are all the more poignant. Their comradeship proceeds from Hal's 'I know you all' (1.2.155) and finally expires in his 'I know thee not, old man' in *2Henry IV* (5.5.43).

By drawing up the theme of 'friendship' from its easy complacency, making his love explicit, Falstaff necessarily exposes it to the raw chill of scorn. So, when Hal says only a Colossus can defend their friendship, he thus implies that friendship places upon him too great a demand. The rejection is a kind of sardonic repudiation of a social contract, in deference to the state, filial duty and self-interest.

### (iii)  Line 132: '*What is honour? A word*'

Having put the frighteners on his comrade, the Prince abandons him. Falstaff is graphically alone on stage. Calling to the departing prince, he takes up Hal's pun on 'owest' and throws it defiantly back:

> 'Tis not due yet – I would be loath to pay him before his day.
> What need I be so forward with him that calls not on me? Well, 'tis
> no matter, honour pricks me on.

Falstaff makes a stoic avowal of survival. Then he opens his catechism. The time for God to take his soul is not yet due, so why go looking for him? He is as puzzled as he is defiant (and afraid). He addresses his rhetorical questions to both the audience and his own conscience in a speech which is a gift for an actor in making repartee with his audience.

Along with all the other discourse markers here, 'Well', in line 128, seems directed towards the audience: the notion of settling death's debt is irrational since honour continues to 'prick', or spur, him on. All the way through his monologue, Falstaff's solicitude swings between doubt and resolution, spurring on and reining back.

The term 'honour' at first glances back to the King's belief in a just cause, backed by divine approbation. Combat is the right and true course of action. This reassuring thought is then undermined by another, that of being pricked off. In Elizabethan English to 'prick off' works exquisitely for Falstaff as a pun: as well as a hint of bawdy, 'prick' can be the act of being stabbed in the battle – but it also refers to the practice of ticking names on a list by pricking a hole next to each (see *2Henry IV*, and Falstaff's use of this 'prick' in the recruitment scene; 3.2.86 on). He accepts, phlegmatically, that honour may yet prick himself on death's muster.

In Falstaff's frenzied sophistry he makes a personification of honour – chiefly by the reality of what it cannot accomplish. Honour rationally cannot set a wounded leg and it cannot relieve the pain or grief of a wound – it is unable to remedy the injuries of the conflict which itself has brought about.

Honour, then, is merely a word, an empty word, filled only with air. Falstaff rates this as a 'trim reckoning', and since a 'reckoning' is but a tavern bill (debt again), honour is only of slight account, something base and – in Falstaff's case – to be utterly ignored. Moreover, Honour is irrelevant to the living and incomprehensible to the dead, those who can feel its point, its 'prick', no longer (134–5).

He queries why honour will not dwell with the living – and his reply is another complex and mocking quibble: 'Detraction will not suffer it' (136). This is not an easy phrase to unpack, but if we remember Falstaff as essentially a man of the living we can find our way through. 'Detraction' is in part a malapropism for 'protraction', so honour will not survive ('suffer') over a long period of time. 'Detraction' also equates with insults or slander, so 'insults will not safeguard honour either' ('suffer', in the old sense of tolerate or stand for). However, I think the gist is clear, that honour, having no lasting appeal, does not spur him to die in its cause.

Falstaff is a tenaciously virile man who has passion only for the living and its cares. A 'scutcheon' is a painted funeral shield, so by likening honour to such a mean kind of funeral frippery, Falstaff eschews 'honour' as a tawdry thing of the dead, a *memento mori*. His soliloquy, begun in fear and loathing, closes in triumphal laughter (and most likely in jubilant applause).

This is the first scene in which Falstaff and the King are found together on stage, though neither acknowledges the other, verbally at any rate. It is interesting to speculate how their mutual reactions could be played. The question might be raised as to why Falstaff is there at all. He mockingly claims that honour 'pricks' him on, but it is more likely that after Hal had enlisted him Falstaff has been swept along in the hurly-burly of battle-mania and undoubtedly by the prospect of remuneration.

As a conscientious objector Falstaff's little speech here steps outside the rising emotion of partisanship, only to discover the commotion raging within himself. The style of the speech aptly expresses his interiority, making the subjective external. His catechism is a kind of 'trim reckoning', slick, pared down to single-word answers, through which the serpentine sense wriggles.

A catechism is a method of instruction introduced by the early Christian Church by which basic dogma and principles of faith are inculcated, especially in children. It proceeds by a lugubrious process of question and answer, akin to rote learning in school.

Here the rhythm of the process produces an antiphonic effect, which is ripe for some droll mockery. On a dramatic level Falstaff is visibly isolated and his irrepressible volubility must thus erupt as auto-interrogation. What emerges is a form of reductive reasoning based on definition and linguistic evasion:

> What is honour? A word. What is in that word honour? What is that honour?

Apart from the airy circularity of this process it tends to produce only negatives: that is, what honour is *not* (Falstaff uses in total eight 'no's and some fourteen negative words in his twelve lines). This negativism, along with the hilarious critique of 'honour', is a facet of the anti-war discourse that Falstaff personifies both at this point and in Part 2.

The interrogative mode here also mimics the penetrative examination of the infamous Holy Office, the Inquisition. And as so often with the Inquisitors, Falstaff's questions set out to discover the precise conclusion he desires. Such a catechism can function only on the level of trite commonplaces, and by the end Falstaff is satisfied that 'honour' has been systematically stripped of all substantive content. He is assured that cowardly self-preservation is after all the prudent course, or as he later expresses it:

> The better part of valour is discretion.
>
> (5.4. 116–17)

The passage present an example of psychomachy, a medieval stage effect in which two voices or angels (representing opposing ideas) vie for control or influence over the main character. Falstaff's subjective wrangling is the struggle between his good angel and bad (though which is the good and which the bad is not easy to specify). His soliloquies elsewhere sometimes take this form, exaggerated for comic effect, and it projects an image of a man in a state of relentless turmoil (for example, see 5.4.110–24 or 2.2.9–23). Here the impression given is again of tormented indecisiveness, but that of a soul wrought less by a moral agonising than by compelling entreaties of self-interest.

We can now summarise what this passage contributes to the play as a whole and why it is important. First, it provides additional insights into Hal's relationship to Falstaff and indicates changes in their relationship which will continue to be developed in Part 2. It also gives us more information about the King's character and it is the first time in the play that he and Falstaff have appeared on stage together, symbolically enacting the twin demands on the Prince's attention and loyalty. In terms of Falstaff himself, it is interesting to see him alone, shorn of the company of the tavern and the battlefield. Of crucial importance are his satirical thoughts on the theme of honour, and how this sets a framework of discussion for the past as well as the future action. This one moment has the power to change the way we see the play as a whole through the subject of honour and interrogating the motives of each of the other three protagonists: Hotspur, Hal and King Henry. In this regard the passage also raises the issue of the 'just war' and personal responsibilities in it.

## Conclusions

Being in large part a sequel to *Richard II*, *1Henry IV* extends and develops actions started in the earlier play. There we saw Bullingbrook as a vigorous radicalising force; here we see him to a large extent a reactionary, dominated by the political situation of which he has been the major architect. The question of his very right to act as king has also stretched into this play and is given spirited articulation by the voices of the Percy faction, backed by force of arms.

Our analysis of the play has centred on its discussion of key themes such as friendship, honour and loyalty (to family, friend or nation), as well as a continuation of the discussion begun in *Richard II* of the topics of kingship and ambition. These have also been at the heart of our examination of the play's major characters.

The rebel leader, Hotspur, together with the towering figure of Sir John Falstaff, are the overwhelmingly dominant presences in the play. They serve as its two most dynamic motive forces, for different reasons and in differing ways. Both attest to Shakespeare's brilliant stagecraft and go a long way to explaining why *1Henry IV* was such an extraordinarily successful text and so massively profitable at the box office.

For many readers and viewers, the most remarkable and engaging facet of the play will be the formidable John Falstaff. He has something uniquely fresh and overpowering to contribute in his variety and dramatic fascination, which spring in large measure from his role as a counter to the milieu and values of the King and Court. A figure of hedonistic misrule, he represents an alternative father-figure and a source of cultural difference for Hal. He is the swaggering antithesis of King Henry's chill Machiavellian Realpolitik. In structural terms the play makes continuous use of the dualism of idealism and pragmatism (for instance, honour versus ambition, symbolised by Hotspur and Henry IV, respectively) – refreshingly, Falstaff transcends yet manages to exploit both strands.

However, in spite of the title name of the play the question still arises as to who is or are the main characters of the play: the King, Hotspur, Prince Hal, Falstaff – all of these? *The first part of Henry the Fourth* is a truly decentred text. Although his name appears on the title page of the playtext, the King himself is hardly in the play much and the action is, in reality, divided between and defined by others around him, chiefly Falstaff and Hotspur. Henry IV is present at the beginning and there at the end but absent from most of the centre. Even when he is present his mind is dominated by what these others characters are up to.

In *1 Henry IV* the nature of King Henry is defined by Hotspur and by Falstaff (acting through the Prince). These represent the double axis of the play. If the play can be said to be about King Henry IV then we can say that his nature and role are largely defined by other characters. We can equally extend this argument to all four of these characters, because the decentring of the play is perhaps a correlative of the profound unrest implicit in its actions.

The comedy of the play arises from its unresolved tensions, especially regarding the King's own sense of identity, as much as from the enigma of his son and the droll antics of Falstaff.

Another question that is often raised queries whether *1 Henry IV* is a discrete, self-contained play. With some slight forbearance about the final scene of the play we can feel that the action which arises from within it (together with what we are reminded of from *Richard II*) is by the end settled aesthetically – though not thematically. If we compare *1 Henry IV* with, say, *Hamlet* or *Julius Caesar* we can say there are as many loose ends here as at the close of most Shakespeare plays. And it can be argued that any chronicle play is going to focus on an arbitrary tranche from the great flow of history and try to make it appear artistically complete.

Within these parameters *1Henry IV* achieves a reasonable sense of closure. Had it not had the adjunct 'Part 1' to its title we may well have felt reasonably satisfied. But, inevitably, Part 2 hovers over it. As Harold Jenkins observes: 'Part I begins an action which it finds it has not scope for but which part II rounds off' (in Hunter, p. 171). On the other hand, if I am correct in saying that King Henry and Prince Hal are defined by their antitheses, Hotspur and Falstaff, then the business of Part 1 is only partly complete because they have not yet successfully emerged as fully complete characters. Falstaff's full dramatic significance (and therefore Hal's) is not realised until Part 2.

## Suggested Work

To broaden your understanding of the play, take another look at 2.3.31–58, in which Lady Percy addresses her husband, Hotspur. What is the function of the character of Lady Percy in this scene and in the play as a whole? Does Lady Percy have a convincing existence of her own apart from her husband? She also appears in *2Henry IV*, where she has a long speech at 2.3.9–44 which you may want to consult for additional pointers. Compare her character with that of the Hostess of the Boar's Head tavern, and try to decide how their roles differ. What does each contribute to the play (in other words, what would be lost if they were omitted?). Try to explain the ways in which their individual speech patterns differ.

# 3

# *Henry IV Part 2*: History as Carnival

Hegel remarks somewhere that all great events and characters of
world history occur, so to speak, twice. He forgot to add: first as
tragedy, the second time as farce.

Karl Marx, *The Eighteenth Brumaire of Louis Napoleon* (1852)

The earliest record of Shakespeare's *Henry IV Part 2* is an entry in
the Stationers' Register for 23 August 1600 by the booksellers
Andrew Wise and William Aspley announcing their intention to
print the play. This, the Quarto, promised a continuation of the
Falstaff legend plus some new directions:

*The*
*Second part of Henrie*
*the fourth, continuing to his death,*
*and coronation of Henrie*
*the fift.*
*With the humours of sir Iohn Fal-staffe, and swaggering*
*Pistoll.*

Shakespeare had probably written the play two years earlier and
had it performed by his acting company at their own playhouse. It is
conceivable that *2Henry IV*, if it had been first performed in 1599,
was the first of Shakespeare's plays to be performed at the Globe,
reconstructed from the old timbers of the theatre (which were lugged
across the Thames in 1598) and opened in July the following year.

About a thousand copies of *2Henry IV* were printed off in the first edition, and (in contrast to the multiple printings of *Part 1*) this was the sole edition during Shakespeare's lifetime. Perhaps this was due to the perennial problem of selling part two of a work which appears to depend on having seen or read part one, though this seems less crucial in Shakespeare's day. For example, Christopher Marlowe's *Tamburlaine Part 2* (quoted by Pistol at 2.4.131–2) capitalised handsomely on his immensely popular *Part 1*. More interesting is the question of whether Shakespeare, while writing *1Henry IV*, had already envisaged a second part to accommodate the bridging section to *Henry V*. Further, is *Part 2* problematic in skewing the structure of *Part 1*, perhaps being simply tacked on, or is it a refreshing new perspective on its characters, extending or deconstructing our previous assumptions?

Without doubt, and with a little imagination, *Part 2* can certainly stand on its own five feet. However, its experiences and internal relationships are made much richer (and more comprehensible) by a close reading of *Part 1* – plus *Richard II*.

Even so, many passages in Part 2 give catch-up references recapping episodes in *1HenryIV*; for example 1.1.105–32 and 1.2.118–19. And as much as anything else, such backward glances imply the idea that history is not exclusively a linear movement but is to some extent circular, history repeating itself, the same anew. Like Henry IV, we never quite escape the ghosts of Richard II and Hotspur, while the words of John of Gaunt (in *Richard II*) resonate through the Henriad, as the second tetralogy is sometimes referred to.

However, Shakespeare does not mechanically extend the world of *Part 1* into *Part 2*, but adds new treats, including the characters of Shallow and Doll Tearsheet. The Prince of Wales's brothers – especially Prince John – are fleshed out, as is the Lord Chief Justice and the Archbishop of York. Moreover, the Hostess of the Boar's Head tavern is at last identified: namely, Mistress Quickly.

Not surprisingly, many of the themes from the previous plays receive extended treatments here. The questions surrounding the legitimacy of Henry IV's kingship persist and we continue to observe the concept of the King's dual nature – man and divine – but with a new departure. The play sees an expansion of the themes of friendship and loyalty, which take on a fresh significance in relation to this play's interest in ambition, apostasy and betrayal. And new topics appear, too, one in particular what we may call the 'versions of historical reality' theme. This takes the form of a 'discussion' of the nature of truth and interpretation, a discussion fundamental to the very enterprise of the history play. Another of the important new themes in *Part 2* relates to the role of Falstaff, central to which is the notion of 'carnival': that Falstaff embodies and projects values which are at variance with those of Henry IV and which become problematic to his son, Prince Hal. The meaning of these new issues should become clearer as we see them emerge from discussions of selected passages.

Note on the text used: *In order to keep playtexts consistent I have again used the New Cambridge edition* – The Second Part of King Henry IV *edited by Georgio Melchiori (1989, updated 2007); Act 4 of the play has been variously edited, and Melchiori's edition divides it into two scenes. To facilitate references for readers using other editions I have provided double citations for Act 4, using the typical format: 4.1.420[4.3.69].*

## Context Passage 1: *The Induction*, 1–40

For the first context passage I have selected the Induction of the play, since in important ways it influences the audience's reading of the play as well as subtly anticipating many of its deviances.

*Enter RUMOUR, painted full of tongues*

| | |
|---|---|
| *Rumour*: | Open your ears; for which of you will stop |
| | The vent of hearing when loud Rumour speaks? |
| | I from the Orient to the drooping West |
| | (Making the wind my post-horse) still unfold |
| | The acts commenced on this ball of earth;                    5 |
| | Upon my tongues continual slanders ride, |
| | The which in every language I pronounce, |
| | Stuffing the ears of men with false reports: |
| | I speak of peace while covert enmity, |
| | Under the smile of safety, wounds the world;                 10 |

And who but Rumour, who but only I,
Make fearful musters, and prepared defence,
Whiles the big year, swollen with some other grief,
Is thought with child by the stern tyrant War?
And no such matter. Rumour is a pipe 15
Blown by surmises, jealousy's conjectures,
And of so easy and so plain a stop
That the blunt monster with uncounted heads,
The still-discordant wav'ring multitude,
Can play upon it. But what need I thus 20
My well-known body to anatomise
Among my household? Why is Rumour here?
I run before King Harry's victory,
Who in a bloody field by Shrewsbury
Hath beaten down young Hotspur and his troops, 25
Quenching the flame of bold rebellion
Even with the rebel's blood. But what mean I
To speak so true at first? My office is
To noise abroad that Harry Monmouth fell
Under the wrath of noble Hotspur's sword, 30
And that the king before the Douglas' rage
Stooped his anointed head as low as death.
This have I rumoured through the peasant towns
Between that royal field of Shrewsbury
And this worm-eaten hold of ragged stone, 35
Where Hotspur's father, old Northumberland,
Lies crafty-sick. The posts come tiring on,
And not a man of them brings other news
Than they have learnt of me. From Rumour's tongues
They bring smooth comforts false, worse than true wrongs. 40

The sardonic Induction is not always included in performances of
*2HenryIV*. But, as I hope to demonstrate, the Induction performs a
vital function both as a threshold to the play itself, setting up expectations and a viewpoint, while also looking back at *Part 1*, where
curiously the word 'rumour' is completely absent. Janus-like, the
Induction looks both ways.

On the other hand, the phenomenon of rumour appears (in a
number of guises) repeatedly throughout *2HenryIV*; for example, at

2.4.70 (the Hostess and the 'swaggering' gossips); 3.1.87 (King Richard's 'perfect guess'); and at 4.2.13[4.4.13] (Gloucester's unconvincing cover-story for his brother). In a drama in which gregariousness plays such a major role it is no surprise that rumorous tongues are prominent among its own 'multitude'.

This opening soliloquy divides thematically into two sections, pausing at line 22, and so we can tackle the speech in two stages.

(i)   Lines 1–22: *'My well-known body to anatomise'*

Rumour opens his account with a brusque command followed by a direct question. On stage alone, part of his task is to capture the attention of a noisy audience, and these sentence-types are highly effective:

> Open your ears; for which of you will stop
> The vent of hearing when loud Rumour speaks?
>
> (1–2)

An actor might stress keywords such as 'stop' and 'loud' and then pause before 'Rumour'. He insists on our listening and then hits us with the first of a series of wryly rhetorical questions. Who is not susceptible to 'loud', or lurid gossip (and in costume terms, what could be louder than a gown of tongues!)? Almost everyone is curious to lend an ear for some tasty morsel of tittle-tattle.

Deftly, he slips in a couple of puns here too: 'stop', the finger-hole on a musical pipe (again in line 17) and 'vent', a word that plays on the French for 'wind' (implying the wind itself – line 4 – or a slit in a man's gown by which the wind may escape!).

The reader clearly knows who this speaker is supposed to be, but for a theatre audience the point is not that straightforward. An actor must work hard here to get the point across and his/her costume should have a stunning visual as well as symbolic impact.

Rumour and rumour-mongering are – he asserts – universal. Like the sun which traverses this 'ball of earth' from Orient to west, rumour is ubiquitous (3–6). Moreover, rumour has been here for all human time, implied in the words 'still' (4) and 'continual' (6). From its start his agile discourse pulsates with lively tropes. Two instances can illustrate this: understatement in 'ball of earth' and oxymoron in 'still unfold' (4; suggesting that rumour's effects are never-ceasing). Furthermore, the 'wind' as his 'post-horse' conveys the express speed of his virulence.

Pointing to the tongues on his gown, Rumour next re-emphasises his ubiquity, in 'every language' (7). Now that he has our attention, he can indulge in some mischievous boasting of how 'slanders ride' upon his metonymic tongue – while the word 'ride' implies a sort of conceited parasitism (6) – that rumours breed on the back of human discourse. Likewise, in his 'Stuffing the ears of men' he boasts of how easily he can cram this gossip like food into a greedy stomach (8).

In the opening eight lines of Rumour's speech his sentences have tumbled along with polished fluency to outline his general character-istics. At line 9 he impudently pauses, ostensibly to confess the truth:

> I speak of peace while covert enmity,
> Under the smile of safety, wounds the world;
>
> (9–10)

He positively gloats over his duplicity. Rumour's skills of deception emulate those of a diplomat who talks of peace to allay suspicion while secretly plotting war. His cunning anticipates that of Prince John in the encounter with the credulous Archbishop at Gaultree in Act 4 (Falstaff of course has a perennial knack for this kind of double-dealing, while Rumour alleges the same of Northumberland at line 37).

His vanity mounts higher in the following lines as he crows 'who but only I', who but Rumour could spread fear of war through a world which is already distressed by other misfortune ('grief'). Shakespeare's allegory swells with pride when he explains how he can turn the tables on people: people both create the rumours and become terrified by them. So reports of war cause people needlessly to prepare defences, 'fearful musters' of troops. As critic James Shapiro explains, 'fearful' refers to the corruption in the muster sys-tem as well as to the concern about hostilities (Shapiro, p. 71). War becomes an expression of or a distraction from social strife at home (note how towards the end of the play the dying king advises his heir to divert attention from the great political grief in England via 'for-eign quarrels'; 4.2.342[4.5.210]).

This rumour of war anticipates the play's actual muster in 3.2 with Falstaff's hilarious inspection of the 'troops'. In the end it is a false alarm and Rumour's comment here is along similar lines when he somewhat cynically concludes, with a dismissive snort, 'And no such matter' (15). The truth is that he and war, personified as a 'stern tyrant', are together brazenly abusing us poor mortals (or exposing the cynicism).

Accordingly, Rumour concludes the first part of his breezy lecture with a monstrous joke on his audience. He reiterates his pipe metaphor, the noisy instrument (15). adding that it is

> Blown by surmises, jealousy's conjectures ... .
>
> (16)

On a local scale, rumours are the speculative inventions of the obdurately anxious – namely lovers – filling the fearful vacuum of uncertainty with worried guesses.

The word 'blown' is especially heavy with meaning. It can, of course, mean the process by which rumours are wafted around, just as the metaphorical pipe itself is played by blowing and closing those stops or vents. But 'blown' can also mean 'polluted' or 'made corrupt', as in the phrase 'fly-blown'. Thus rumours are not simply neutral but become distorted and in turn corrupt their listeners.

Deriding his audience, he declares that rumour is such an easy thing to spread that even the blunt monster, the 'wav'ring multitude' of the gregarious public before him, can do it; they are 'my household' (22). It is a perfect moment for some rowdy repartee directly with the audience.

During the hectic course of his dissertation Rumour stops himself twice, as if inadvertently becoming caught up in his own hurtling 'conjectures'. Both times he steps out of character to make jokes, deviously pretending that these asides are actually facts, whereas of course all he does is further distort the framework of truth:

> But what need I thus
> My well-known body to anatomise
> Among my household?
>
> (20–2)

If we are to assume the whole speech is rumour, then this is all an outrageous hoax.

It is worth remembering that reading this passage is by no means the same as watching it enacted, for the simple reason that it is not until line 11 that this bizarre orator makes clearer who he is. He declares that he is speech itself (2), tongues (6 and 39), ear-stuffer (8), smiler (10), a whistle or pipe (15), deception (9–10) and all-round bringer of chaos. He compares himself to the sun (3) as well as to the wind (4 and 16). Rumour is fast, pervasive and trenchant. He is linked with other eloquent talent: slanders, jealousies, falsity, wounds, fear and noise. To facilitate confusion he works in league with war, exaggerating false alarms and civil panic. All fine negatives. As Warwick later confirms:

> Rumour doth double, like the voice and echo,
> The numbers of the feared.

> (3.1.96–7)

His flair for disruption recalls similar Shakespearean tricksters like Puck (*A Midsummer Night's Dream*) and Ariel (*The Tempest*) – although these spirits differ in remaining under the scrutiny of higher authorities. Furthermore, Rumour is less a figure of destiny than a psycho-sociological phenomenon, an allegory of human insecurity in the face of power and danger.

In terms of costume, Rumour's fantastic cloak of tongues suggests the wardrobe of carnival, a visual allegory of the forces of mischief, provocatively challenging the prevailing order (in this he shares the subversive values of Falstaff and the rebelliousness of the Percys). This disruptive facet is one shared with and essential to the seditious comedy of the play as a whole (critic François Laroque interestingly sees rumour as a 'complex device to materialise time under the form of carnival pageantry'; Bloom, p. 212).

Evasive, shifty, arrogant ('who but I?'), Rumour is a playful deadly sin, an antihero who brags that his mischiefs are joyously negative, embracing neither motive, nor reason, but pure pointless devilry:

> And no such matter

> (15)

And yet, paradoxically, his oratory is fiendishly rational, and marked by exquisite coherence.

### (ii)  Lines 22–40: *'smooth comforts false'*

At line 22 Rumour turns to apply his remarks to what the audience had come to watch. After all, they had stumped up their pennies expecting something more about a gallant king, some tasty political intrigue and plenty of bloody swordplay. So, 'Why *is* Rumour here?'

Of course, he himself does not get around to answering this, not yet anyway, not until he has set out a brief history of Act 5 of *1Henry IV*. He claims at line 28 that his 'office' or duty is to spread misinformation. This is only one of his 'offices', and another is here to recap for those who have already seen *Part 1* and to put newcomers in the picture. He runs 'before' the King's victory over Hotspur at Shrewsbury, 'before' meaning previous to the victory or preceding accurate reports of that victory (see lines 34–5). As Rumour himself notes in line 28, this section places him in an invidious position, since although by nature a deceiver, he is now obliged by this office to speak the truth.

The truth – according to *Part 1*, anyway – is that King Henry

> Hath beaten down young Hotspur and his troops,
> Quenching the flame of bold rebellion
> Even with the rebel's blood.

> (25–7)

This is an interesting statement because the words 'rebel' and 'rebellion' had hardly figured at all in *Part 1* (I count twenty occurrences in *2Henry IV* but no more than six in *Part 1*). Their rebellion is 'bold' in the sense of 'shameless' or 'disgraceful'. Following in the wake of *Richard II* the idea has persisted that the Percys were not indeed the rebels, since Henry IV had dethroned the rightful, divinely appointed King Richard. Who, then, is the rebel and who the righteous? In line 32 the King's 'anointed head' obliquely hints that Henry is not divinely appointed, merely blessed by secular authority (i.e. himself).

After joking that it is not Rumour's job to be spreading the truth, he boasts that he will broadcast the falsehood of Prince Hal's death – 'Harry Monmouth fell' – and that the King, also Harry, has been slain (note too that under this version of history Hotspur is still described as 'noble'). His use of the chatty diminutive 'Harry' for both Prince and King attests to his judicious alliance with the royal establishment.

As the play itself confirms, such rumours are spreading virally from the battleground of Shrewsbury throughout the north of England as far as Lord Percy's stronghold, Warkworth Castle. The epithets 'worm-eaten' and 'ragged' clearly carry metaphorical power that Northumberland is defeated, crestfallen. These words also embody a moral tone, especially in the light of Rumour's royal sycophancy – that the Percy clan as well as the 'rebel' cause itself as 'worm-eaten', rotten. This inference is supported in the following lines by the punning descriptions 'old', 'Lies' and 'crafty-sick'. 'Lies' and 'crafty-sick' imply 'deception', that Lord Percy is shirking, shamming illness to avoid battle, a point which was rumoured in *Part 1* as well and is confirmed here in 2.3 of *Part 2*.

Rumour contemptuously boasts exclusive rights on the Shrewsbury story while the messengers ('posts') exhaust themselves ('tiring on') in delivering his falsehoods. In a speech replete with jaunty ironies Rumour goads his listeners with mounting impudent scorn. He ends his scathing audacity on a smug aphorism that

… smooth comforts false, worse than true wrongs.

(40)

Rumour's chiasmic final couplet brings his soliloquy to a close in a spiral of thorny complexity. We really ought not to trust any of it, but his word is proved truthful in the play's opening scene. His 'smooth comforts' bring to their listeners a sense of illusory reassurance, paradoxically worse because the shock brought about by the eventual revelation is even more painful.

We can ask here what the overall effect is of paradoxes such as this – another appears in line 10 – together with his use of oxymorons (lines 4 and 19), and puns (lines 2, 35 and 37). One effect is the general aura of uncertainty, side by side with a feeling of evasive detachment. The highly fluid tumble of Rumour's discourse, with its nimble and cunning tropes (sometimes bordering the surreal), presents us with a performance of bizarre protean subtlety. Two enduring impressions of the speech are, first, it shares an outrageous joke on the subject of gossip, and then, more seriously, it problematises the terms 'truth' and 'falsehood' for the rest of *2Henry IV*.

It may seem odd, but we should also ask what Rumour's importance is to the play as a whole. My answer to this is that Rumour has at least two functions: a thematic function and a dramatic function.

One important reason for Rumour's discourse is that it introduces some of the play's key themes, including truth and deception, rebellion and history, and he discusses the notion of textuality, all the world being a text. The theme of truth versus deception occurs in the opening scene but also later, with many instances of unreliable sources and distortions. For instance, when Westmoreland comes to parley with the rebels at Gaultree, he first talks of the need for truth in appearances (see 4.1.34, 37) while later his brother John will dupe them by a deception after first giving his word (see 4.1.294[4.2.66].

Although rumours are not of course inherently false, Rumour himself warns us not to trust to words. Conversely, at the comic muster in Act 3 Falstaff believes that the tag names of the recruits should truly reflect their inner nature (3.2.89ff.) – but Falstaff is himself a shifting, elusive quantity.

But of course this is not the final story. Rumour's soliloquy gives us a good warning about 'history', the documentation and memory of past events. Rumour himself points up the two versions of the Battle of Shrewsbury, drawing attention to the significance of the reporter's point of view. In the first account of the battle, Hotspur is the 'flame of rebellion' (26), while later he is 'noble Hotspur' (30). Rumour's discourse reveals that personally he has prudently accepted the royal version as authoritative.

Thus, in his account of versions of history Rumour draws attention to the power of 'spin', since the two versions refer to the same previous event. Lexical choices like 'noble', 'bold', 'worm-eaten' and 'crafty-sick' confirm the speaker's preferences. Falstaff pointedly cautions 'believe not the word of a noble' (4.1.403[4.3.51]); the Prince of Wales will also betray his outward show of comradeship when he

rejects his former devoted friend in Act 5. 'True' and 'false' as modifiers have, far from being absolute, become fluidly relativistic,
negotiable.

In the same camp with rumour is reputation – indeed the two are
almost synonymous. The passage refers obliquely to this in epithets
like 'noble', 'bold' and 'crafty-sick', foregrounding the idea that it is
rumour among people that creates reputation. In other words, it is
public approval (and its obverse) rather than truth or falsehood that
elevates a figure, while revisionist accounts of history – such as
Shakespeare's own here – realigns and influences the later reception
of people and events.

So, in *1Henry IV*, as the usurper King Henry becomes swiftly
honoured as a worthy fellow, and in *2Henry IV* the defeated Percy
clan are vilified as rebels. Falstaff, at least before we meet him, is a
man constructed almost wholly of rumour. Reputation, like truth, is
convertible by rumour (though Rumour strives to place himself
beyond public opinion).

This view of reputation as fluid and relative is a typically
Renaissance concept. In this, honour, grace and virtue are understood as contingent qualities, conditional on public approval – like a
modern honours system – unlike the medieval position, which is
more likely to regard them as religiously fixed properties inherent in
a certain disposition, or perhaps to be acquired by selfless deeds: 'for
there is nothing either good or bad but thinking makes it so' (*Hamlet*
2.2.249–50). Hamlet vocalises the modern, Renaissance view of
character as mutable.

Turning now to the dramatic function of Rumour, on a quite ele-
mentary level a prologue is handy as a means of settling a rowdy
audience. And while this Induction does have strong thematic value,
Elizabethan latecomers – delayed perhaps by a slothful ferryman or
by obstructive shoppers on London Bridge – would not miss the
play's opening scene. With his agile flair for comedy, along with his
affinities with conflict, chaos and mischief, Rumour is an exciting
conundrum. He speaks as a man of the people, an ideal interface
connecting the two different experiences of *Henry IV*.

Rumour's crucial dramatic role, then, is to set up the play's unrelenting relish for the absurd. He is a sparkling counterpoint to its

sober political currents and intrigues, yet remains as lord of misrule over a farce in which after all the ballyhoo no one is killed and only pride and honour are offended. Even his appetite-whetting promise of 'fearful musters, and prepared defence' is disappointed by Falstaff's laughable rustic parade and Prince John's bizarre swindle in Gaultree Forest.

Why, then, did Shakespeare not simply assimilate Rumour as a character within the mainstream play? The answer lies in the essential carnival nature of Rumour, which in spite of setting the facetious tone, precludes the possibility of his being a character in the play: by definition he is detached from the truth of reality, which in this case is the play itself. This is exactly how his irony succeeds. By appearing at the start his misrule precedes and colours everything that happens after it.

In simple dramatic terms, Rumour is both a warm-up comic and a portal into *2Henry IV*. 'He' plays very little explicit part after Act 1. I have already mentioned how Rumour resembles Janus, the Roman god of doorways and beginnings, and although he links both parts of *Henry IV*, he effectively obstructs the flow between them, since he breaks the continuity by standing outside the two plays, mediating the experience before it has happened.

Rumour, like literature, presents us with *versions* of truth, versions of history which are revealed as much through subtle lexical choice as through direct statement, as we have noted above in the partiality of Rumour's epithets. Along with the many ironies in this Induction, these conflicts between the versions, truth and falsehood, generate much of the tension in the speech.

This notion of 'versions' of the 'truth' (Rumour forces us even to guardedly put the word 'truth' in inverted commas) bears most vividly on the general theme of history. How does rumour or myth or legend get converted into truth or history? Verification is one method, by consulting the Chronicles – though we should be mindful that these are also versions. The truths of a culture are those either confirmed by a licensed source or which pragmatically reflect a political bias. Rumour reminds us that Shakespeare too presents only a version of history.

In her dazzling essay on 'Shakespeare's Histories and Counter-histories', critic Alison Thorne draws attention to the importance of

Rumour in this context, 'flagging up the play's indebtedness to popular tradition' (in Cavanagh et al., p. 50). She notes the high number of instances in the play in which 'high political state history' is

> displaced by the meanderings of the oral tradition in which the past is typically reconstituted in anecdotal form through the informal medium of rumour, hearsay, gossip and personal reminiscence. (Cavanagh et al., p. 49; see also my discussion of Thorne in Chapter 6)

The printed version of history usually gets valorised over the spoken. Because of the politics and economics of the business of publication, the printed word has been the privileged version of those groups wealthy and powerful enough to control it. However, in *2Henry IV* Rumour – the medium of the poor and illiterate – has been the vehicle of news for the peasant villages between Shrewsbury and Northumberland, filling in the gaps of knowledge, refracting the truth. And now Shakespeare himself 'runs before' his Rumour.

Rumour does more than signal the start of a new play, crucially he signals the start of a new attitude to history itself.

## Context Passage 2: 1.3.85–110

The second passage for analysis I have taken from a speech near the end of Act 1 spoken by Richard Scroop, Archbishop of York. To get a sense of the context in which the passage occurs it will be useful to trace events since the Induction.

Paralleling the first scene of *Part 1*, *2Henry IV* proper opens with a setting in which an old patriarch receives tenuous reports from a distant source. Here at the ancient family residence of Warkworth Castle the ageing Lord Percy receives a report ('certain news') from his ally Lord Bardolph of his son Hotspur's glorious victory at Shrewsbury, routing the King's army (cf. *Induction* line 29ff.). Warkworth is pulsing with rumours and alarms concerning Hotspur's fate until eventually Morton presents a first-hand account of his defeat and death. At first demoralised, Northumberland later resolves to inflict revenge by combining with the army of the Archbishop of York.

Meanwhile, on a London street Falstaff rants and thunders against the doctor's announcement that he is riddled with pox as well as gout (these early scenes are suffused with imagery of decay, ageing and decline). He is rounded on by the Lord Chief Justice, reminding Falstaff of the summons for the Gad's Hill robbery (see *1 Henry IV* 2.2). With typical bravado Falstaff pleads exemption on grounds of military service – then begs a loan of £1000 for expenses.

Rumours abound and the tension increases as Scene 3 focuses attention on the rebels at York preparing for battle. Although their forces number 25,000 they remain uncertain of Northumberland's commitment to their cause:

*[The Archbishop's Palace at York]*

| | | |
|---|---|---|
| *Archbishop*: | Let us on, | 85 |
| | And publish the occasion of our arms. | |
| | The commonwealth is sick of their own choice, | |
| | Their over-greedy love hath surfeited: | |
| | An habitation giddy and unsure | |
| | Hath he that buildeth on the vulgar heart. | 90 |
| | O thou fond Many, with what loud applause | |
| | Didst thou beat heaven with blessing Bullingbrook, | |
| | Before he was what thou wouldst have him be! | |
| | And being now trimmed in thine own desires, | |
| | Thou, beastly feeder, art so full of him | 95 |
| | That thou provok'st thyself to cast him up. | |
| | So, so, thou common dog, didst thou disgorge | |
| | Thy glutton bosom of the royal Richard, | |
| | And now thou wouldst eat thy dead vomit up, | |
| | And howl'st to find it. What trust is in these times? | 100 |
| | They, that when Richard lived would have him die, | |
| | Are now become enamour'd on his grave; | |
| | Thou that threw'st dust upon his goodly head | |
| | When through proud London he came sighing on | |
| | After th'admired heels of Bullingbrook, | 105 |
| | Criest now: 'O earth, yield us that king again | |
| | And take thou this!' O thoughts of men accursed! | |
| | Past and to come seems best; things present, worst. | |
| *Mowbray*: | Shall we go draw our numbers, and set on? | |
| *Hastings*: | We are Time's subjects, and Time bids be gone. *[Exeunt]* | 110 |

Significantly, this passage was not printed in the Quarto of 1600 and it is not difficult to appreciate why, presenting as it does a seditious churchman fomenting rebellion against the sitting monarch. If we ask why the passage (and the play) should have been relevant to Elizabethan audiences then we have our answer exactly there – the parallels between a jittery Tudor administration and the unstable regime of Henry IV are at least tacit, and, in the right hands, downright incendiary. In 1596 there had been a series of popular riots in English rural areas over steeply rising corn prices, about which the Archbishop's discourse casts a warning for Globe audiences.

A preliminary reading of the passage delivers a firm impression of the Archbishop's astringent tone of voice and some very interesting issues immediately show up. One item of the diction that catches my eye from the outset is the repetition of the adverb 'now', appearing in lines 94, 99, 102 and 106. In each case this is preceded with a statement about the past, and the effect is to shuttle the audience tersely between the two moments; namely before and after the ascent of Henry IV. Furthermore, this term 'now' seems to perform a structural role, acting as the nodal points of the Archbishop's tirade, and consequently it allows him to stress this word with particular force. With these possibilities in mind we can begin to probe the details.

The Archbishop's opening words – 'Let us on' – are intended to steer the general's attention to the planned fight with Henry by declaring their warlike intentions (the 'occasion of our arms'). Until this moment they have spent the scene in speculation, with Bardolph's long-extended building metaphor straining their attention. Ironically the Archbishop himself veers off on his own private hobbyhorse, on what he regards as the capricious loyalties of the common people:

Their over-greedy love hath surfeited ...

(87–8)

The 'commonwealth' is the state, which has become 'sick' by the mob's 'own choice' of new king. The Archbishop claims that, having formerly loved and preferred King Henry over Richard II, they have now grown weary of him. Note the familiar Shakespearean imagery of the appetite to express extremes of desire, now cloying with excess of usage. We can imagine that an actor playing this role would here emphasise the modifier 'common'.

The imagery of sickness and greed both here and in the rest of this speech chimes with that of Falstaff (pox and gout) in the previous scene. Indeed, the play as a whole is much preoccupied with decay and ageing, decline and death. So we see a 'crumbling' Falstaff, decrepit recruits, an infirm Lord Chief Justice, aged Silence, and a sick and dying king: the visual trope for the kingdom, John of Gaunt's 'sceptred isle', is now in moral as well as vital decline (see *Richard II* 2.1.37ff.).

Here sickness is a metaphor for a kingdom riven by unrest, factionalism and civil strife – all of which accord with Carlisle's prescient warning in *Richard II* (see 4.1.141–2). His prediction refers to Henry Bullingbrook's 'crime' or 'sin' in deposing the rightful king, and the Archbishop's word 'sick' carries moral resonance, since for him the body politic is diseased. The Archbishop regards himself as the specialist who will 'purge' the diseased land – this is especially evident in his speech at 4.1.54–66, which is the pendant to this one. There, although he denies being the physician to the 'infected' land, he has become fixated on sickness, envisioning himself as a crusader, expunging its disease.

In the next line, 'habitation' (89) resumes Bardolph's 'building' image from earlier in this scene (and perhaps we can even hear Rumour's 'household' in the word). 'Giddy' is a half-rhyme with 'greedy', both of which, together with 'unsure', imply unstable, restive, a populace not to be trusted. We should expect biblical phrases from a churchman, even one so worldly as the Archbishop, and lines 89–90 gloss an idea from the New Testament (*Luke* 6:49), while lines 103–4 remember *2 Samuel* 16:13.

If we are surprised at his martial attitude, then we may equally be jolted by Bardolph's transparent snobbery – though this is of its time. 'Vulgar heart' (90) underlines the theme of 'common' and reinforces the sense of the people being dominated by feelings instead of reason, an idea taken up in the following line with 'fond Many', 'fond' being a favourite Shakespearean condescension, here meaning 'stupid' or 'frivolous':

> O thou fond Many, with what loud applause
> Didst thou beat heaven with blessing Bullingbrook,
> Before he was what thou wouldst have him be!
>
> (91–3)

These lines create quite a strong visual and aural image of the clamorous London poor, cheering on their favourite as he processes to receive the crown. Alliterative line 92 reminds us that in approving Henry they defied God's choice of Richard II, the sanctified ruler, and this image reappears strikingly in lines 104–5. In reality these humble Londoners had little influence and merely applauded the populist Bullingbrook, doing so before they understood his true nature (see *Richard II* 1.4.24–36).

The consonant /b/ of line 92's alliteration beats through the following lines, and its plosive quality permits the Archbishop to belt out his invective against the common people. 'Now' (line 94) announces the present reality of nausea at their over-indulgent acclaim. By referring to them as the 'beastly feeder', he merges two common Shakespearean ideas of loathing: they resemble beasts and are driven by greedy appetite ('desires'; line 94). It is interesting to note that in *Richard II* York – an ally of the Archbishop – also uses the terms 'greedy' and 'desires' in depicting the London rabble in their reception for Henry Bullingbrook (*Richard II* 5.2.13).

In line 98, the importance of the phrase 'royal Richard' may not be instantly apparent, but it carries some important weight. The epithet 'royal' implies that King Richard II was the lawful king ('regal' and 'legal', 'royal' and 'loyal' deriving from the same semantic root; the King is literally the law). It implies that Richard comes of the rightful, God-ordained line, which Henry offended (see Chapter 1). Henry himself has only the 'bless' of the mob (line 92). Consequently the artful Archbishop signals yet again his contempt for Henry.

Line 103 develops this idea, yet in an oblique way. By throwing dust over Richard's 'goodly head' they not merely befoul but also degrade a king, God's appointee, and so deny his divinity. For a churchman this would naturally carry extra theological nuances. 'Goodly' here means 'virtuous', of course, but is also synonymous with 'godly'.

The insubordinate, ungodly rabble of London is next epitomised, in line 99, as a common dog that eats its own vomit. Within the power structures of the period the Archbishop finds it abhorrent that the lowest should impinge on the highest. Yet, presumably, these are of the same yeomanry and peasant stock from which his own soldiery is mustered. Doubtlessly valuable as tillers of the tilth or as infantry, they ought to recognise their lowly station in the order of society. This is the beginning of the Archbishop's particular version of history (as anticipated by Rumour).

There is within the Archbishop's soliloquy an unmistakable air of grave tension. His attacks on the commoners (there are more to follow) resemble a fixation, as of something gnawing at his sensibility. Moreover, this speech characterises the mood of the play as a whole, being in a constant state of stress and turmoil ('giddy and unsure'), a nervous anxiety that stems from Rumour's disconcerting overture. The substratum of the play appears to be in foment.

Technically speaking, the Archbishop's discourse is not a soliloquy, but the degree of interiority in it closely resembles one. It lays bare his innermost disquiet. Nevertheless his discourse likewise comes across as largely spontaneous, since his phrasal constructions are so baggy: the simple conjunction 'and' occurs at least seven times, giving the impression of thoughts and emotions converging but loosely connected, structured by the impulses which continually return his attention to the *idée fixe*.

Line 100 returns to the 'giddy and unsure' theme, uncertainty and concern:

What trust is in these times?

A rhetorical quotation, this is not so much answered in the remainder of the Archbishop's speech as extended and instanced. His question has at least two interpretations: that today there is no longer any such thing as trust or loyalty, and that these times are volatile and unpredictable.

He illustrates his scepticism in subsequent lines. Those fickle, arrogant ('proud') Londoners now revere their once-reviled king, Richard:

> Criest now: 'O earth, yield us that king again
> And take thou this!' O thoughts of men accursed!
>
> (106–7)

However, there is no evidence in the play for their turn-coating, and at worst only indifference (and recall that Northumberland and his son Hotspur were once the staunchest of Henry Bullingbrook's allies; see *Richard II* 2.3.45–50).

Until these closing lines of his 'soliloquy' the rhythm of the Archbishop's speech is unusually regular. Nevertheless, as the memory of his dead King resurfaces and his indignation rises, the metre of his lines breaks down markedly (by contrast, Mowbray and Hastings both speak in regular blank verse, suggesting highly judicious or resolute counsels).

The ghost of the past King stirs while Shakespeare clearly revisits his words of *Richard II*, where the Duchess of York describes the former King's demise:

> Where rude misgoverned hands from windows' tops
> Threw dust and rubbish on King Richard's head.
>
> (*Richard II* 5.2.5–6)

Like Shakespeare, the Archbishop now finds strength, plus resolution, by looking back. He closes aphoristically:

> Past and to come seems best; things present worst
>
> (108)

His line conceals the fact that Scroop's hero, Richard, was no saint and in the earlier play he is depicted as rapine in terms of Bullingbrook's lands, a dissolute squanderer in whose crown 'a thousand flatterers sit' (*Richard II* 2.1.100). Ironically, the Archbishop's discourse is more likely to recall the sins of that deposed monarch than those of his successor, Henry. Yet another version of history.

Impassive Mowbray refocuses their attention on the immediate, the practical business of organising the muster of troops. Ironically, given that the Archbishop's speech refers so much to the word 'now', his meditation itself dwells on the dark past. Hastings's metaphysical commonplace that 'We are Time's subjects' economically reminds them that they are victims of Time's past while deftly urging his grace to get a move on (it might retain echoes, too, of Richard's sombre lament, 'I wasted time and now time doth waste me', *Richard II* 5.5.49; compare also in the present play 3.1.44–5 and 4.1.104).

The metaphysics of Hastings's line touch on issues in the play at large. The theme of time lies at the very core of the rebel sense of resentment. History is to blame. This is borne out by the large number of ties between the Archbishop's speech and previous plays in the Henriad, especially *Richard II*. In fact it is not really possible to do full justice to his soliloquy without some familiarity with the earlier play.

The Archbishop's speech emphasises a view of history as a kind of ineradicable memory in which nothing is lost or swealed away. Like the workings of a Greek tragedy, we feel here that a perceived sin cannot easily be expiated but rolls implacably on over time until it is finally remitted. Thus in these history plays we find generations of characters appearing in a complex of relationships. Mowbray himself exemplifies this feature: son of the Duke of Norfolk who was banished by Richard II and whose valet was none other than the young John Falstaff (see 3.2.20–1 of the current play). Meanwhile, the name of Mortimer, whom the rebels hold to be the rightful heir to the throne, trundles inexorably through all the history plays like a restive ghost. They are all time's subjects.

Because of this persistence of time, the Archbishop understands it as a guarantor of social order and degree. In this matter he contradicts Rumour, who beholds only discord and rebellion in its operation.

In his introduction to the Arden edition of *2Henry IV* A.R. Humphries offers some very salient points on this theme of time in relation to Hastings's insightful remark: 'the play embeds itself in a deep layer of time. Time has two main aspects – the present as it presses towards the future, the past as it revives the present' (*2Henry IV* Arden2, p. lii). The first of these aspects refers to both the force of the rebels' ambition to oust Henry IV and the King's efforts to thwart them in favour of his son as future king. The second refers to the unrelenting tendency of the past to impede both of these.

With this in mind, Hastings's epigram is unmistakably fatalistic and, recalling Rumour, posits that mankind cannot be its own masters. Caught in the necessary workings of time, man cannot be free. This is not a metaphysical thread that Shakespeare develops here to any great extent but it is an important dynamic in the comedy of the play. Absurdly, we watch these figures making plans and striving to bring them to fruition (the 'hatch and brood of time'; 3.1.85), all the while conscious that they will be thwarted, certainly in the cosmic sense. King Lear famously deconstructs the chimera of human free will:

> As flies to wanton boys are we to the gods,
> They kill us for their sport.
>
> (*King Lear* 4.1.178–9)

Even the Archbishop seems aware of this susceptibility of the will to become thwarted when he acknowledges the flair of the 'fond Many', the vulgar commoners, to frustrate his own best-laid schemes. L.C. Knights comments on this propensity:

> The world of *King Henry IV*, Part II, ... is a world where men are only too plainly time's subjects, yet persist in planning and contriving attempts by hook or by crook to further their own interests.
>
> (Knights, p. 48)

What does the passage tell us of the identity of this turbulent priest, Archbishop Scroop? Is he an insufferable bigot? Or do you perceive him as a man of deeply held political convictions and loyalties? A zealot of sorts, with deep-rooted intensity? Among the rebels in this scene he is the one who acts as a spokesman, making him appear their leader, too, and indeed, he comes across as a man of unyielding conviction who carries the other generals along with him. Here Mowbray and Hastings defer to his rank and command, possibly as a consequence of his church role. After the above extract we do not meet the rebels again until 4.1, by which time the Archbishop has become the de facto leader of their army.

It may seem anomalous to modern audiences that a Christian archbishop should be chief protagonist among military men. It is a role that attracts comments throughout the play from both sides. As a churchman he is equally likely to surprise us both by his misanthropy and by his bellicosity, and to many this may even seem an incongruous, faintly bizarre confederacy.

We have noted his misanthropy, evident in his fuming denunciation of the common people. He becomes increasingly manic, impiously venting his wrathful spleen on a generally abstract target. His intolerance towards his 'flock' may come over to purists as unchristian, but Shakespeare is reminding his audience of the hypocrisy among contemporary churchmen and that ministers have rarely been dogmatic in observing Christ's own teachings. To a contemporary Protestant audience the sight of a monstrously corrupt and hypocritical Catholic prelate could have presented a gratifying endorsement of their own apostasy.

Our Archbishop here is a warrior in all but name and vestment. His scolding of Henry IV's vulgar supporters displays no overt reference to God but, as we have noted, it is cross-veined with religious citations and allusions. The imagery of his reproach has unmistakable, almost palpable moralistic overtones, while a good many deadly sins slither through it: avarice (88), desire (94), gluttony (98) and pride (104). He fulminates with undisguised anger, demonstrating scant charity, but perhaps line 108 holds out some hope ('to come seems best').

The Archbishop's sharply purgative slant is one element in the play's composite theme of disease and catharsis that includes the King's cleansing the land of rebellion and Prince Hal (as King Henry V) eventually harrowing Falstaff too. This regularising impulse contrasts with Falstaff's (and Rumour's) characteristic fondness for disorder. As we noted in Chapter 2, many critics interpret Falstaff as a figure of carnival (for instance see Graham Holderness's *Shakespeare Recycled*). In many ways, Archbishop Scroop is the antithesis of Falstaff: sober misanthropist, condescending snob, warmonger, a repressive and compulsive advocate of order and degree. If we understand Falstaff as representing Carnival, then we may be willing to regard the Archbishop as its antithesis, Lent: austerely puritanical, forbidding, ruthlessly unforgiving.

## Context Passage 3: 3.1.1–39

Following the Archbishop's tirade against plebeian frailty, Act 2 opens in Mistress Quickly's lowly Eastcheap tavern, the Boar's Head, with its spirited repartee steeped in a rich vernacular. Quickly commissions Fang and Snare to arrest Falstaff for breach of a promise to marry her and his failure to repay a loan, but Falstaff slinks out of it, even securing a further loan.

In 2.2 Prince Hal, now beginning to regret his neglect of his father, makes his first appearance in the play. Exchanging comic banter with Poins, the two concoct another practical joke on Falstaff. Meanwhile, with the prospect of war gathering, the focus switches to Northumberland, where Hotspur's widow passionately bewails her husband's death at Shrewsbury and persuades the Earl to escape north, thereby abandoning the rebels.

Back at the Boar's Head (2.4), Prince Hal and Poins, disguised as barmen, play their feeble joke on Falstaff, but are interrupted by Bardolph and Peto announcing news of the imminent military campaign in the North. Falstaff makes his affectionate farewell to the 'ladies' of the tavern.

In the wake of the hearty clamour at the finish of Act 2, Act 3 at first begins in nocturnal hush. King Henry enters in his nightgown, accompanied by a page:

*King*:     Go, call the Earls of Surrey and of Warwick;
           But ere they come, bid them o'er-read these letters
           And well consider of them. Make good speed.

                                                    *Exit [Page]*

           How many thousand of my poorest subjects
           Are at this hour asleep? O Sleep! O gentle Sleep!          5
           Nature's soft nurse, how have I frighted thee,
           That thou no more wilt weigh my eye-lids down
           And steep my senses in forgetfulness?
           Why rather Sleep liest thou in smoky cribs,
           Upon uneasy pallets stretching thee                        10
           And hushed with buzzing night-flies to thy slumber,
           Than in the perfumed chambers of the great,

> Under the canopies of costly state
> And lulled with sound of sweetest melody?
> O thou dull god, why liest thou with the vile,          15
> In loathsome beds, and leavest the kingly couch
> A watch-case, or a common ''larum-bell?
> Wilt thou upon the high and giddy mast
> Seal up the ship-boy's eyes, and rock his brains
> In cradle of the rude imperious surge          20
> And in the visitation of the winds,
> Who take the ruffian billows by the top,
> Curling their monstrous heads and hanging them
> With deafening clamour in the slippery clouds,
> That, with the hurly, death itself awakes?          25
> Canst thou, O partial Sleep, give thy repose
> To the wet sea-son in an hour so rude,
> And, in the calmest and most stillest night
> With all appliances and means to boot,
> Deny it to a king? Then happy low lie down,          30
> Uneasy lies the head that wears a crown.
> 
> *Enter WARWICK and SURREY*

*Warwick*:   Many good morrows to your majesty.
*King*:   Is it good morrow, lords?
*Warwick*:                            'Tis one o'clock, and past.
*King*:   Why, then, good morrow to you all, my lords.
      Have you read o'er the letters that I sent you?          35
*Warwick*:   We have, my liege.
*King*:   Then you perceive the body of our kingdom
      How foul it is, what rank diseases grow,
      And with what danger near the heart of it.

Act 3 Scene 1 is a short scene, but operates as a pivotal *ricorso*, quiet and meditative, squeezed between two knockabout Falstaff episodes. It is the still point at the very heart of the play, counterpointing Falstaff's extrovert ribaldry with its intense introspection. It is, moreover, the King's first appearance in the play that bears his name.

Many of the scenes in *2Henry IV* have counterparts in *Part 1*, but this scene has an important corollary *in Richard II*, namely 5.5. There the King, ousted by Henry, finds himself in persecuted isolation, constrained to contemplate his mortality and his basic humanity, using similar words and ideas to Henry. For example:

> Sometimes am I a king
> Then treasons wish myself a beggar
>
> (*Richard II* 5.5.31–2)

In *1Henry IV*, King Henry is the first figure on stage and the first to speak. He is important there, at the heart of the important business right through to the Battle of Shrewsbury at the close. Here he appears in only three scenes and in each he appears sick and attenuated in stature. Emerging on stage here, this forlorn figure in a nightgown may not at first be recognisable as the King, the most powerful man in England. Perhaps expecting a self-assured, even self-righteous monarch, we encounter instead a weak, sickly figure wracked by guilt and inadequacy. The moment presents a striking contrast with the Archbishop's brashly assertive monologue, full of a terrible conviction.

My preliminary reading of this passage throws up some lucid impressions: the agitation of the King, some surprisingly visual and lyrical images, and in the soliloquy some important recurring themes. The King's soliloquy obviously focuses on psychological insights while his dialogue with Warwick speaks of the physical body and 'rank diseases'. I propose to orchestrate my analysis around four key items of diction: 'nurse' (6), 'crown' (31), 'uneasy' (31 and 10) and 'body' (37).

(i)   Lines 1–17: '*in the perfumed chambers of the great*'

As we watch Henry approach us on stage it is important to remember that this is the man who, as the cunning schemer Bullingbrook, assembled an alliance of most powerful backers, drew the common people ('fond many') to his side, and outwitted the anointed King and his confederates. And this the man that in his chamber quivers:

> *King*:   Go, call the Earls of Surrey and of Warwick;
>            But ere they come, bid them o'er-read these letters
>            And well consider of them. Make good speed.
>
> (1–3)

As well as fetching the King onto the stage, this business of the letters is dramatically important in quickly establishing the official, public man in his role of king. His opening utterances are all imperatives – 'go', 'call', 'bid', 'consider', 'make' – he is in command, despatching official documents. At the end of the extract, Warwick's responses to the King have a similar effect and force: 'your majesty' and 'my liege' remind us that these courtiers owe fealty to him, whatever rumours we have heard.

So we observe here how Henry the mortal man is framed, encased even, by his official public role. And within we observe the private, more vulnerable human being. Perhaps this is why the scene may have been censored, since it presents a royal personage almost bare, an ordinary man with arms and legs, and a conscience, very much like the rest of us (or as King Lear describes himself, a 'bare forked animal'; *King Lear* 3.4.103).

After the Page leaves on his mission the first thought of the King's may at first be taken as paternal empathy, care towards the multitude of paupers in his kingdom:

> How many thousand of my poorest subjects
> Are at this hour asleep?
>
> (4–5)

Kingship has sometimes been thought of as fatherliness, the kingdom's subjects small helpless children. But what follows makes clear that the emphasis is not on the 'subjects' but the word 'asleep'. His rhetorical question is followed up by a cry of anguish, personifying sleep as a god:

> 'O Sleep! O gentle Sleep!
> Nature's soft nurse, how have I frighted thee ...
>
> (5–6)

Possibly he is thinking here of Hypnos, the Greek god of sleep, but notice how his question is formed to suggest a sense of his own guilt. The repetition of the word 'sleep' as well as the exclamation marks allude to the King's tormented frustration.

Interesting, too, is his representation of sleep as a nurse, a curative figure. Macbeth likewise thought in these terms, describing sleep as nature's 'balm of hurt minds' (*Macbeth* 2.2.38–9) – and we will have more to say below on this connection. He begins to point up the contrast that while the poorest are asleep he has insomnia, that it is somehow *unnatural* for him not to sleep, and so there is something deeply wrong. His reference to 'nurse' takes up a recurrent motif in the play – of sickness and disease – and he himself refers to this later in the soliloquy, at line 38. As a curative 'nurse', sleep is given a moral tenor, since the King strongly implies a connection between his failure to sleep and the 'rank diseases' in the kingdom.

Frustration is compounded into despair in the following line in his despondent fear that sleep will 'no more' close his eyelids. We can make of this at least two points. The first is a technical note: this quaint image of sleep weighing down eyelids is what is called a 'kenning', a highly imaginative phrase describing something usually mundane (there is another example in line 31). The other point is that if sleep will not close his eyes then the only means left to do so is death, deepening his sense of despair (see line 25).

Then follows a series of strikingly lyrical images:

And steep my senses in forgetfulness

(8)

The whispering alliteration of this line captures the intense longing for sleep, while the word 'steep' conveys a notion of complete abandon, the oblivion of 'forgetfulness'. Equally, the word 'forgetfulness' implies a desire to escape both from the cares of kingship and from the guilt that simmers away under this soliloquy.

'Steep' is part-echoed in 'Sleep' in the next line, 9, where the King begins to make explicit his central concern: why is it that the lowliest poor can sleep in their smoke-filled hovels ('cribs'), stretched out on 'uneasy pallets', the crudest type of straw bed? Their slumber is 'hushed' or soothed by 'buzzing night flies'.

It seems unnatural again that those in the filthiest slums should have the advantage over the 'perfumed chambers of the great'. The word 'great' in this simile refers not to the famous or successful, but simply those at the top of the chain of being, the nobility, those who can afford to lie

> Under the canopies of costly state
> And lulled with sound of sweetest melody.

(13–14)

This is a curious phrase. 'Canopies' indicates on one level the expensive beds or 'couch' of the wealthy. The term also implies protection, safety or assurance, and so the King ought to be able to sleep well here. But the phrase 'costly state' rubs hard against this, not just literally in the great expense of building, but pointedly in the high cost of acquiring and defending his present 'state' or situation as King: in other words, the murder, deposition and civil war which have made enemies of his people (what the Archbishop refers to as the 'habitation giddy and unsure').

It is worth pointing out how, over these lines, the King makes a three-point antithesis of his own lot with that of the poor; so he contrasts perfumed chambers with smoky cribs, his kingly couch against uneasy pallets, and the 'sweetest melody' in opposition to those buzzing flies.

It remains inexplicable to him, leading to a fierce outcry at the climax of this first part of his soliloquy:

> O thou dull god, why liest thou with the vile,
> In loathsome beds, and leavest the kingly couch
> A watch-case, or a common 'larum-bell?

(15–17)

The god of sleep is 'dull' in the sense of being inattentive to him, or dead, as well as simply sluggish. 'My poorest subjects' have become the 'vile, / In loathsome beds'. The modifier 'dull' echoes 'lulled' in the previous line and introduces the alliterative /l/ over these lines. This alliteration contrasts strongly with the earlier whispers (or hisses), allowing the actor to snarl out this mini-climax with ferocity. This intensity is also enabled by the strong adjectives here: 'vile', 'dull', 'loathsome' and 'common'. It is matched by the King's gnawing repetition of the theme of injustice as well as of phrases such as 'liest thou ' (lines 9, 15 plus 'lies' in 31).

'Watch-case' is an interesting item. In terms of a timepiece this is, of course, an anachronism in Henry IV's fifteenth century (the earliest watches begin to appear in the early 1500s). However Shakespeare was probably familiar with them, the case acting – like 'canopies' – as a protective shell resembling that around the King (cf. *The Tempest* 2.1.12).

Then there is another significant meaning of 'watch-case', especially because in Shakespeare 'watch' and 'sleep' are closely related. The two words are antithetical; for example, from Hamlet, 'some must watch while some must sleep' (3.2.267). 'Watch' is a synonym for 'care', that is, 'attend', 'concern' or 'worry'. So a watch-case typically represents a space in which one should feel safe from harm but instead, for the King, has become a metaphorical cell of anxiety.

Moreover in falconry – in which Shakespeare was well-versed (see line 19) – to 'watch' is to *prevent* a bird from sleeping. All of this encapsulates precisely the King's dilemma, constantly on the watch, robbed of sleep, and on edge, expecting at any moment the kind of emergency implied in the word ''larum' or alarm bell (cf. *Macbeth* 2.2.69–71 and *Hamlet* 2.2.148–50).

(ii)  Lines 18–31: '*Uneasy lies the head that wears a crown*'

Conventionally, on the Elizabethan stage, a soliloquy is assumed to intimate to the audience the true inner thoughts, feelings and motives of the speaker alone on stage, and is therefore regarded as truthful. However, here we can see that the form does not in reality exactly match the consciousness behind it, because for one thing the King speaks in regular sentences. Furthermore, although he is in acute turmoil, he manages to conceive the most dazzlingly lucid and lyrical images. These are particularly apparent in the next section of his soliloquy:

> Wilt thou upon the high and giddy mast
> Seal up the ship-boy's eyes, and rock his brains
> In cradle of the rude imperious surge ...

(18–20)

The matrix of his febrile mind somehow creates brilliantly stark pictures.

The King continues by wondering how the sea-boy up in the crow's nest, 'high and giddy' in a violent storm and rocked by mountainous ocean waves ('the rude and imperious surge'; line 20), manages to sleep, while he, 'in the calmest and most stillest night' (28), is forced to remain wide awake. 'High' switches their relative positions, since absence of sleep now makes the King poor. The adjective 'giddy' gives a nod towards the Archbishop's speech just discussed and, as there, it carries the same connotation of unrest (the King himself is also giddy with worry).

Even in this 'imperious' storm the cabin boy can so easily doze off that his eyes must be sealed up, referring once again to falconry and the practice of sewing up ('seeling') a young bird's eyelids during its early training (cf. *Antony and Cleopatra* 3.12.12). His 'cradle' is a sea hammock, yet another example of bed imagery. The verse here is beautifully sinewy, winding round the almost palpable alliterative /r/ sounds in these lines, mimicking the rolling swell itself.

Those sounds are then exchanged for wide-open assonances of 'ruffian billows', 'monstrous' and 'clamour' (lines 22–4) in accord with the wind-blasted clouds. The metaphor 'ruffian' extends the imagery of rough poverty while evoking the theme of aggression, and rebellion (a 'visitation' – line 21 – is a violent onset of conflict here). Shakespeare's vivid depiction of the warring marine elements is astonishing for its compactness:

> Curling their monstrous heads and hanging them
> With deafening clamour in the slippery clouds ... .
>
> (23–4)

It is worth noting too, the effect of participle endings (-ing) hereabouts: 'curling', 'hanging', 'deafening'. These permeate the tempest with an impression of overpowering relentlessness, a point emphasised by the long, mazy sentence structure, winding and condensing over lines 18–25. The extract is a foment of sounds and motion: from 'frighted' and 'buzzing' through 'rock' and 'surge', to 'deafening clamour' and 'hurly' (almost all the verbs are in the present tense, once again giving the impression of constant unease).

The storm at sea is clearly a mental marinescape, a powerfully creative projection of the storm booming in the King's own troubled mind – we may even be reminded here of other Shakespearean storms like that in *The Tempest* or King Lear's 'cataracts and hurricanoes'. Reading the word 'hurly' (line 25), who is not also put in mind of Macbeth (and *his* sleepless nights after regicide)?

'Slippery' in line 24 extends the imagery of instability, set up by words such as 'uneasy', 'giddy' and 'hurly'. The very elements seem unloosed and mutinous until this amazing image is brought to a startling climax, when even 'death itself awakes' (25). This memorable personification links up with line 5, where the King fears that now only death may close his lids.

With the climax of the storm comes a sudden change in the point of view, from lyricism to explicit interrogation. In one complex question the King returns obsessively to the repeated issue of 'partial Sleep' (26). Perhaps there is a pun here on 'partial' ('biased' as well as 'incomplete'). His rhetorical interrogation resembles something more inquisitorial than a simple enquiry: once more, how can sleep be granted to this boy, 'sea-son', in the most uncongenial environment, when he himself, in the most conducive setting, writhes in sleepless agony?

His rhetorical questionings draw the observer towards the inevitable conclusion that the problem is less rooted in the external world than in his tumultuous, guilt-ridden inner world. But of course it is in the nature of insomnia to thwart cool reason, and of vanity to impede wisdom. Ironically, by denying repose to the mighty King Sleep turns the tables, reducing the King to a disconsolate minion.

In the final line of his soliloquy he seems to achieve a position of despondent resignation:

Uneasy lies the head that wears a crown.

(31)

This aphoristic sentiment is given added gravitas by its reversed syntax. It is a line succulent in sound and sense. Altering the normal word-order helps it to bring the speech to a conclusion with a line that is metrically highly regular, thereby implying the King's final acquiescence. But this word-order also helps to give emphasis at the end of the line to the key phrase 'that wears a crown'.

Let us examine this phrase in more detail. First, the word 'a'. Not a big word, but what does it imply here? Clearly he is saying uneasiness can afflict *any* king, not necessarily this one. He suggests that this heavy responsibility comes with the territory. Yet, it is another evasion of responsibility, since the cause of his insomnia lies deeper than general kingship, onerous though that may be.

On a simple level the phrase in line 31 is another example of a kenning, equating to 'anyone who is king'. But it is significant on a literal level, for the reason that the word 'wears' may remind us once more that he is not the true king; he simply dons the crown, rather than possesses it in the sense that an anointed king would.

So, the evasion in this final phrase actually draws attention to the cause of his sleeplessness: to become king, the wearer of the crown, Henry had to depose the rightful king and deny his heir Mortimer. And given that, it is of course not the 'head' that is uneasy but the mind, or the conscience. For the Elizabethans the conscience is the golden, the quintessential competence of the sovereign being, that ordinary people lack. His son – as Henry V – argues a similar point on the eve of Agincourt:

> ... every fool, whose sense no more can feel
> But his own wringing. What infinite heart's ease
> Must king's neglect that private men enjoy.
>
> (*Henry V* 4.1.242–3)

In the above extract, when Henry IV uses the adjective 'Uneasy' in line 31 he does not of course use it in the same sense as at line 10. It is a word that might describe the climate of the whole play. From Rumour's 'smooth comforts false' and Fastaff's disease through to the Epilogue's 'My fear is your displeasure', the whole surface is unsettled with, for instance, Falstaff's shameful past finding him out, rebels cheated of battle at Gaultree, and Hal's rejection of his former ally. Together with its decentred universe, the text exudes deep restlessness.

Something is seriously amiss, rotten, or has what the King calls 'rank diseases' (line 38). His reign is out of joint, implying some deep-rooted defect. Just as the geographical extensions of kingdom are unstable and under threat, so the internal, the King's mind, is in comparable disarray.

For the first time in both parts of *Henry IV* we are presented with Henry the man, divested of his state and public panoply, the carapace of persona lifted (lines 4 to 31). We have generally seen him imperious in military or political council, and scolding his son. Now, his outward garments removed, the soliloquy pares him down to his intimate being.

A modern production may even dispense with the nightgown in order to show us someone essentially identical to his 'poorest subjects'. The scene clearly emphasises his mortality. The next time we see him – in 4.2[4.4] – he is 'exceeding ill', carried in a chair, so in terms of the accoutrements of kingship he is not only in physical and mental decline but, in a symbolic sense, already dethroned. Act 3 Scene 1 serves as a symbolic anticipation of the prince's removal of the crown in 4.2[4.5].

The King's deliberations become so wholly turned in on himself that we could be forgiven for believing that he was in fact sleepwalking. Neither fully asleep nor wide awake, he is already as monarch losing his grip on real affairs and, in the remainder of 3.1, he broods on the past and the shrinking likelihood of a visit to the Holy Land. Shifted from the centre of the play, together with his dwindling vigour, the 'uneasy' head appears less and less engaged in the mainstream of the drama.

Shakespeare's Macbeth – in effect another regicide – famously reports the voice of his conscience spooking him as

> Macbeth does murther Sleep ... Sleep, that knits up the ravelled sleeve of care ...
>
> (*Macbeth* 2.2.35–6)

In *2Henry IV* care is epitomised in both its aspects within the figure of the Prince, his 'unthrifty son'. In the role of father, Henry recoils at the reports of his dissolute life with Falstaff (his 'barren pleasures'; *1Henry IV* 3.2.41), while as King he frets for the health and future of his kingdom. These are not new. The King utters the opening line of *Part 1* introducing the keynote of care with:

> So shaken as we are, so wan with care ...

In the intervening period from 1.1 to 3.1, both the care and the wan-ness have become exacerbated, so much so that the Prince himself later recognises this when he scorns his kingship, the crown, as 'O polished perturbation! Golden care!' (4.2.153[4.5.21])

This 'golden care' extends to include care of his kingdom, or at least concern for its power-structure, a hierarchy that reaches from Doll Tearsheet near its base to himself at its apex. But he never seems to feel it genuinely his own.

The deposition of Richard has undermined the very ontology of Henry's kingship. If, as the rebels believe, Mortimer is the true heir, then Henry is merely the man that '*wears* the crown'. Ironically, by postulating that if sleep gives repose to sea-boys and the vile poor, yet denying it to himself, Henry inadvertently sets up a syllogism in which the inescapable conclusion is that he cannot really be a king.

(iii)  Lines 32–9: '*good morrows*' and '*good morrows*'

When Warwick and Surrey enter the stage the effect of their greeting is to intrude external reality on a trancelike mind-space. They represent the outside world returning to haunt the King. It thus also marks a change from the private to the public Henry, and the diction points accordingly: majesty, lords, liege:

*Warwick*: Many good morrows to your majesty.

The reference to time in this and in subsequent lines ('morrows', 'one o'clock', 'past') has the effect of suddenly thrusting the reality of time into the King's mental space, where previously his thoughts seemed to have been outside real time (for example, he is unaware how late it is).

The late hour stresses the state of emergency felt by the King. What could these letters relate to? In the dialogue following this extract, the King's mind is very much consumed with the recent history of deposing, rebellion and the defections of former allies, the essence of which is encapsulated in lines 37–9:

Then you perceive the body of our kingdom
How foul it is, what rank diseases grow,
And with what danger near the heart of it.

Warwick's truncated, or *catalectic* line 36 before this seems to suggest that he defers to his liege, inviting the King to develop his statement. The King uses the metaphor of the sick body to dramatise the dire condition he finds the commonwealth to be in (recall the Archbishop's words at 1.3.87). The kingdom is in a perceived crisis of danger, having become corrupted at its centre, the inescapable conclusion being that he, as the heart of this body-state, is morally corrupt (in addition to being physically ill).

The imagery of sickness in these lines reflects the clearly delineated thread of sickness or decline that runs through the whole course of the play. The King's sleeplessness is now to him clear evidence of this corruption which has been putrefying under the idle show of 'perfumed chambers', sweet music and ease.

Something is rotten in the state of England and its source comes down to two possibilities: his own sin of deposition and the gnawing tumour of the rebels inside the body of the state. The King's reference to the 'body of our kingdom' is an allusion to the contemporary political theory of the 'body politic'. In a court case of 1562 Queen Elizabeth's lawyer argued in relation to Edward VI:

> For the King has in him two Bodies, viz, a Body natural, and a Body politic. His Body natural is a body mortal, subject to all Infirmities ... But his Body politic is a Body that cannot be seen or handled, consisting of Policy and Government ... .
>
> (quoted in Dutton and Howard, p. 128)

This important concept plainly lies behind the words of the above extract (especially lines 37–9), and it was a belief widely held in the Early Modern period. One development of it is that the king's body was understood as a microcosm of his kingdom, and inherent in this is the belief that the corpus of the king metaphorically embodied a form of harmony for the realm, his person uniting the physical limbs of the country as well all its human components. Thus, the workers may be envisaged as the hands of the state, the king its heart, his council the brains, and so on (a slightly different version is expounded in Shakespeare's *Coriolanus*: 1.1.95). From this issues the notion of the royal 'we', referring to the two aspects in one person.

Some critics have felt this scene contributes little to the play and could therefore be dropped. However, I have tried to make the case that neither this scene nor the above speech could be excluded without significantly unbalancing the build-up of the narrative. Most important, the extract tells us much about the King's state of mind, both in its content and its form, fitting these into the broader context of the preceding plays of the Henriad.

The form of the King's soliloquy is set by the two principal climaxes in lines 15 and 26 and their cadences. It has a fairly baggy construction – consistent with its moment – and the clauses (mostly straggling questions) tend to develop as impromptu ideas, piling up and continually relapsing to the same nagging themes while evading the main cause.

Given this free flow of thoughts, what then gives the passage cohesion, if it has any? This flow of thoughts is structured organically by the mind of the speaker, the King, and it is his voice, with its consistent viewpoint and emotions that hold it together. The audience is drawn in and onwards, partly out of sympathy for this forlorn figure and partly by the expectation of a revelation or an admission regarding the past, one which could in some way affect the status of his kingship (and of his heir). We have come to realise that Henry is either too narrow or too myopic to understand the value of either. And this is his tragedy.

## Context Passage 4: 5.5.21–55

Following the previous extract, we observe the maturing friendship between the two old Justices Shallow and Silence towards whose eccentric wistfulness Falstaff becomes increasingly attracted. The middle sections of the play are absorbed with the advancing threat of the rebels, which finally collapses with Prince John's cunning trick in Gaultree Forest. After the declining King's lament over Hal's failure to reform, his son visits the Court and dramatically takes up the crown from his dying father (who at last appears to express contrition for his deposition of Richard). In marked contrast, Falstaff's scenes continue to supply comic vigour, especially in the recruitment episode (3.2), while the bucolic sections at Shallow's grange depict provincial respite from the claustral intrigues of court. News of

Prince Hal's accession summons Falstaff's crew to London with drooling expectations of generous sinecures:

| | |
|---|---|
| *Falstaff:* | But to stand stained with travel, and sweating with desire to |
| | see him, thinking of nothing else, putting all affairs else in |
| | oblivion, as if there were nothing else to be done but to see him. |
| *Pistol:* | 'Tis *semper idem*, for *obsque hoc nihil est*; 'tis all in every part. |
| *Shallow:* | 'Tis so, indeed                                                    25 |
| *Pistol:* | My knight, I will inflame thy noble liver, |
| | And make thee rage. |
| | Thy Doll, and Helen of thy noble thoughts, |
| | Is in base durance and contagious prison, |
| | Haled thither                                                       30 |
| | By most mechanical and dirty hand: |
| | Rouse up Revenge from ebon den with fell Alecto's snake, |
| | For Doll is in. Pistol speaks nought but truth. |
| *Falstaff:* | I will deliver her. |
| | *The trumpets sound* |
| *Pistol:* | There roared the sea, and trumpet clangour sounds.                  35 |
| | *Enter the KING and his train* |
| *Falstaff:* | God save thy grace, King Hal, my royal Hal. |
| *Pistol:* | The heavens thee guard and keep, |
| | Most royal imp of fame. |
| *Falstaff:* | God save thee, my sweet boy. |
| *King:* | My Lord Chief Justice, speak to that vain man.                      40 |
| *Justice:* | Have you your wits? Know you what 'tis you speak? |
| *Falstaff:* | My king, my Jove, I speak to thee, my heart. |
| *King:* | I know thee not, old man. Fall to thy prayers. |
| | How ill white hairs becomes a fool and jester! |
| | I have long dreamt of such a kind of man,                           45 |
| | So surfeit-swelled, so old and so profane, |
| | But, being awaked, I do despise my dream. |
| | Make less thy body hence, and more thy grace, |
| | Leave gormandising, know the grave doth gape |
| | For thee thrice wider than for other men.                           50 |
| | Reply not to me with a fool-born jest, |
| | Presume not that I am the thing I was, |
| | For God doth know – so shall the world perceive – |

> That I have turned away my former self;
> So will I those that kept me company.                                    55

Even a superficial reading of this extract immediately offers up some key impressions; for instance, the general mood of turmoil, as tension builds towards the climax of Henry V's chilling rejection of Falstaff in line 43. His infamous denial represents the emotional and thematic climax to the play as whole.

The diction of the passage is crucial in generating this curious sense of churning turmoil, especially in its early part; words of action and sound are prominent – 'stained', 'sweating', 'thinking', 'putting', 'inflame', 'rouse', 'speak', 'roared'. The feeling of mounting anxiety is unmistakable as Falstaff and his associates muster in anticipation, having journeyed expeditiously from Shallow's Gloucestershire home.

As I reread the passage, certain thematic words also lift off the page; for example, 'desire' (21), 'awaked' (47) and 'grace' (48). These items have such a strong topical charge that I have decided to organise my discussion of the extract through them. For the purpose of analysis the extract divides reasonably into two movements; first, the section prior to the King's arrival (lines 21–35) then the King's reaction to Falstaff's greeting (lines 36–55).

(i)   Lines 21–35: '*sweating with desire*'

This phrase describes well the state of Falstaff's longing to meet his old friend. And 'stained with travel' implies that he has not yet spent on new clothes ('new liveries') the £1000 sponged from Justice Shallow. His mind has heeded little else, putting all other business into 'oblivion', or neglect. Falstaff is entirely focused on the business of meeting the new King – partly out of ties of old friendship, mostly for the chance of currying favour and promotion, and has already promised Shallow a position of influence at court (as well as implying road-dust, 'stained' may reflect dimly on the ethics of their enterprise.

The fact that Falstaff is having to wait at the side of the royal route implies of course that he has not been granted direct access to the King. However, it may equally denote uncertainty concerning his current relationship with the new King.

Pistol, elusive as ever, answers in Latin. He often says things because they sound rhetorically impressive, for effect, making him appear here legally authoritative though slightly nutty. His first phrase, *semper idem*, means 'nothing changes'; Falstaff does not change (with heavy irony for later), while *obsque hoc nihil* is slightly more metaphysical, 'apart from this there is nothing' (though he mistakes *obsque* for *absque*). Perhaps he means 'we put our whole trust in Falstaff', which, in addition to adducing Falstaff's unfailing charisma, confirms Pistol's guile.

The gist of Pistol's histrionic, euphuistic oratory (beginning at line 26) is that Doll Tearsheet has been arrested and 'haled', dragged off, to pestilential ('contagious') prison. 'Rude and mechanical' in line 31 implies that she was roughly treated by ruthless, impersonal guards. Pistol is probably attempting to provoke Falstaff, and his next perplexing line confirms this idea:

Rouse up Revenge from Ebon den with fell Alecto's snake

(32)

This is typical of Pistol's abstruse musings, a quibbling Byzantine style of discourse. He often gives the impression of quoting obscurely from other plays or classical works, as here. He affects to be scholarly but his contributions generate more heat than light. Here, the fact that he is exceptional among the petitioners in using verse adds to the aura of learnedness, yet his verse is quirky.

The substance of the line is to incite Falstaff to Revenge, like Alecto, one of the classical Furies, agents of vengeance especially against the disobedient. It is nevertheless an interesting line since the settling of scores is something also on Hal's mind. On the other hand, Pistol's florid oration has the important function of striking a trenchant contrast with the King's steely forthright verse.

After, Pistol's rambling jabber, we may feel that Falstaff's response sounds limply prosaic:

I will deliver her.

Is he indifferent to his paramour's plight? Or is he simply distracted? Or is this in fact a phlegmatic assertion of his resolve, a fiercely adamant determination to exact revenge?

So an atmosphere of holiday jesting and sanguine expectancy jostles among the supplicants preparing to greet the newly-crowned Henry V. Expectations have been so much hyped up that their petitions seem a mere formality. This is why I believe Falstaff's word 'desire' in line 21 is such a defining term for this early part of the scene. His retinue is here for one purpose, and the early part of the extract amplifies the hopes and cupidity of Falstaff's party.

Desire is a pervasive force here. Falstaff's motive in travelling to London is the desire to exercise vicarious power through his friend Hal, in the hope of nepotistic appointments, which would empower him to exact revenge on the Lord Chief Justice ('the laws of England are at my command'). Shallow's loan of the £1000 represents his own desire for high office, because

a friend i' th' court is better than a penny in purse.

(5.1.25–6)

This heightening of optimism in turn drives the excitement of the occasion, which is due in part to Falstaff's familiar bravado becoming translated into certainty. At the same time it does also suggest a depth of genuine feelings, reinforced during the King's appearance in lines 36, 39 and 42 with what James Loehlin describes as 'beatific wishes' (Loehlin, p. 116).

As mentioned before, Falstaff appears much older, goutier and poxier than the man of *Part 1*, though his wit and guile remain sharp enough. This is the last scene in which we observe Falstaff – he is referred to in *Henry V*, but in that play he is off-stage, present only in reports of his decline and death. Throughout *Part 2* there has been a strong sense of doom, of a net gradually closing on his freedom, and 5.5 is a kind of disorderly farewell to the old libertarian, his star falling somewhere over the walls, out of sight. There have been a number of hints about Falstaff's separation from the Prince, beginning in 1.2 in which he crosses swords with the doggedly steadfast Lord Chief Justice, who prays:

Well, God send the Prince a better companion

(1.2.156),

which turns out coincidentally, in 5.5 at least, to be himself.

## (ii)  Lines 36–55: '*Presume not that I am the thing I was*'

The arrival of the King's party is announced by 'trumpet clangour'. Falstaff makes appropriate obeisance before the King: the theme of majesty demands it and his wit demurs:

> God save thy grace, King Hal, my royal Hal.

How does Falstaff deliver this line? Is he genuinely deferential, or sardonic? Does he bow, and if so, how? With exaggerated flourishes, with painfully gouty jerkiness? With unguarded and unfeigned cordiality? It is interesting to note that Falstaff used the identical phrase 'God save thy grace' of Hal when first we met them in *1 Henry IV*, at 1.2.13. He certainly mouths the conventional sycophancies in the early part of the line and then he unbuckles with a more proprietorial '*my* royal Hal'. His greetings become increasingly familiar, up to 'my sweet boy' in line 39.

The King suffers a string of salutations until their performance is cut short: 'God save', 'guard', 'keep', and again 'save'. Complaisant maybe, but conventionally so. When at last the King speaks, it is not to reply directly to his former ally but to give a command to the very officer Falstaff had hoped to bring down. The King cuts him cold, dismissing Falstaff as 'that vain man'. 'Vain' here can mean foolish and worthless or idle, as well as conceited (but all of these are pertinent), and his petition too is vain.

The Lord Chief Justice is similarly impersonal, imputing stupidity in the man whom he well knows to be among the most cunning. The Lord Chief Justice is here the antithesis of the bumbling, shambling Justices Shallow and Silence. He is the very opposite of the raffish Falstaff, in possessing a rigorously abstemious sense of order and terrier-like pursuit of justice. He has pursued Falstaff since at least the Gad's Hill robbery in *Part 1*, and he will later issue the warrant for his arrest and incarceration.

The Lord Chief Justice's realignment is significant too in that he graphically sanctifies Hal's new regime, since formerly he was Henry IV's minister. The fact that it was this Justice who had once stalked Hal signifies the Prince's new apostasy. He symbolises continuity of royal administration, holding out the possibility of stability (another contrast with Falstaff's more erratic lifestyle) while settling the realm on a new rigour.

After Falstaff's impassioned plea, from or to 'my heart', the King deigns to acknowledge his presence, though not his identity. Falstaff's appeal to the 'heart' rather than the head has usually succeeded with Hal. Note his reference to 'Jove', a pagan supreme god frequently associated with pleasure. Falstaff's shift of ground is all one with his wily dexterity. By significant contrast the King prefers the Christian 'God' (line 53), and, by extension, 'grace' (48; on which we have more to say below). The King's new scheme is characterised by order, reason and honour, not the feelings:

I know thee not, old man.

(Contrast Hal's shrewd aside, 'I know you all', in *Part 1* 1.2.155.)

The King insults his former ally, by recognising his old age while denying his history, a history which has been formed and shared with Hal (he repeats the word at line 46, and the idea at 44 and 49). Because of its emotional and spiritual implications this private cadence transmutes into a profound dramatic climax. The carnival of Falstaff here ends and social discipline commences.

Line 4 is a wilful line, its ten mortifying monosyllables like a bell tolling Falstaff's death-knell. It is an desolating sentence of exile from the King's care. The denouncement evokes Peter's denial of Christ (*Matthew* 26:70–4), carrying similar finality as well as overtones of expediency.

The new Henry denies the old Falstaff by first denying the old Hal. The old Hal would have understood the ludicrous notion of Falstaff falling to prayers. The short hammer-blow of denunciation is followed by the new King's insulting dismissal repudiation:

How ill white hairs becomes a fool and jester!

(44)

The line is ambiguous, depending on whether 'ill' is read as an adverb or adjective, but the general humiliating thrust is clear.

The cold inflexibility of the King's attitude is mirrored in the spareness of tropes in his speech. However, the anaphoric repetition in line 46 ('so ...') is an exception and cleverly varies his rhetorical method by introducing an extended sentence, one that again catalogues his ex-friend's shortcomings. After demeaning the man, he explains the reason for his 'knowing not' Falstaff: his previous life with him is now rationalised as a dream, an illusion that he despises. Realism once again breaks into idealism, as line 47 makes clear.

We should be careful not to take the King's line 47 too lightly, as a throwaway line, but recollect how in Act 3 his father was unable to sleep or dream and that this was judged an unhealthy condition. The problem is a commonplace: what is dream and what reality, what is true history and what deception? The King attempts to deny the history that was Falstaff, to deny his own self that was Hal and to make a tabula rasa of his own history (thereby reducing his experience to the status of a rumour).

When the King says that he is not what he once was he is in effect reproaching his former self as a separate and corrupt entity. He comes across clearly as guilt-ridden yet, oddly, simultaneously crediting the 'fool' Falstaff with sole responsibility for this. The gaping grave to which he alludes in line 49 is in reality the Hell's Mouth, a familiar stage fixture in medieval morality plays, the ultimate destination for the Vice, the traditional role that Falstaff has so closely resembled at times in *1 Henry IV*.

'Fool-born' (51) and 'fool and jester' (44) summon up images in marked contrast with the important word 'grace' in line 48. In fact the only positive theme in these middle lines is that of urging Falstaff to cultivate grace. It is important because the word carries with it a whole cluster of moral, religious and social connotations cognate with ideas of kingship.

A half-echo of 'grave', 'grace' is the quintessence of gravity. In simple terms it refers to Hal's new order of reason and discipline (these elements are reflected in the highly regular verse of his speech here). He has abandoned the emotional logic of Falstaff's world in favour of the cerebral logic of court and politics, exchanged feeling for logocentrism as the new basis of knowing. The new king regards this

transition as essential to his conception of kingship. So, early in
*Henry V* the Archbishop of Canterbury remarks:

> The king is full of grace and fair regard.
>
> *(Henry V* 1.1.22)

This statement confirms Hal's repudiation of Falstaff as a prerequisite to his metamorphosis as King. Later in the same scene the King himself avers:

> We are no tyrant, but a Christian king
> Unto whose grace our passion is as subject
> As is our wretches fetter'd in our prisons ...
>
> *(Henry V* 1.1. 240–2)

('our wretches' by then of course include both Falstaff and Doll Tearsheet).

Grace thus entails honour and decorum, performing an act out of selfless obedience to an ideal order of duty, medieval in its origins (the notion of honour briefly links the King with Hotspur, the epitome of honour in *1Henry IV*). It is to a large extent an idealised state of existence, transcending the bodily realm for a semi-spiritual condition of virtue and service. With this reference to the ideal of grace, *Henry V* signals an intended return to a medieval mind-set and its principles (which his father had so vigorously eschewed in *Richard II*).

The King's references to the old man's 'white hairs' and the grave make explicit Falstaff's mortality. In effect the King sentences his old comrade to death, and this reminder of mortality prompts us that all along, Falstaff has been denying and eluding mortality through his glittering wit and 'timeless' friendship.

Over the two parts of *Henry IV*, this is the last of Hal's three practical jokes. At each point he has disguised himself for mock humiliation of Falstaff. However, this time, wearing the crown to mask his former self, the joke sticks. In *Henry V* (where Mistress Quickly has married Pistol), Pistol in his distinctively baroque mode reports of Falstaff:

> His heart is fracted and corroborate ...
>
> *(Henry V* 2.1.124)

that is, his heart is broken and corrupted. The Epilogue of the current play makes a hazy allusion to this, but Mistress Quickly herself later points a decisively knowing finger:

> The king has killed his heart.
>
> (*Henry V* 2.1.88)

(This makes a telling contrast with the end of *1 Henry IV*, where the 'dead' Falstaff springs into life again.)

Was the rejection of Falstaff a sudden decision made after the crowning of Henry V? Or had it been envisaged even from the outset of their association? The key speech is Hal's soliloquy in *1 Henry IV* 1.2. Following his duplicitous scheme to rob Falstaff after the Gad's Hill caper, he confides:

> I know you all, and will a while uphold,
> The unyoked humour of your idleness. ...
>
> (155–6)

concluding:

> ... So when this loose behaviour I throw off,
> And pay the debt I never promised,
> By how much better than my word I am ... .
>
> (168–70)

Conversely, some critics believe that at the end of *2 Henry IV* Hal has been coerced into rejecting Falstaff, that he does so in tears. Nevertheless it would seem from the above that the rejection was premeditated even at that early point, stringing the 'fat knight' and his accomplices along for selfish ends: namely, an edifying experience of the *demi-monde* of Eastcheap. Warwick certainly believes so, as when he springs to the Prince's defence with the King:

> The Prince but studies his companions ...
>
> (4.2.68[4.4.68])

and in time will 'Cast off his followers'.

That Hal could be so calculating, so insensibly cold, is perhaps illustrated by his reaction to his apparently dead father (in 4.2[4.5]): instead of experiencing or expressing grief his spontaneous impulse is to slip on the crown. On the eve of the coronation he announces a sea-change in his life, declaring 'the tide of blood in me ... now doth it turn ... (5.2.128–30). And yet we should not be surprised, because in the Henriad as a whole defection has been a recurrent and destabilising motif: Northumberland, Douglas, Hotspur and Glendower all shift allegiance, as does Bullingbrook, Hal's father.

This passage, then, is important for many reasons. One is that it advances the plot of *2Henry IV* by drawing the central relationship of Falstaff and Hal to its dramatic and emotional resolution. From the point of view of Hal's life and the second tetralogy as a whole it marks a profound turning point and transfers the focus of attention towards *Henry V*, the next play in the cycle. It represents a surprising epiphany of the character of Hal and in so doing it casts more light onto his conception of kingship.

In *Richard II* the right to the throne became a discussion between the principles of divine sanction (Richard) and pragmatism, the best man for the job (Henry Bullingbrook). Strictly speaking, in *2Henry IV* Hal has no lawful right to the throne, either by divine sanction or by any remarkable political action (as in the case of his brother, John). He succeeds merely by right of primogeniture, being the eldest brother. We have seen this theme rumble along from *Richard II* and it will re-emerge in Shakespeare's *1Henry VI*, where Mortimer's historic claim is once more reiterated – and its backlash rumbles on through to *Richard III*.

From the point of view of the Elizabethan audience, in a period when the topic of the English succession was becoming increasingly urgent as Elizabeth aged, the accession of Henry V here appears satisfyingly peaceful. The sequel, *Henry V*, would reassure them that the succession – in terms of its stability – had taken the right route.

## Conclusions

Ever since the First Folio of Shakespeare's collected plays, published in 1632, *2Henry IV* has been designated a 'History play'. But in this chapter I have tried to argue it also as a comedy, and more particularly a play of carnival. In what ways, then, is the play a comedy, and how can it be said to be 'carnival'?

Like most Shakespearean comedies, *2Henry IV* has no life-threatening disaster and its tone is, on the whole, light. But, of course, a comedy needs more. On one level there is what we can term the comedy of human frailty, of human life itself. The comic tone and nature of the play are initiated by Rumour's facetious Induction and sustained by, among other things, the magnetic wit of Falstaff, lord of misrule. There are light comic interludes too, like the one in Shallow's orchard and the major tavern scene with Mistress Quickly and Doll Tearsheet.

In *2Henry IV* we observe a world of human folly, of age, disappointment and abandonment. It is a contingent world in which its people are continuously the subject of mutability and caprices of fate, creating an atmosphere of near absurdity. Ancient Greek theorists sometimes defined comedy as the clash of *eros* and *thanatos*, drives of desire, sex and eroticism on one side and the finiteness of human time, or death, on the other. In comedy human desire is frequently thwarted by human limitations, including death itself or its loitering immanence.

These two dimensions give rise to two important principles in Shakespearean comedy: fertility (from sex) and rebirth, and its associated concepts of change and return (that is, return from death, real or figurative). All of these are discoverable in *2Henry IV*. In fact the figure of Sir John Falstaff embraces all of these features. A man driven by appetite (including the need of human friendship), he is the play's essential creative vitality, though it must said that there are others at work in its many plots. Symbolically reborn at the end of *Part 1*, the 'Manningtree ox' becomes the sacrificial ox in *Part 2*, the fatted calf, immolated in the process of rebirth of his 'son' King Hal. His rejection by the reborn Hal forces him to confront the mortality which he has both evaded and celebrated in his search for love. The play itself is a return, extending the ongoing business of *1Henry IV*, while the tropes of *Richard II* are constantly being revisited and recycled: history repeating itself with a difference.

As Rumour initiates the comedy, so does he its carnival. Beginning with his fantastic cloak of tongues, a visual allegory of carnival, he introduces the framework of subversion for what follows: those forces of sedition and mutability that provocatively challenge or threaten the established order in the play's hierarchy extending from the tavern to the court. Rumour implicitly announces the insurgent values of the play in a multiplicity of forms: embracing, for example, Falstaff's anarchic counter-culture, the reborn mutiny of the Percys, the unpredictable vitriol of Archbishop Scroop, the Gaultree wangle, a confused King and Hal's climactic tergiversation. The play is a pageant of carnival virtues: evasiveness, change, insurrection, reform and reaction, interrogations of language and truth. Still, nowhere is there despair, and this is the comic surprise: the human project goes cheerfully and absurdly on.

In the end these perturbations, relentlessly threatening to burst through the membrane of the play's formal order, appear to be held in check. Even so, the play derives much of its great fascination from the constant tension arising from this danger and the humane absurdity of attempts at its correction.

## Suggested Work

To obtain a broader grasp of the play, it would be valuable to analyse one of the scenes in which Falstaff appears with Mistress Quickly and/or Doll Tearsheet (that is, 2.1 or 2.4). In particular, try to determine what your chosen scene contributes to the play as a whole, in terms of characters, themes and the nature of the relationship between the women and Falstaff. Identify the conflicts and tensions in the scene. How does that scene advance the play as a whole?

Analyse the speech of these women and of Falstaff and note how it differs from the language of Prince Hal or of the Archbishop of York. Try to explain what the function of these women is in *2Henry IV* (how is this different from the role played by, for example, Lady Percy in 2.3)?

# 4

# *Richard III*: History as Problem Play?

He cried in a whisper at some image, at some vision – he cried out twice, a cry that was no more than a breath – 'The horror! The horror!'

Joseph Conrad, *Heart of Darkness*, Ch. 3

*Richard III* can be approached both as the final part in a sequence of four history dramas, staging the Wars of the Roses, which begins with *1Henry VI*, or as the final instalment in the whole eight-play sequence which starts with *Richard II*. However, like *Richard II*, it can readily be read or seen as a fully self-contained, autonomous play.

*Richard III* is an intensely rich and complex drama, and yet amazingly it is generally numbered among Shakespeare's earliest plays. As usual, however, precise dating of the composition or first performance of Richard III is not easy – even the basic chronology of Shakespeare's earliest works is problematic. But what we can say with some confidence is that the play belongs to the early period of Shakespeare's writing career, in the same general phase as *King John* and *A Comedy of Errors*. We do know that the first printing of the play was in 1597 (the 'first Quarto'), and that it was regularly reprinted over the next half-century. This Quarto version is a much leaner text than that printed in the collected plays of Shakespeare, the 1623 Folio, and most modern editions of the play follow this later version.

The character of Richard, Duke of Gloucester figures in two plays of the first tetralogy, briefly in *Part 2* then more extensively in *Part 3*. Since *Richard III* extends and intensifies the action of that sequence, it is well worth the effort of first familiarising yourself with the intricate relationships in those dramas (especially as so many actions, grievances and resentful motives in *Richard III* are unfinished business from the *Henry IV* plays). This may also help make more sense of the bewildering phalanx of Edwards, Richards, Elizabeths and Yorks in the current play. The characters themselves are grimly conscious of the long shadow of history that pursues them into *Richard III*.

In very brief terms, *3Henry VI* chronicles the violent struggle for the throne and for family ascendancy, chiefly among the Lancastrian and York factions: Henry VI is forced into accepting the young Duke of York as his heir. However, Queen Margaret, continuing to struggle on behalf of her son Edward, Prince of Wales, captures, torments and murders York. Soon after, York's sons, Edward [IV] and Richard [III], overcome the Lancastrians at Towton, where Henry VI is captured, leading to the coronation of Edward IV. At the Battle of Tewkesbury the Lancastrians are finally defeated, Edward the Prince of Wales is stabbed to death and Henry VI is murdered by Richard [III] in the Tower of London. This protracted chain of feuds and vengeance – prophesied by the Bishop of Carlisle in *Richard II* – fizzes and boils to its momentous denouement in *Richard III*.

In *2Henry VI* Richard has a passably minor role, but it is in *Part 3*, when he speaks his 'marrow bones' soliloquy of 3.2, that he begins to emerge from his obscure shell as the recognisably venomous, scheming and ruthless egotist of his eponymous play.

The action and consciousness of *Richard III* are clearly dominated throughout by the play's engrossing title character, who is present on stage for almost every scene in the play. And the play has many other important and expressive individuals, including Queen Elizabeth, Hastings and Lady Anne. Yet, especially fascinating are Margaret, former queen of Henry IV, the Duke of Buckingham, and Richard's brother, Clarence.

I have enquired whether *Richard III* can be regarded as a 'problem play' in order to get away from the idea, again, that we should consider the play as belonging to just one genre. Shakespeare's plays are often classified into groups such as Comedies, Histories, Tragedies, the Roman plays and Late Romances. On the other hand, some of his plays do not fit wholly into any one of these genres and these are usually referred to as the 'problem plays'. The three dramas which are most often thought of in this way are *All's Well That Ends Well*, *Measure for Measure* and *Troilus and Cressida*, and these were all written at about the same phase in Shakespeare's life. Other plays cannot be neatly categorised, and the truth is that each play is ultimately of its own kind, *sui generis*. Like *Richard II*, *Richard III* seems to be closer to tragedy than to any other genre, as though the historical trappings existed chiefly to provide a context to a tragic study. But we may also feel that *Richard III* evades this easy classification too, since it has strong elements of black comedy. This ambivalence extends to (or is derived from) the destabilising of power by Richard, and this presents another source of problem in the play's tragedy. Our examination of the play will attempt to draw out these elements of 'problem'.

In addition, *Richard III* develops our discussion of the themes of kingship, tragedy and language and Shakespeare's thesis of history. Furthermore it brings in some new and stimulating subjects, including the place of women, nature and the relationship of will and providence, and Machiavelli and the ethics of power.

To scrutinise these issues in relation to Shakespeare's technical approach I have chosen four important passages from the play for analysis, and the first is extracted from the opening speech by Richard himself.

## Context Passage 1: 1.1.1–31

ENTER *RICHARD DUKE OF GLOUCESTER*, *solus*

*Richard*:   Now is the winter of our discontent
            Made glorious summer by this son of York,
            And all the clouds that loured upon our house
            In the deep bosom of the ocean buried.
            Now are our brows bound with victorious wreaths,          5
            Our bruised arms hung up for monuments,
            Our stern alarums changed to merry meetings,

Our dreadful marches to delightful measures.
Grim-visaged war hath smoothed his wrinkled front,
And now, instead of mounting barbed steeds          10
To fright the souls of fearful adversaries,
He capers nimbly in a lady's chamber
To the lascivious pleasing of a lute.
But I that am not shaped for sportive tricks
Nor made to court an amorous looking-glass,          15
I that am rudely stamped, and want love's majesty
To strut before a wanton ambling nymph,
I that am curtailed of this fair proportion,
Cheated of feature by dissembling nature,
Deformed, unfinished, sent before my time          20
Into this breathing world scarce half made up,
And that so lamely and unfashionable
That dogs bark at me as I halt by them,
Why, I, in this weak piping time of peace,
Have no delight to pass away the time,          25
Unless to spy my shadow in the sun
And descant on mine own deformity.
And therefore, since I cannot prove a lover
To entertain these fair well-spoken days,
I am determined to prove a villain          30
And hate the idle pleasures of these days.

A typical answer to the question of 'what is the importance of the above opening speech?' is to say that it 'sets the scene'. It may tell us much about many things, but setting the scene is not one of the things it does. The reason I refer to this is that Richard appears to be speaking in a vacuum. The truth is there is no scene. His words appear to emanate from a disembodied voice, as if he were asleep, or in darkness (the opening few words seem to imply that he actually prefers the dark, while on stage he is often clothed in deepest black, his natural 'colour', and conventionally of vice itself). He is alone, too ('solus'), which is characteristic of this creature of social detachment. While – as here – Richard enjoys alienation, it is only among people, machinating with them, that he comes vigorously alive and vigilant.

As usual, I have decided to approach an analysis of the passage by breaking it down into sections which are grouped roughly around common subjects or points of view, anchoring each section on what seems to me to be key signal items of the diction. Accordingly, for the purposes of analysis we can look at Richard's speech in three phases.

(i)   Lines 1–13: '*made glorious summer*'

Richard opens the play with the dogmatic adverb 'Now', as though suddenly wishing to draw the whole audience towards and into his confidence. His first line is intentionally ambiguous. Out of context it reads simply:

> Now is the winter of our discontent ...

In fact, of course it is not winter, not for the royal Court, anyway. The former period of unhappiness, wintry war or 'discontent', is now turned into a glorious, summer-like season of peace and harmony. It is in Richard's nature to deceive us and the characters of the play. Yet in a sense it is a period of 'discontent' – namely for Richard himself, and he will explain how further on.

The man who has brought about the transformation is Richard's brother, King Edward IV, son of the Duke of York and triumphant victor in the Wars of the Roses. Some editors have 'sun' instead of 'son' here (though when heard in the theatre they are virtually punning homophones), and this plays on the emblem of the sun that appeared on the York family arms (together with that of a boar).

All the melancholy ill fortune that had beset 'our house' or family is now buried deep, forgotten. Notice how Richard is already setting up a rhythm of contrasts, counterpointing metaphors of winter and summer, discontent and glory, military and civil. In spite of what he says later, he is extremely adept at speech and in the techniques of seduction, and even at this early stage he is trying to lure us, the audience, into his own 'bosom'. As Phyllis Rackin expresses it, Richard 'reaches out to seduce the audience by the sheer energy and dramatic force of his characterisation' (Rackin 1990, p. 64). Park Honan goes further in noting this effect: 'He is even endearing up to Act 4' (Honan, p. 142).

His deftness in the arts of oratory mean that he is particularly brilliant in his choice of the perfect word. Conflict has dogged the nation since the time of Richard II, like a period of unrelenting attrition. That is in the past, and in line 5 he brings us back to the 'now' of the victorious celebrations. 'Now' is what interests him – and how it can control the future (more on this shortly). 'Wreaths' can have a double meaning, of course, and the word hints at classical Rome or Greece, of which there are more reminders to come. The next few lines describe the transformations which Edward's victory have brought about: weapons become ornaments, military musters are replaced by parties, legs once used for marching are now dancing.

Richard's lyrical depiction of *Pax Edwardiana* is more akin to the stuff of Shakespearean comedy. Grim war has become translated as if by magic into a scene of pleasure. Richard again employs a personification: here 'war' is used as though it were a person, and yet it still looks somehow impersonal, as if we do not quite see the face of the ex-soldier who now dances ('capers'; line 12):

He capers nimbly in a lady's chamber
To the lascivious pleasing of a lute.

(12–13)

This seems at first a delightful line, evoking flirtation and love-making, with nodding delicacy and humour. However, as this image takes shape over the next few lines it performs at least two things. Richard seems to have drifted away from his general vista of happy England to fix on what becomes for him a kind of erotic fantasy. Leering from a distance at the couple on the stairs, suffused with the seductive harmonies of the lute, towards the private chamber, he observes in his mind's eye, at a distance, like a prurient voyeur. Richard watches and notices everything.

The other related strand here is that Richard is incapable of regarding affectionate human relations in anything but terms of political manoeuvring or lust. His use of the word 'lascivious' reminds us of the same word used lecherously by *Othello*'s Iago ('the gross clasps of a lascivious Moor'), for whom love was no more than lust, 'the beast with two backs'. There are further points of contact with Iago.

In this opening 12 lines of the play Richard has managed to set in motion a great range of ideas and images. History itself is to be a key player here. Although he talks of the present, most of the verbs are in the past tense, denoting what has happened to bring 'us' to this moment, to this 'now'.

As such, certain interesting, meaningful words stand out here. The simple noun 'sun' (and we may hear 'son') is an important and complex motif in the play as a whole. It is an indication of Richard's skill in discourse that his words so often swell their meaning to such an expansive metaphorical significance that he compels us to tread warily in forming our conclusions. 'Son' is a timely reminder of the importance in the play of family, especially in terms of royal ascent. 'Sun' too is interesting because it will sparkle – if only as a memory – through the play alongside its converse, shadow, a word much used by Richard (see line 26, where the pun reappears, and note the louring 'clouds' in line 3), These prepare for the oscillation of light and dark throughout the twisting action.

I have already drawn attention to the adverb 'now'. It is another pointed word and, like sun/shadow, it resonates with its antitheses 'then' and 'to come'. Richard cannot escape his past any more than we can, but it has brought him to this moment, and he not only knows this but despises it, since it has placed him in the shadow, forced him to be a spectator as the sportive lovers waltz on up to bed. The past has deformed him. But 'now' is what he is all about and where he is – not history, or lineage or received principle, but now and 'me'. The word 'now' appearing three times in the extract is insistent, like a psychopathic compulsion.

A third item that catches my eye is the pronoun 'our'. The first 13 lines of the passage are focused on this word, where the next few turn ominously to 'I'. The repetition of 'our' lets us know how heavy is his rancorous irony (he is, of course, parodying the royal 'we'), and this pronoun is repeated so often it draws into it other half-rhymes: 'are', 'alarums', 'adversaries' and 'loured'. Gradually, the whole opening drones with the burring growl of Richard's ire. 'Our' is, in fact, the other people, the ones he sets himself apart from – 'adversaries' – but whom he will use and abuse for the end of 'self'.

## (ii)  Lines 14–27: '*Cheated of feature by dissembling nature*'

Where the opening section began with 'Now' and tumbled forward, ostensibly in overtures to the delight and beauty of this 'glorious summer', the skipping tempo is suddenly tripped and arrested by the halting word 'But' in line 14. This switches the attention from the 'sportive tricks' of others to the crabbed and cramped speaker himself.

The next few lines are marked by a catalogue of the deformities and abuse suffered by Richard: shaped, made, rudely stamped, curtailed, cheated, deformed, unfinished. All of these are passive verbs, giving the unmistakable impression of a man who has been a casualty of both capricious Nature and callous History, none of his own doing. After talk of summer fun, we are at this point urged to feel sympathy for this cheated and deformed victim. As before, however, each word has been deftly selected for its political or metaphorical potency.

Richard believes he lacks the kind of physical beauty to attract women, not being shaped or stamped so. Thus, even if he had the 'tricks' they would not work. What does this word 'tricks' imply? The cunning ploys of seduction, the smooth tongue of a charmer? Like 'lascivious', the word 'trick' implies lovemaking reduced to the deceits of stratagems of lust, such as a man who learns by rote some 'knockout' chat-up lines. Furthermore he concedes that he lacks 'love's majesty' (16) and could not entice a randy whore, a 'wanton ambling nymph' (17).

'Tricks' could refer to nature, too, in its having played a sick joke on him. It may equally be applied to Richard himself in regard to tactics later formulated for his vengeance on cruel nature.

He is not made to 'court an amorous looking-glass'. This seems to me to be a line especially rich in connotation. On the one hand, it does typify Richard's cunning in self-effacement (see 3.7 for the epitome of this in Richard's amusing encounter with the Mayor). He concedes that he is unsightly, and, yes, he could not woo a nymph, and in doing so he transfers the epithet 'amorous' to the mirror, his 'looking-glass'.

Mirrors are a recurring image in *Richard III*, fulfilling a number of functions. Here the mirror is, of course, a constant reminder to the speaker of his deformed physique, and his words appear to say that he cannot bear to look at himself (the mirror up to nature). On the other hand, there is a strong idea throughout the play that he is constantly watching himself, observing with approving smugness.

Another of Richard's complaints is that he is 'curtailed', or falls short of 'fair proportion' (18). He falls short of Elizabethan ideals of beauty and feels it acutely. This important line is followed by a similar one of momentous possibilities:

Cheated of feature by dissembling nature

(19)

With this line Richard now begins to attribute a cause, an agency behind his misfortune: namely, nature. What exactly we may infer from that word 'nature' we can leave for fuller discussion below, but for the present we can note those key verbs 'cheating' and 'dissembling', for ironically these describe the active narrative of Richard himself throughout the play.

Notice how 'dissembling' takes up the internal rhyme of 'nimbly' and 'ambling', reinforcing the impression that he is a most accomplished orator. The word means deceitful, pretending, and just plain mendacious, and it is among the most characteristic of his traits. Ironically, it is a tribute to his mesmeric powers that everyone in the play (with the exception of the slow-witted Lord Mayor of London) is aware of this even while he works his conspiracies. Indeed young Prince Edward has picked it up, asking of his grandmother:

|  | Think you my uncle did dissemble, grandam? |
| --- | --- |
| *Duchess of York*: | Ay, boy. |
| *Prince*: | I cannot think it. |

(2.2.31–3)

Richard is cheated of 'feature' only in the sense of lacking masculine beauty, and as for his character and his speech, no one would describe him as plain.

Above all, it is his deformations that are Richard's distinctive trademark, and he is usually portrayed on stage as a hunchback, with a twisted body, and 'lamely'. Thomas More (whose account of Richard was strongly influential on Shakespeare – see Chapter 5) describes Richard as having his left shoulder higher than his right, while in *3Henry VI*, Richard provides a more picturesque description of his appearance:

> [Love] did corrupt frail Nature with some bribe,
> To shrink mine arm up like a withered shrub;
> To make an envious mountain on my back,
> Where sits Deformity to mock my body;
> To shape my legs of unequal size ...

(3.2.155–9)

He comes across as a man much fixated on his body – witness the weight of 'body' imagery in this speech. In spite of his shrinking from the looking-glass, this Duke of Gloucester takes a quasi-erotic gratification in sporting his deformities, sneering with a kind of inverse pride.

'Sent before my time' is interesting, because in addition to implying that he is physically premature, he is also temperamentally out of joint with the English Court. Later references confirm this view that, although a premature baby, he was was born with his teeth already 'finished', as his nephew Prince Edward volunteers during his flight to sanctuary:

> They say my uncle grew so fast
> That he could gnaw a crust at two hours old.

(2.4.27–8)

(Queen Margaret postulates that he got his teeth early in order to bite sheep!)

This speech of Richard's is heavily concerned with time. He recounts to others his own hapless position in time – a victim of birth, of family, of God, of just plain bad luck. But the clarion word 'Now' in line 1 operates as an oblique but terrifying warning that Richard puts everyone on notice that he proposes to seize the time, to force time to work for him.

Lines 14–27 are taken up with one prolonged, complex sentence. Richard artfully grips our attention verbally by suspending his key main clause through mazy, anaphoric phrases ('I that am ...'), and a thumping beat of past participles, to reach the climactic line 25:

[I h]ave no delight to pass away the time ...

It is to the dazzling credit of the speaker that at no time do we feel that this beautiful, compact oratory is flagging, overindulgent or drifting off. It is a most daring overture to the play, a masterpiece of cunning seduction from an arch-dissembler.

He takes no delight to pass away this 'piping time of peace', because simmering away beneath this invective against his cursed plight is the imperative of action. We feel instinctively with each blistering notch of protest that he is not merely whingeing about his lot but he is drawing us forth towards some terrible retribution.

And there is no time to lose: 'Unless to spy my shadow in the sun'. About this line a number of significant possibilities spring out. He watches his shadow repeatedly to remind himself of its horridly distorted shape, perhaps to ratchet up his irritation (and at 3.4.67–8 he finds disfigurement a profitable pretext to his conspiracy). Additionally, if we cast back to the opening and the talk of 'son/sun' we can see that Richard stands in the shadow of his brother King Edward IV, sun king, and so his inborn inferiority can itself be cast as a 'deformity' (27).

Furthermore, a shadow is another kind of mirror, like the 'looking-glass' of line 15, suggesting this strange narcissistic tendency to halt and become self-absorbed. Graham Holderness goes further, suggesting even that Richard 'roots his self-consciousness in the externalised image of his own shadow' (Holderness 2000, p. 81).

Not surprisingly, this narcissism of mirrors and shadows extends to actions of the play itself. Often, throughout this intense drama Richard can be observed spying from a distance, while his agents carry out his instructions (this opening soliloquy is an indictment of the society that compels him to live apart from it; see also 1.3.266–7). A great many of his hallmark soliloquies are taken up with a perverted delight in his own machinations, as if his identity were in fact divided between Richard the doer and Richard the watcher.

(iii)  Lines 28–31: '*I am determined to prove a villain*'

The flagrant audacity of his declaration is early corroboration of our suspicions about Richard. All the tortuous, emotive history of his deformity is now seen as a sanction for the revenge to be exacted on those sportive caperers, ambling nymphs, ladies of Court and sons of York.

The form of the speech up to line 31 is arranged around three verbal coordinates: 'Now ... But ... Therefore', and my analysis has tried to follow these. Distilled down to these three points it is not difficult to see how this opening reads like a philosophical argument, a dialectic, with major premise, minor premise and conclusion. It also resembles a legal contract (especially with all its subordinate clauses and multiple connectives). It is as though Richard were setting down to us a bond or a compact to be agreed with the audience, pulling us in as consenting parties to his scheme, yet also arbitrators as to its determination. It is a contract of defiance.

The third part winds up this extract by neatly casting back (or 'descanting') to previous lines. Line 28 looks to the lovers of line 12; line 29's 'well-spoken days' connects with the 'glorious summer' of 2; while 31 repeats an idea of 25, of passing away or idling time.

In lines 18–19 Richard bemoans the condition of being cheated by 'dissembling nature', and to understand what is meant by this phrase we need to explore it further – especially as in Early Modern literature 'nature' has a variety of different yet interrelated meanings.

'Nature' could refer loosely to a deity, for instance, the creative and regulatory principle in the world and the universe ('Mother Nature'). Richard is also alluding to his physical features, distorted by forces of nature before and since his birth. Related to this is the notion of his own 'nature' as his personal being, body, mind, identity, and so on: in other words, the entity behind the title 'Duke of Gloucester', political, domestic, secret. In this latter nuance, of the whole Richard, he himself concedes a difference between body and spirit, or mind – between his repellent body, 'rudely stamped', and his astonishing intellect mirrored in the brilliant masterpiece of this opening speech.

At the same time, Elizabethan audiences were well apprised of the contemporary orthodoxy that the natural body mirrored the moral nature of the soul within it. Putting it simply, it was held that a misshapen body reflected a morally corrupt mind.

But perhaps the most interesting interpretation of 'nature' is its metaphysical dimension: nature as personal life-history. In the opening 25 lines of his soliloquy Richard outlines some of the forces and influences in his world that have brought him to this point: political and private history, wars, the misfortune of his body and its alienating effect, plus the natural world (in the emblematic shape of those barking dogs!). There are other causal forces catalogued later, including genealogy, 'blood', relationships, accidents – determinants beyond even Richard's control.

Some people prefer to identify this causal nature as 'destiny', a form of determinism, nature as the great bundle of forces driving us passively along. On the other hand, in lines 27–31 Richard switches from the passive to the active voice:

And therefore, since I cannot prove a lover ...
I am determined to prove a villain ...

He determines to direct his own life, to exercise free will against natural forces.

Furthermore, this strident assertion entails key ethical implications. By imposing his will in the world, breaking out of the apparent solipsism here, Richard becomes ethically autonomous, thereby taking full responsibility for his villainous actions which will, in turn, work as a catalyst on the 'glorious summer' of Edward's Court.

In some other Shakespearean tragedies – such as *King Lear* and *Macbeth* – it is possible to argue that the hero is compelled to act by being determined through those external forces which lie beyond their power (including 'divine Providence'). These activate their powerful chemistry by operating through internal forces such as ambition, vengeance and temperament, as well as an individual's nature. And yet we are still justified in asking whether Richard's misanthropy is a cause or an effect.

Shakespeare presents us with what Jorge Luis Borges calls a 'history of the mind'. This opening speech resembles a solipsism, that is, a subjectively controlled domain. It is a world of seething rancour into which nature, history and humanity will tumble – and Richard will have his revenge on the whole pack of them.

## Context Passage 2: 1.3.143–80

Richard completes his opening soliloquy by boasting that he has set in motion a strategy which will drive a wedge between his brothers, King Edward IV and Clarence, resulting in the latter's imprisonment. To distract suspicion, he impugns the Queen, Elizabeth, and when Hastings is released, opportunistic Richard nimbly turns him too against the women of the Court. Richard's second soliloquy boasts that, with the King's death imminent, his next move will be the outrageous dare of wooing the widow Lady Anne.

In 1.3, as Anne weeps over the corpse of Henry VI en route to Chertsey, she is joined by Richard, whom she blasts for his past 'butcheries'. Astonishingly, by subtle shifts he seduces her, turning detestation to compliance ('Was ever woman in this humour wooed?'). The next scene confirms King Edward's rapid decline in health, and Queen Elizabeth fears for her young son Prince Edward, now under the guardianship of Richard, 'Protector'. Talk of the devil, and in bursts Richard, challenging Elizabeth, provoking her into an acquiescent denial of any part in the imprisonment of Hastings and Clarence. As Richard and Elizabeth continue to wrangle, Margaret slips in unnoticed and begins to deliver her asides:

| | | |
|---|---|---|
| *Rivers*: | My lord of Gloucester, in those busy days | |
| | Which here you urge to prove us enemies, | |
| | We followed then our lord, our sovereign king | 145 |
| | So should we you, if you should be our king. | |
| *Richard*: | If I should be? I had rather be a pedlar. | |
| | Far be it from my heart, the thought thereof. | |
| *Elizabeth*: | As little joy, my lord, as you suppose | |
| | You should enjoy, were you this country's king, | 150 |
| | As little joy may you suppose in me. | |
| | That I enjoy, being the queen thereof. | |

| *Margaret [Aside]:* | A little joy enjoys the queen thereof, |
| | For I am she, and altogether joyless. |
| | I can no longer hold me patient – |  155 |
| | Hear me, you wrangling pirates, that fall out |
| | In sharing that which you have pilled from me. |
| | Which of you trembles not that looks on me? |
| | If not that I being queen, you bow like subjects, |
| | Yet that by you deposed, you quake like rebels. |  160 |
| | Ah, gentle villain, do not turn away. |
| *Richard:* | Foul wrinkled witch, what mak'st thou in my sight? |
| *Margaret:* | But repetition of what thou hast marred, |
| | That will I make before I let thee go. |
| *Richard:* | Wert thou not banished on pain of death? |  165 |
| *Margaret:* | I was. But I do find more pain in banishment |
| | Than death can yield me here by my abode. |
| | A husband and a son thou ow'st to me – |
| | And thou a kingdom – all of you allegiance. |
| | The sorrow that I have by right is yours, |  170 |
| | And all the pleasures you usurp are mine. |
| *Richard:* | The curse my noble father laid on thee, |
| | When thou didst crown his warlike brows with paper |
| | And with thy scorns drew'st rivers from his eyes, |
| | And then, to dry them gav'st the duke a clout |  175 |
| | Steeped in the faultless blood of pretty Rutland – |
| | His curses then, from bitterness of soul |
| | Denounced against thee, are all fall'n upon thee, |
| | And God, not we, hath plagued thy bloody deed. |
| *Elizabeth:* | So just is God, to right the innocent. |  180 |

A glance over this extract makes clear the general atmosphere of conflict and escalating tension, until, that is, when Elizabeth intervenes to try to ease the hostility. With the internecine Wars of the Roses still fresh in the characters' minds, we should not be surprised that the lexis of war and its personal traumas should be foregrounded. After a closer rereading of the passage, some items of diction strongly invite larger discussion, and the three words that especially caught my eye are 'should' (line 146), 'curse' (172) and 'God' (179, 180). The reason these stand out is that they seem to point a reading towards interesting thematic strands. A closer examination can be facilitated by splitting the passage into two sections, along its natural seismic line, at 155/156.

(i)   Lines 143–53: *'So should we, if you should be our king'*

Rivers's speech here is in reply to Richard's acrimony about nobles switching their allegiance during the Wars. Rivers's argument represents values which are alien to Richard's, predicated as they are on an absolute principle: that subjects owe a duty of fealty to the 'sovereign king'. Of course the passage (and the history plays as a whole) focuses on the difficulty of knowing exactly who that may be, and thus the dangers in expressing allegiance to a king who becomes ousted and/or killed (the theme of 'owing' – 'ow'st' in line 168 – is recurrent in this play).

Typically, Rivers begins with deference to Richard, 'my lord'. He is tactful about the controversial civil wars, describing them as 'those busy days' – in which outrages were committed by each side. He also draws attention delicately to Richard's tactic of holding these wars in the forefront of his memory ('urge' meaning to 'remind'), 'to prove us enemies'. This is consistent with Richard's strategy of dividing the English Court into factions, the easier to destroy it.

Rivers's diplomacy stems from his courtly skill in language. Thus he builds on this oblique censure with one further judicious comment:

We followed then our lord, the sovereign king.

(145)

He hints perhaps that there *is* such a thing as a sovereign, or absolute ruler, and the word 'followed' implies this principle of obedience. Neither of these are features that Richard himself will observe.

But I think Rivers's next line, with his use of the modal verb 'should', is especially interesting. The word appears twice, with different meanings: the first means 'ought', while the second is subjunctive, expressing possibility, 'may' ('we ought to follow you in case you may become king').

Instead of treating Rivers's throwaway line as a jest (that Richard as king is just too implausible), Richard is momentarily and uncomfortably distracted. His dismissal of the idea, though intended to allay any aspersion, accidentally draws attention to his secret ambition. 'Heart' and 'mind', body and spirit, should eject the thought entirely, but these in fact refer to Richard's desire and purpose.

The word 'should' ricochets throughout the following lines like a joke, pointing up its vacuity in these days of negotiable values. Elizabeth replies in a typically unreal language. Her sense is simply put: there's no fun in being the monarch. However, she expresses it in a strangely ethereal rhetoric (she has a proclivity for sublimating her deepest grief into heightened poetical rhetoric; see, for instance 2.2.39ff.). Interlacing the phrases 'a little joy' and 'you suppose' through her four lines produces a mazy fabric of dreamlike anaphora and a teasing symmetry of ideas. The metre is perfectly regular, and she creates a balance in each line by interposing a caesura in both:

> As little joy / may you suppose in me.
> That I enjoy / being the queen thereof.
>
> (151–2)

Queen Elizabeth and Queen Margaret both have a proclivity for non-natural or heightened speech, which at times implies an alternative level of reality, not necessarily referring to the immediate moment. At other times their affected formal language is reminiscent of the Chorus in Greek and Latin tragedy (more on this later).

The throne is a curse. Elizabeth's prophetic lines are disregarded by Richard, but they invite Margaret to step out of the shadows. Until line 156 she has been a disengaged, perhaps disembodied observer of the exchanges between those on stage, counterpointing the main dialogue with a pointed commentary:

> *Margaret [Aside]:*   A little joy enjoys the queen thereof,
> For I am she, and altogether joyless.
> I can no longer hold me patient ...
>
> (153–5)

What has not been very apparent is to whom she addresses her 'asides'. Is she speaking directly to us, or only within herself, like a frustrated spectator, here? The other characters have been oblivious of her while she stands apart from them, perhaps even above them (see line 162).

(ii) Lines 156–80: '*The curse my noble father laid on thee*'

Then, without warning, Margaret steps forward from her spectral recess to intervene, because the cursed crown had been her husband Henry VI's, until the Plantagenets 'pilled', that is, 'stole' it (an abbreviation of 'pillaged'). Until this moment she has been standing outside the action, but on her entrance, the play takes on a new complexion, drawing in historical and even mythical overtones. Stepping forward, her first utterance is significantly a command, surprising and seizing the attention. She compares the ruling group to 'pirates' who fall out over the shares of the booty. She sustains the momentum by next posing a confrontational question:

Which of you trembles not that looks on me?

(158)

It is as though a ghost had materialised before them, and they do seem to respond with genuine shock, as her description over the next few lines implies.

In Elizabethan convention, ghosts returned to haunt for a number of reasons; usually to point to hidden treasure or possibly to reveal information about the future (as in 5.3, on the eve of battle), or to address an injustice (as the ghost of Hamlet's murdered father does). Margaret draws attention to what she considers an outrage: she is '[a queen] by you deposed'. Perhaps she casts an accusing finger around, but in any case she does catch Richard in the act of slinking away.

Calling him a 'gentle villain' (161) seems odd at first sight, but 'gentle' can mean 'of the nobility' (hence, a sort of upper-class gangster). However, 'villain' is also a spelling of the Middle English 'vileyne', a serf or scoundrel, lower even than that 'pedlar' disdained by Richard himself. Thus her insult is a complex yet bitter class smear, though in comparison with all the other tags flung at Richard (devil, dog, spider, cacodemon, cur, and so on) it is mild stuff.

However, his reply confirms that her barb really has found its tender mark:

Foul wrinkled witch, what mak'st thou in my sight?

(162)

It is easy for Richard to denounce Margaret as a witch (a common enough slur in contemporary England). It is an opportune insult for Richard to throw, since in one breath it disqualifies her from this circle. Later, as she continues to scold him, he similarly despatches her with 'Have done thy charm, thou hateful, withered hag' (1.3.213).

When he asks her what she 'mak'st' in his sight, this perhaps extends his allegation of her as a witch, as though performing a spell. However, she nimbly casts this back at him, converting his word into a pun on the proverbial 'make and marr' (162), and adding a third meaning, that she will 'repair' the injury done by his family (she repeats this technique throughout her asides in the early part of this scene: see, for instance, line 110).

She is a harrowing presence, warning Richard that she will complete her reparation 'before I let thee go' (164). Given the horrors that Richard is capable of, these are fearlessly menacing words. Whether or not we go along with the description 'witch', she does retain some power over him, and this is rooted in knowledge, particularly an acute awareness of the past (his murders of her husband and son), but also of his personality. While in martial terms she is now a spent force, she nevertheless holds him steadfastly through his terror of woman.

He reminds her that she was 'banished on pain of death' (at the end of *3Henry IV* she is ransomed home by her father the King of France). Margaret concurs but is less afraid of dying in England, which she regards as her rightful home ('my abode'), than of the sterility of lonely exile – as she hinted in line 154.

Later in the scene, after Margaret exits, Richard appears to express a modicum of sympathy for this, her lot, and the husband and son he has taken from her:

I cannot blame her, by god's holy mother
She hath had too much wrong, and I repent ...

(1.3.306–7)

Almost certainly he is dissembling yet again, to impress and 'seem the saint when most I play the devil', a conclusion that seems corroborated by Rivers's ingenuous admiration for his Christian virtue!

The rest of Margaret's speech traces an intriguing interplay of pronouns whose importance is not perhaps immediately clear. She switches in her address between 'thou' and 'you' and Richard replies with 'thee'. This variable personal pronoun is indicative of the status of the addressee, and in the extract it works as a subtle code. In Elizabethan English (though not thoroughly consistent) the vocative 'thou' or 'thee' is used by a superior to an inferior, and conversely, 'you' is employed by an inferior to show respect to a superior (see Chapter 1, Context Passage 3 for other examples of the thou/you exchange in *Richard II*).

Accordingly, at the start Rivers and Elizabeth address Richard, as Duke of Gloucester, as 'you' (lines 144 to 151). Margaret speaks to the group using the plural 'you' (156–60), but she addresses Richard as 'thou', thereby maligning him as a subordinate (163–4), and he throws this insult right back at her in line 172 on. This highly subtle interplay of grammar is characteristic of the bitter sparring of these two fiercely imposing speakers. Decoding her speech, Margaret asserts that Elizabeth the current Queen owes her the kingdom, in addition to obedience and 'all the pleasures', comfort and ease, therefrom.

Although he has nothing to fear materially from Margaret, this confrontation marks the first bloodless challenge to Richard's ambitious progress. It is a psychological wound that she strikes into him, detaining and then making him starkly acquainted with true danger.

However, Richard's response to all her aggression is to remind her of the humiliation of his own father, Richard Duke of York, then a general in the Lancastrian army, captured in *3Henry VI* by Margaret (1.4). After mocking him with a paper crown she had stabbed him to death, but not before he could lay a curse on her, that she should one day find herself in the same plight as himself.

Hence Richard speaks from a long-held grudge, and we may feel his complaint is well rehearsed. The word 'curse' (172) is exactly apposite here and it is a word and idea with a long reach, in and beyond *Richard III*, through all of the history plays. In containing a grudge, history's perennially unfinished business, it emphasises the legacy of the past for the present, and on into the future (cf. Lady Anne's words at 4.1.67). Additionally, it is coherent with the imagery of witchcraft – which, if condemning Margaret, also incriminates Richard the 'black magician' (1.2.33). The word 'curse' calls attention to the persistence of memory, personal and familial, in the continuing tit-for-tat cycle of violence, usurpation, murder, atrocity and revenge. So long as the 'curse' of memory endures, History will never end.

Crucially, these lines thrust to the heart of the question of what actually motivates Richard in seeking to eliminate his rivals. He springs here to the defence of family in the remembrance of his father. He does so in an effort to deflect from himself that attention which Margaret has tried to fix onto him and his father. But this does not necessarily imply that he is motivated out of family honour – since his family is presently in power, this is not a viable consideration. And yet the passage does highlight this tremendous quality of clan loyalty that has been a constant force in the Histories.

His rejoinder to Margaret has the incisive effect of pointing up the symmetry in the history of the two families ('mirror' again). Each side has lost fathers and sons, often brutally, as in the case of young Edmund Rutland (Richard's older brother: line 176), and there will be no end to the cycle. Of course, Richard's cardinal object here is not to rehearse some fine point of historicist metaphysics – his purpose is to neutralise Margaret's line of attack, and at the same time to expose the futility of atavism, repeatedly referring to the past to validate present action.

I have referred already to Richard's mastery of language. It is an important facet of his enduring appeal for audiences. Here his blocking tactic attests to his agile cunning, with facts swiftly to hand (his resemblance to a lawyer is surely no accident). Ever alert to the rhetorical force of sound, he accentuates his keywords with assonance and alliteration (crown/brows, faultless/pretty/Rutland; all/fallen) and smartly rounds off with a rhyming couplet.

Brazenly, he attributes the decline of the Lancastrian fortunes to a righteous God. Elsewhere, Richard does not give the impression of being a devout believer in God, and his conduct more resembles

Renaissance humanism. This is a notion widely held in the Early Modern period that though under the sphere of God's aegis, mankind is free to act and will be judged only in death, neither by the Church nor by any providential intervention. If Margaret symbolises the past, then Richard shapes himself as the present, the Renaissance New Man.

Since his humanism denies the possibility of divine intervention on earth, his offhand reply to Margaret (in line 179) is simply another expression of political rhetoric. Outrageously, since history is written by the victors, then the Godhead too must be subject to their revisionary definitions:

> And God, not we, hath plagued thy bloody deed.
> *Elizabeth*:   So just is God, to right the innocent.
>
> (179–80)

Elizabeth, in a trusting reverie, draws out the inference in Richard's words. Her childlike trust in God links her with the innocent Rutland and with the other victims of infanticide in this play, while her simple faith is a counterpoint to the merciless, self-centred pragmatism of Richard and his cronies.

Margaret herself foreshadows Providence, though her role is simply choric, that is, to prophesy rather than to bring about a resolution. Some critics such as W.H. Clemen go further to think of her in mythological terms, likening her role to the avenging Nemesis, Greek goddess of retribution (Clemen, p. 48). And Edward Dowden is of course right in describing her as the terrible Medusa-like queen (in Cartelli, p. 304).

Why, then, is this passage important? In terms of dramatic perspective, this passage, like many others in *Richard III*, gives the context and causes which have brought us to the present state of affairs. It is significant in giving more distinct information on Richard himself, especially in the way he encounters women. His character comes into clearer definition as a result of his engaging with a forthright woman such as Margaret. Measuring this interaction against his 'seduction' scenes with Lady Anne reveals that while Richard has mettle, he is far from inviolable.

The clash between them adds some interesting information about his political views, and the challenge of Margaret tests out both his and her views on history. This extract derives almost all of its exhilaration from the collision of its two chief personalities (it is difficult to believe that in some eighteenth-century productions Margaret was omitted altogether). This foregrounds the deep enmity in the unresolved tension arising from their two hostile lines of descent. These extend back to the Wars of the Roses reaching back to *Richard II*, and forward to converge violently on the field of Bosworth in Act 5. The language of both protagonists here is remarkably nuanced and highly flavoured, and Elizabeth's heightened verse prepares for the antiphonal exchanges enacted by herself, with Margaret and the Duchess of York (in 2.2 and 4.4).

In many different ways Shakespeare rewrites history in *Richard III*. One of the important rewrites involves Queen Margaret, who had already died in exile in 1482, before the historic events of the play. He must therefore have regarded her as carrying some symbolic drive or imbuing the play with thematic strength, and this extract provides us with some clues as to exactly why. It begins by providing a window onto Margaret's eminently compelling identity, together with some idea of the role of women in the play. A fully coherent character, she also has the prickly dramatic role of opening up and confronting Richard with the past and his own moral infirmity.

In this scene, as in 4.4, she is both a formidably realistic and symbolic presence. As an obdurate figure from the years of the *Henry VI* plays, she stands for a past that cannot be denied or ignored. She will not go away, and her knowledge as well as her undaunted courage unnerve Richard. She also creates a dangerous change of focus, of pace and of tone, contesting those clandestine conspiracies that her antagonist has set in motion.

In the past these characteristics may have been understood as conventionally masculine – let us not forget that she was a ruthless warrior in the Lancastrian army at St Albans. It is for this that Richard and other male characters box her up as a witch. Dorset warns that she is a 'lunatic' (1.3.254), while Rivers wonders 'why she's at liberty' (1.3.305). She carries around so much emotional electricity that after she exits this scene, Buckingham exclaims timorously:

My hair doth stand on end to hear her curses

(1.3.304)

At frequent intervals throughout the play, characters dolefully note the fulfilment of her curses-cum-prophecies and then rue her 'advice': for example, Grey at 3.3.14–16 and Hastings at 3.4.91.

Is Margaret really a witch? Richard talks of her 'charm' and of her as a 'hag', and a 'foul wrinkled witch', but these are generally phatic expletives. The answer will pivot on how we define 'witch', if there is such a thing – as the sixteenth century believed there was. She does not appear to influence events, and her eloquent 'curses' function more like predictions, 'prophesies', insights or what we may term 'prehistories'. For this reason she is presented as a woman intimately acquainted with a realm beyond the local present that Richard finds unnerving, *unheimlich*, generating fear and challenge to his all-embracing control. Perhaps we should think of her in terms of a visionary or classical sibyl.

Famously she is described by Richard's father as a 'tiger's heart wrapped in a woman's hide!' (*3HenryVI* 1.4 137). This is said immediately before she stabs him to death and he adds with awestruck truculence:

> Women are soft, mild, pitiful, and flexible;
> Thou stern, indurate, flinty, rough, remorseless ... .
>
> (*3HenryVI* 1.4.141–2)

But most of the women in *Richard III* are made by Shakespeare to conform to the first part of York's characterisation (Rackin argues that most of women of the play are victimised, 'play no part in the affairs of state, and seem to spend most of their limited time on stage in tears'; Rackin 2005, p. 49).

## Context Passage 3: 3.5.72–109

The third passage I have chosen for detailed analysis is the concluding section of Scene 5 in Act 3. However, before launching into the passage it will be very useful to make a brief résumé of the course of events since the previous extract (in 1.3).

After the departure of Margaret, Richard meets the contract killers tasked with the murder of Clarence. Before they arrive Clarence describes his frighteningly prophetic dream, and then his killers allege that the King, his brother, has sanctioned his murder.

In Act 2 the dying King is comforted by the belief that he has managed to reconcile all warring factions – but Richard lurks ominously at the side. A switch in tone comes with Clarence's children innocently affirming their trust in God and honest Uncle Richard. However, once again optimism turns to lamentation with news of the King's passing away, so that Uncle Richard and his trusty henchman Buckingham rejoice in the prospect of a new king, namely young Edward, who is promptly summoned from Ludlow.

A brief interlude follows (2.3) in which some prescient citizens voice their mistrust of Richard together with their anxieties for the nation's future. In the meantime, the arrests of Rivers, Grey and Vaughan panic Queen Elizabeth and the Duchess of York into seeking sanctuary.

Act 3 begins with the arrival of Prince Edward into the guardianship of Richard. The Lord Cardinal is coerced into breaching the protocol of sanctuary so that the boy-princes can be united within the menacing confines of the Tower. Now in effective political control, Richard forces the pace, setting about ridding his ranks of former royal allies: Hastings is seized and the three nobles held at Pomfret are summarily beheaded.

In Scene 5, Richard and Buckingham appear theatrically in 'rotten armour' to impress the credulous Lord Mayor. With unabashed dissembling, they affirm steadfast loyalty to the Princes, evidenced by Catesby's timely presentation of Hastings's freshly severed head:

| | | |
|---|---|---|
| *Richard*: | Go, after, after, cousin Buckingham. | |
| | The Mayor towards Guildhall hies him in all post. | |
| | There, at your meetest advantage of the time, | |
| | Infer the bastardy of Edward's children. | 75 |
| | Tell them how Edward put to death a citizen | |
| | Only for saying he would make his son | |
| | Heir to the crown, meaning indeed his house, | |
| | Which, by the sign thereof, was termed so. | |
| | Moreover, urge his hateful luxury | 80 |
| | And bestial appetite in change of lust, | |
| | Which stretched unto their servants, daughters, wives, | |
| | Even where his raging eye or savage heart, | |
| | Without control, lusted to make a prey. | |

|  | Nay, for a need, thus far come near my person: | 85 |
|  | Tell them, when that my mother went with child | |
|  | Of that insatiate Edward, noble York | |
|  | My princely father then had wars in France, | |
|  | And by just computation of the time | |
|  | Found that the issue was not his begot, | 90 |
|  | Which well appeared in his lineaments, | |
|  | Being nothing like the noble duke, my father. | |
|  | Yet touch this sparingly, as 'twere far off, | |
|  | Because, my lord, you know my mother lives. | |
| *Buckingham*: | Doubt not, my lord, I'll play the orator | 95 |
|  | As if the golden fee for which I plead | |
|  | Were for myself. And so, my lord, adieu. | |
| *Richard*: | If you thrive well, bring them to Baynard's Castle, | |
|  | Where you shall find me well accompanied | |
|  | With reverend fathers and well-learned bishops. | 100 |
| *Buckingham*: | I go, and towards three or four o'clock | |
|  | Look for the news that the Guildhall affords. | |

*Exit Buckingham*

| *Richard*: | Go, Lovell, with all speed to Doctor Shaw. | |
|  | Go thou to Friar Penker. Bid them both | |
|  | Meet me within this hour at Baynard's Castle. | 105 |

*Exit Lovell*

|  | Now will I go to take some privy order | |
|  | To draw the brats of Clarence out of sight, | |
|  | And to give order, that no manner of person | |
|  | Have any time recourse unto the princes. | |

*Exeunt*

In the first part of this passage (to line 94), the main thrust consists of Richard issuing detailed instructions to his willing adjutant, Buckingham, on the poisoning of Edward's reputation and suitability as king. In the second we see the range of attention broaden to include pointers to the relationship between these two men. To see how these two parts relate to each other, let us delve into their details.

(i)   Lines 72–94: '*without control, lusted to make a prey*'

One of the chief features which identifies Richard in this play must be his great skill in anticipation. He is brilliant at second-guessing other people's movements, perhaps even before they themselves do. Here he sets Buckingham the task of heading off the mayor, who has just departed. Speed is of the essence: 'after, after' and 'in all post' conjure up the urgency to act immediately. The Mayor has departed with a favourable impression of the Duke, which he will report back to the citizens at the Guildhall, but Richard wants to follow this up immediately, not allowing the Mayor to mellow this view, keeping up the momentum and the stress.

The tension is also evinced by the fact that most of this first section is taken up with imperatives to Buckingham: 'Go ... infer ... tell ... urge ...come near', and so on. He leaves his listener with little leeway except to act, as he wishes to constrain the Mayor in the range of his possible responses to the new situation.

Recall also that these two are still adorned in 'rotten armour' which now looks perfectly absurd, histrionic, yet attesting to Richard's thorough groundwork. He means to leave nothing to chance, and the armour was intended to make them look like victims of an assault.

Addressing his lieutenant as 'cousin' does not imply they are related, being a term of affection. Clearly Richard draws Buckingham into his confidence, yet with some slight flattery, as though he were more of kin and less than kind. The mayor is hurrying ('hies him') to the Guildhall, government house, and this represents one of those rare occasions when Richard depends on the goodwill and support of others, here the London. Then comes a revealing conditional:

> There, at your meetest advantage of the time ...

(74)

Clearly he trusts Buckingham unquestioningly, since he mandates some decisions to his discretion, for him to judge the moment. Further, this line seems to me to sum up an important facet of Richard, the opportunist, having a keen eye for (or actually creating) that optimal moment for action, and to have some course of action up his sleeve in anticipation of the advantage. He is also well apprised of the fact that the speed of events makes an opportunity fleeting, to be either seized or lost.

What Buckingham is to 'infer' – about Richard's own brother – is most shocking. First, that Edward the king is impulsive, given to reckless and egregious reactions. This is illustrated by his execution of the landlord of the Crown who, making an unhappy blunder, had suggested his own son would be heir to the 'house' or business. The point of the story (which Shakespeare gleaned from his source, Sir Thomas More) is to throw doubt in the Mayor's mind about the suitability of Edward as king (and his account stresses the word 'citizen' to bring home the apparent danger).

But worse is to follow. As I discussed in Chapter 1, Shakespeare's use of the noun 'appetite' is almost always used pejoratively. It usually refers, as here, to lust and failure to curb it, suggesting a character's lack of restraint. It is invariably used about a situation of moral compromise in which reason becomes a hostage to sexual lust. The sense here is translucent: insatiable in appetite, Edward is not merely moved by lust but oppressed by it, 'his hateful luxury', which is always hunting for new deviations ('change') in sexual outlet:

And bestial appetite in change of lust … .

(81)

Edward's carnal appetite, unfulfilled by his wife, has become pointed at their 'servants, daughters, wives' with a 'raging eye or savage heart', ferociously desperate to achieve a receptive mate, predatory in desire, with more than a hint of bestiality.

In the context of 'appetite' Richard's contention that Edward desires 'without control' (84) is a crucial point here. For any Renaissance prince the condition of being without discipline is heinous. Perhaps above all, the Court valued decorum, if only as a show: in metaphorical terms the head must rule the heart. Clearly, Richard's gossip strikes at the heart of Edward as a man of honour but also as supreme leader, a man seemingly ruled not by impartial reason but by his appetite, like a beast of the field. The ironies of this in terms of Richard himself are of course quite voluble.

Yet most shocking of all is the allegation that Edward has indulged in incestuous relations with Richard's own mother. The man is clearly out of all control – allegedly. The accusation should not detain us because we understand it is the fabrication of a febrile and pernicious imagination. If it outrages our sensibility it is most likely out of wonder that he could ransom his own mother's reputation to his appetite for power.

Richard's note to Buckingham about the arithmetic relating to the baby's gestation is ironic, because 'computation of time' (89) has been a key element in his own strategic machinations (in addition to touching on the sensitive topic of his premature birth). The counterfactual concerning Richard's paternity is the bodily evidence

> Which well appeared in his lineaments ...
>
> (91)

It is possible that the 'issue' – or son – that Richard descants on is himself (although in historical terms almost certainly impossible). But even if it is not, the word 'lineaments', or physical features, reminds us of Richard's disfigurement, as unnatural as the supposed incestuous offspring of Edward would be to the Elizabethan audience. Moreover, the word 'issue' reminds us of 'lineage', literally perhaps, but also figuratively in the sense that an accident of birth has denied the throne to Richard. Nature up to its devilish tricks again.

Has Richard spontaneously dreamed up these allegations about his own family or 'house'? Unlikely, I hear you say, and the rhythm of the verse appears to support your conclusion completely. Until line 78, where speed is critical, the metre is irregular in almost every hurried line. But at line 79 the metre all at once settles into a composed rhythm, as far as line 99, when its fluency becomes once more ruffled by the shift towards action.

(ii) Lines 95–109: '*I'll play the orator*'

Richard rounds off his instructions to his aide with a delicate piety about his mother. It serves to remind us just how deeply into Richard's trust Buckingham has been permitted to penetrate. Buckingham's assurance acknowledges this, his choice of address in 'my lord' expressing due deference (it echoes Richard's in line 94). In the period that Richard has confided in him, Buckingham has been eager to demonstrate his submissiveness. Note the personal pronouns again: each addressing other respectfully as 'you'.

'I'll play the orator ...' reminds us how much they are playing roles, dissembling, creating narratives, as Richard does with his account of Edward's libido. The 'golden fee' is of course the crown, the ultimate goal for Richard, and it reminds us and perhaps Richard too that mercenary Buckingham also hopes for a reward: the earldom of Hereford and all of Edward's household property (3.4.199; he himself is playing out a role: that of stalwart to Richard, and for a handsome fee). Buckingham is to escort the Mayor and his train to Baynard's Castle, London home of Richard's mother the Duchess of York, where Gloucester will give a masterly theatrical performance (in 3.7) as the devout ascetic, attended by 'reverend fathers and well-learned bishops' (100).

As Buckingham dutifully exits, Richard calls over other instruments of his will to muster the churchmen. Lovell is to fetch the Mayor's brother, Doctor Shaw (sometimes spelt 'Shaa'), and Ratcliffe – addressed as 'thou', an inferior – is to fetch the Augustinian Provincial, Friar Penker. Both of these clerics are historical figures, well known as champions of Richard.

It is impossible to overlook how feverishly energetic Richard's tactical brain is here. His adrenalin surges as he deploys all the necessary factors and players to force his will on the situation. He combines the manipulative skills of the puppeteer with the tactical acumen of a military general, marshalling his forces in the arena in readiness for the next phase.

Having set Buckingham, Lovell and Ratcliffe on their assignments (Catesby meanwhile is the lookout up on the battlements), Richard has saved for himself the more official undertakings. He must legally divert from parental intervention the children of both his brothers Clarence and of King Edward, because individually these stand between himself and his goal as the next in line to the throne. He spits out their names contemptuously with sneering assonance (brats, Clarence) and alliteration (on /r/ and /t/) in

To draw the brats of Clarence out of sight ...

(107)

Why is this passage as a whole important? Although in terms of stage action not a lot happens, the scene is significant in its contribution to the gathering rush of energy working towards the first climaxes: the murder of the Princes and Richard's coronation in Act 4. It is crucial in preparing for the scene in which the Mayor accepts Richard, and it builds on 3.4, where the nobles debate the coronation of young Edward. The passage develops further our understanding of Richard's identity, in his swift response to 3.4 together with his intention to inhibit the advancement of both sets of nephews and niece. Above all, from a critical perspective, it keeps the spotlight firmly on the ethics of Richard's plans.

Although the crown may seem to be Richard's ultimate goal – at any price – he appears to derive as much of a frisson from the process itself, the frenzied brainwork and manipulation entailed in the journey towards it.

This absorption in the process goes a good way to explain why Richard appears so unscrupulous about killing the obstacles in his route. His sophistry has occasionally claimed that murder is to the profit of the victims – though without much conviction, admittedly (1.2.110; and note 1.4.238). But as the passage above tells, Richard becomes especially provoked by total immersion in his own machinations, feeding off its high-octane vapours.

I mentioned above that Richard resembles a military general. We can just as readily compare him to a theatre director, or perhaps an author. W.F. McNeir, writing about the many masks of Richard, speaks for many who have observed this feature:

> Richard III acts for two audiences: his dupes and accomplices in the
> play which he directs and us in the theatre. We become his confidants
> in crime through his soliloquies.
>
> (McNeir, p. 167)

Equally feasible is to compare Richard to an author. Not only an actor and director, but also author and narrator, one who manipulates his people across the landscape of the play. If, as I posited earlier, we conceive of the play as his solipsism, then everyone is Richard; in Act 5 he himself gives a suggestion of this when he cries out in the throes of battle:

> What? Do I fear myself? There's none else by.
> Richard loves Richard, that is, I am I.
>
> (5.3.185–6)

If we travel further along this solipsistic path, then the ineluctable conclusion is that the landscape and its figures are a projection of

Richard's own executive mind. Our passage highlights his drive in this game towards total control over all the other players. This drive becomes obsessive, and it may account further for his hatred of Margaret as a 'witch', since she represents not only a defiance of his rule but possibly a rival puppeteer/author in his highly elaborate game.

Within the scope of the play itself, then, what we see is Richard imposing the order of himself onto the disorder of life as he sees it. (In spite of all its horrifying acts, the play never collapses into chaos, because its world is under the rigorous control of its powerful central personality.) This he does by simplifying its life as well as himself: nothing could be simpler than doing away with troublesome neighbours (the trick is getting them to agree to it!). On the other hand, within the broader ambit of this, the first tetralogy, Richard could be understood as subject to a much greater scheme, which we should call 'history'. Yet if we accept this greater causal entity, it would diminish Richard's accountability here.

And what does the passage tell us of Buckingham? Buckingham is of vital importance to Richard as his chief confederate. Would Richard have succeeded without Buckingham? Not so readily, I think, since as a subaltern the latter does not merely take orders but seizes the initiative in this scene (boasting, too, of his own skill in dissembling). He sups and sleeps at Crosby House, so Richard must feel at ease with his company. Indeed Richard flatters him richly as 'my other self ... my oracle, my prophet...'.

Having said that, Buckingham is not a Richard Mark II. He is less a protégé; we do not see him plot on his own account, and he is loyal – fatally so – to Richard who, in return, finally dismisses him as 'dull brained' (4.4.36), then has him beheaded. In Richard's eyes he is undone by the crisis of conscience in the matter of Prince Edward's murder.

## Conscience and Machiavelli in *Richard III*

This is a good point at which to discuss some of the ethical issues in the play. We have noted already that Richard resolves, then publishes to the world his intention to be a villain (see Context Passage 1). In theatrical terms he is eager to identify with 'the formal Vice, Iniquity' of the medieval morality plays (see 3.1.82–3; Chapter 2, Context Passage 2). His mother is mortified by him:

> He is my son, ay, and therein my shame …
>
> (2.2.29)

She later describes her two dead sons as her princely mirrors cracked in pieces, and that Richard is her 'but one false glass' (2.2.109; extending the play's 'mirror' imagery).

Many critics have glibly dismissed Richard with terms such as a monster, wicked, poisoned, atheist, amoral, villain or unscrupulous tyrant. He is a tyrant, certainly, but most of these other terms are simply subjective labels of acute disapproval. He does not strike me as amoral – he understands the morality of his actions and he has a terrifying grasp of the dire effect these actions have (see, for instance, his disclosure at 4.2.64–5).

E.M.W. Tillyard is typical of his period in speaking of Richard's 'wickedness' (Tillyard 1944, p. 206). However, to claim that Richard is wicked or evil is to evade the issue by resorting to religious concepts with little or no moral content. For instance, if 'wickedness' or 'evil' are properties, where do they originate, are they contagious, or is one born with them? 'Diabolic' seems to imply that someone was under the influence of the Devil. If true, these should rationally diminish Richard's accountability and increase our sympathy. Monster? Monsters are not normally capable of such bewilderingly dazzling strategy, organisation and execution, along with metaphysical reflections on their actions. Richard's exceptional nature tests our vocabulary to exacting limits.

A humanist, Richard does appear to believe in God, though typically he claims to clothe his naked villainy:

> With odd old ends stol'n forth of holy writ
>
> (1.3.337)

But he does not believe in obeying something the others call 'conscience', although Buckingham does believe (and shows) he possesses such, and Margaret cries out for its vengeance:

> The worm of conscience still begnaw thy soul!
>
> (1.3.220)

But Richard transcends such desperate goading:

> Conscience is but a word that cowards use,
> Devised at first to keep the strong in awe.

(5.3.311–12)

Is he perhaps a 'maniac', as some would have it? Psychotic? There seems to be some paranoia, and the question of the psychological causes for his actions seem to me a highly promising dimension. However, taking that route may make us veer away, if only slightly, from the idea of Richard's *conscious* motivation. Instead, some readers have opted to see the origins of Richard's behavioural doctrine in the writings of Niccolò Machiavelli.

Born in 1469 in Ferrara, Italy, Machiavelli has had an enormous if occasionally quirky influence on western political thought. Educated in Bologna, he spent much of his career in the Florentine diplomatic service of the Medici, the powerful banking family. His writings, founded on observations of other small Italian city-states, the Vatican and France, set out to explain the rise and fall of principalities and republics. His most celebrated book is a short treatise, *Il principe* (*The Prince*), written in late 1513, the ideas of which spread rapidly throughout Europe. Since the first English translation did not appear until 1640, *The Prince* was more commonly read and circulated via plagiarised manuscripts.

Machiavelli's separation of political conduct from spiritual values was highly polemical and naturally attracted the scorn of the Church, which denounced him as a pagan and an opportunist. In the words of Roger Ascham, the contemporary English theorist, he was guilty of 'promoting whatever is best for profit and licentiousness'. The result is that the man is often demonised as a ruthless pragmatist, sponsoring the policy of 'the ends always justify the means'. However, this is a principle which Richard Gloucester appears to embrace wholeheartedly in his determination to achieve the crown by any means and at any cost.

Interestingly, in his 'marrow bones' soliloquy of *3Henry VI* Richard finally declares that he will 'set the murderous Machiavel to school' (3.2.193). In other words, he will set out to pursue his vengeful ambition using any measures available, regardless of all conventional morality.

A detailed study of Machiavelli is beyond the scope of our study, but one quotation in particular may give the flavour of his self-help guide intended to advise princes on how to hold on to power, from Chapter XV of *The Prince*:

> If a ruler who wants to act honourably is surrounded by many unscrupulous men his downfall is inevitable. Therefore a ruler who wishes to maintain his power must be prepared to act immorally when this becomes necessary.
>
> (Machiavelli, pp. 54–5)

At some point, then, an individual would be justified in acting against established morality, here the canons of medieval nobility and the teaching of the Bible. Richard's (and Machiavelli's) ways of thinking and acting amount to a quantum leap away from the absolute duty-principles of honour and Christian charity which his fellow-courtiers continue to observe.

Is Richard, then, amoral, or immoral? From our point of view, there is only one possible answer. But from Richard's it is less than simple, because he appears to thoroughly transcend the question of 'right and wrong' – the question itself does not even arise. And yet he is acting in accordance with some tacit contract, a contract that rejects the conscience. I think we can find an answer by focusing on the Will, which is conceived of by Richard as the key to selfhood. And the thoughts of another philosopher could help here: Friedrich Nietzsche (1844–1900).

Nietzsche's views on ethics are peppered through his many works, but one book in particular condenses his unstructured thoughts, *Beyond Good and Evil*. Especially interesting is Part Five, 'On the Natural History of Morals', in effect, jottings, a 'Prelude' rather than a fully formulated system.

Nietzsche believed that ever since Aristotle, mankind had suppressed the 'dangerous' drives such as sex, free will, instinct, rapacity, ambition and guile, replacing them with 'prudence'. Reason is thus opposed to nature and natural urges, desires and the Will. An individual's nature, Nietzsche claims, is a more reliable source of authentic ethics because it respects an individual's particular circumstances, including their own history. To achieve this ideal of authenticity, one should reject the imperatives of the herd and the received morality and formulate one's own independent and original thinking. The individual must rely solely on the Will, and the Will is the key to someone achieving an independent identity. Thus, the Will, not science, nor God, nor parents, is the only source of truth and action (Nietzsche 1886).

Like Machiavelli, Nietzsche has been denounced at times as a fanatical Antichrist. On the other hand, elements of his philosophy have been tremendously influential on twentieth-century continental philosophy and on numerous writers, including D.H. Lawrence, George Bernard Shaw, James Joyce and Henrik Ibsen. Where I think Nietzsche is relevant to our discussion is in terms of how Richard III conceives his own universe of action.

Nietzsche's 'Will' is not simply the determination to achieve one's ambition or desire, though it does encapsulates these. 'Being human' can be described as having a will. The Will is knowledge of one's self through which values and desire become known, and become projected into the world as a unique and dynamic identity. One person becomes distinguished from another by the expression of each will.

These ideas seem to me to help describe what is happening inside Richard's single-minded drivenness. Seen from the viewpoint of unimpeded ambition, Richard Gloucester is the pure embodiment of a preternatural will. The imperative verbs in the above passage relating to this, such as 'go ...infer ... tell ...' are a spontaneous expression of this will, his absolute conviction in his actions. Richard the man is tightly identified with this will, and watching the play is like observing a raw, pure muscle in action. It is the extreme assertion of selfhood through the Will, the absolute expression of authentic morality with all its horrifying outcome, a morality that is contemptuous of the 'herd' around him.

So when Richard declares 'I am determined to play the villain' this expression of his 'will' is the ultimate form of acting because the word 'villain' is not in reality his. He steals words like 'villain', 'inquity', 'conscience' and 'Vice' from the world of 'bad morality' in order that we can understand him – he has no words for himself. There are none. His 'will' is the existence of a domain beyond good and evil, where there can be no words, only madness and oblivion.

## Context Passage 4: 5.3.180–209

In 3.2 at Baynard's Castle, Richard assumes his priestly garb. He is out to deceive the Mayor and citizens over his religious devoutness and thus his eligibility for the crown. Next, at the start of Act 4, with Richard's coronation imminent, Elizabeth is barred from visiting her sons in the Tower. Dorset is urged to flee and join Richmond in exile in France, while Buckingham too plans escape, following the murders of the Princes and Lady Anne.

In 4.4, a chorus of Elizabeth, Margaret and the Duchess of York bewail the loss of their sons or husbands. When Richard proposes he marry her daughter, Elizabeth is stung into bitter opposition. The pace begins to quicken with reports of Richmond's forces in increasing strength, swelled by defectors. However, Buckingham is captured and executed.

The two armies meet and set up their camps on Bosworth field where, on the eve of battle, the two commanders are visited in their sleep by ghosts of Richard's victims (whose spectral manifestation is another point of contact with *Macbeth* and *Hamlet*). In turn each spirit greets Richmond with the promise of victory and life, and Richard with despair and death.

The final passage for analysis is taken from 5.3 as Richard recoils from his vision of these apparitions, waking him with a chilling start:

| | | |
|---|---|---|
| *Richard*: | Give me another horse! bind up my wounds! | 180 |
| | Have mercy, Jesu! Soft, I did but dream. | |
| | O coward conscience, how dost thou afflict me? | |
| | The lights burn blue. It is not dead midnight. | |
| | Cold, fearful drops stand on my trembling flesh. | |
| | What? do I fear myself? There's none else by. | 185 |
| | Richard loves Richard, that is, I am I. | |
| | Is there a murderer here? No. Yes, I am. | |
| | Then fly. What, from myself? Great reason why: | |
| | Lest I revenge. What, myself upon myself? | |
| | Alack. I love myself. Wherefore? For any good | 190 |
| | That I myself have done unto myself? | |
| | O, no. Alas, I rather hate myself | |

For hateful deeds committed by myself.
I am a villain. Yet I lie, I am not.
Fool, of thyself speak well. Fool, do not flatter.                195
My conscience hath a thousand several tongues,
And every tongue brings in a several tale,
And every tale condemns me for a villain.
Perjury, in the highest degree,
Murder, stern murder, in the direst degree,                       200
All several sins, all used in each degree,
Throng to th' bar, crying all 'Guilty! guilty!'
I shall despair. There is no creature loves me,
And if I die no soul shall pity me.
Nay, wherefore should they, since that I myself                   205
Find in myself no pity to myself?
Methought the souls of all that I had murdered
Came to my tent, and every one did threat
To-morrow's vengeance on the head of Richard.

It is difficult to overlook the great sense of personal turmoil in Richard's lines. Also evident is an intense complexity of feeling, which modulates line by line, sometimes even word by word. Several forceful words leap off the page, words which encapsulate the intensity of this moment and the turbulence in the character's mind: 'mercy' (line 181), 'loves' (186), 'pity' (204, 206) and 'vengeance' (209). It is a crucial, climactic point in the play and I would like to structure its analysis along the lines of its four-phase structure, which closely tracks the changing focuses in Richard's mind.

(i)   Line 181: '*Give me another horse! bind up my wounds!*'

Richard, we are told, 'starts out of his dream', that is, from the dream-state peopled by the ghosts of his victims. This opening line anticipates one of the most-quoted lines of the play, exclaimed by Richard at the climax of the Battle of Bosworth (5.4.7). The play teems with such uncanny anticipations, prophecies and curses, as well as legacies – each moment is suffused with or is defined by the weight of other moments.

Note too how Richard is still commanding, despatching orders, 'Give', 'Bind up' and then, in the following line, 'Have mercy.' He is in control and desperate to maintain power. Yet the line is also pessimistic, anticipating loss, even disaster. Ironically, it is Richmond who will met-aphorically 'bind up' those wounds inflicted on the English Court.

These opening lines are of crucial importance for both the audi-ence and the director because they suggest the identity of Richard in a way that his soliloquies do not. Not quite conscious, they reveal Richard in an unguarded moment of genuine feeling. As such they are more true than even the soliloquies because even though the lat-ter are intended to be veracious, Richard still uses them to perform to us, presenting his own version of himself.

Truthful these words may be, but how does he deliver line 181? Imperiously? Desperately? In a traumatised way?

(ii) Lines 181–95: '*myself upon myself?*'

It is in this unguarded moment that Richard uncharacteristically begs mercy from Jesus. There has previously been little evidence of a Christian God in action or devout belief in it. He appeases his despair with the realisation that the ghostly display was all a dream, chastising his 'coward conscience' as the cause of this illusion, not the spirit of vengeance itself (compare his curt remarks on 'coward' conscience at 5.3.311–12). However, the fact that the candle lights 'burn blue' sug-gests that these worrying spectres may still be lingering about his tent. Accordingly he comforts himself they must be illusions, not ghosts, because it is not yet midnight, the hour when ghosts begin to walk (cf. *Hamlet* 1.4.3). He begs for them to be merely a 'timorous dream', an invention of his dissembling conscience.

At this point, line 185, the concord of his mind begins to crack open. Who is he talking to here?

> Richard loves Richard, that is, I am I.
> Is there a murderer here? No. Yes, I am.
>
> (185–6)

To himself, yes. But he speaks as if there were two of him, as there were in the opening soliloquy of the play, when he flaunted his nar-cissism, mirror and shadow (see also 1.2.259). He loves himself

(190), as 'there is no creature loves me' (206). Richard current also loves Richard past, there is no regret, no remorse.

When he says 'I am I', it seems of course to be a tautology, and it is, but perhaps more than this. He cannot divide off the murderer from the conscience (some editions print here 'I and I', which may stress the separation in his mind between the doer and the thinker). One side asks if there is a murderer and the other side of him – the dissembler – denies this: 'No' – alluding to the perjurer in line 199. Yes, replies the forthright conscience, which cannot deny but which Richard has suppressed. The appearance of the ghosts, too, betrays the presence of the murderer (among their many functions ghosts could, of course, reveal wrongdoings).

This catechism, of question and answer, is another example of the dramatic technique of psychomachy, the externalisation of conscience as two voices (sometimes personified as opposing angels) in a searching examination of a character (see Chapter 2).

Richard momentarily considers the possibility of flight but registers immediately the impossibility of flying from the indivisible conscience:

Then fly. What, from myself? Great reason why ...

(188)

Notice here the recurrence of the /aɪ/ sound, relentlessly reiterating the presence of the 'I' persona as if Richard were subliminally struggling to hold together his psyche in the face of persistent splintering. Also note the complex internal rhyme in the passage, again based chiefly on the /aɪ/ sound. Many of the lines have end rhymes ('murdered' / 'Richard', 'degree' / 'me', 'myself' / 'myself'). The whole complexity of repeated phonemes and words creates a dizzying convulsive network of sound to underscore the torsion in Richard's crisis.

Many of the lines in this phase have balanced or symmetrical phrases: 'Richard love Richard', 'I am I', 'myself upon myself'. Although these appear semantically to suggest unity of personality, in expressionistic terms they actually highlight schisms within it: what is and what ought; what was and what should have been.

Richard's statements of self-love have the ring of desperation as well as solipsism once more. His self-love is consoling in the face of deepening melancholy. Splitting his identity into two aspects does offer the possibility that his life may have pursued an alternative, more virtuous path:

> ... any good
> That I might have done myself
>
> (190–1)

Is this a hint of conscience and the belief in the other course that the other 'Richard' might have followed? It is hard to imagine, and yet he follows this with reflections of self-hate for those 'hateful deeds committed by myself' (193).

In what sense are these deeds now 'hateful'? We imagine he refers to murder, cruelty, mental torture and chaos. However, does he intend to say that these are 'hateful' in the social sense, the source of other people's suffering – what *they* find hateful? Or is it that in reality Richard's conscience overriding his Machiavellian half, in other words, that he himself at last finds these actions hateful? This may not seem a significant point but it will arise when we come to consider the degree to which Richard's ending can reasonably be termed 'tragic'.

(iii)  Lines 196–206: '*I shall despair*'

At first the state of Richard's consciousness appears to worsen. His conscience is not solely one voice, but 'a thousand several tongues' (196). These are the tongues, metaphorical voices, of his victims.

If we look at the metre of the lines in this speech we can register that in the latter part (lines 181–95) almost every line is irregular, clearly reflecting the agitation of their speaker. But at line 196 the rhythm of the lines suddenly settles to a more regular cadence, at first, anyway. It is as though the brief gap between lines 195 and 196 has enabled Richard to break out of the circularity of the earlier phase. There are now fewer of those self-harming interrogations, and in their place simple statements begin to dominate, slowing the tempo.

His first words in this phase, 'My Conscience', establish the new tone and direction. Intense anxiety stressed by speculative, incoherent utterances subsides into statements of self-knowledge. He now replaces the word 'dissembling' (an earlier source of pride) with the guilt-laden 'perjury', setting up the courtroom imagery with its accusatory 'several voices', and culminating in their

> Throng to th' bar, crying 'Guilty! Guilty!'
>
> (202)

Every word of their indictment is aimed at himself.

From a condition of terror and self-pity in the first 16 lines Richard proceeds through self-knowledge and the possibility of penitence, and on to finish in despair, at line 203:

> I shall despair. There is no creature loves me …

He knows full well that his followers, now diminishing in number and fervour, were all along purely mercenary in their support. This once untouchable, vaunting superman posits his own death on the battlefield on the following day and the likelihood that this will result in the death of his immortal soul: 'no soul shall pity me' is a coldly terrifying prospect, even for this Renaissance humanist, since the phrase 'no soul' includes God and thus the certain judgement of damnation. It is from this that Richard's unguarded exclamation in line 181 ('Have mercy, Jesu!') derives its significance – for all his bluff tyranny he still shrinks back to God and His redemptive sovereignty.

### (iv) Lines 207–9: *'Methought'*

The effect of the final three lines of the passage is to increase the dreamlike quality of what has preceded them. The language of the first two lines plus the final three is of a different order from the middle 26, making the central phrases appear to originate in a different consciousness. The word 'Methought' confirms this – as when in *A Midsummer Night's Dream* Titania emerges from her enchantment with 'Methought I was enamoured of an ass.' Richard, now adopting very plain speaking, says that he can hardly believe the disputation that his conscience has just led him through. He is waking, and it is as if he had lived through the middle 26 lines in a nanosecond, while the final three are in hyper-slow motion.

The passage demonstrates again Richard's capacity for stepping outside and apart from the action. He is actor, stage manager, author and puppeteer, yet here he is somehow unable to detach himself from the corrosive torments now visiting him. How does he speak these tormented lines on stage? Is he standing? Lying down in his tent? Or is he kneeling? How he appears on stage can substantially affect our interpretation of these words.

At first Richard comes over as incoherent. Then the intensity mounts and with it, his anxiety. He becomes frightened, possibly remorseful, and even despairing. The chief driving energy of the speech emanates from within Richard himself, his deep reactions to the apparitions that represent his body count. Technically, the dramatic force of the passage is generated by the emotions in conflict and the short, desperate statements and questions.

We need to consider why this passage is important in the context of the play as a whole. In terms of topics, the speech focuses again on power, past actions and the moral question of 'villainy', but it also at this late stage introduces hints of the theme of 'humanity'. Significantly, it touches on the possibility of insight and remorse, and these are threatened by the surfacing of Richard's incipient grief. It presents Richard's agitated response to the indictments of the ghosts, immediately prior to this speech, and to the desertion of his 'supporters'. For the viewer there arises the possibility of Richard's anguish, the reassurance of his suffering and the prospect of justice.

Of course, it tells us even more about Richard, at the same time confirming some previous conclusions. From early on we have been made aware of his pathological inability to empathise with his victims, that he is unaware even of the humanity of others, such as when he proposes marriage to Lady Anne and to Queen Elizabeth's daughter – he cannot even comprehend their response to his horrendous crimes against them.

We can reasonably ask what it is from within that drives this individual called 'Richard'. There is a strong suspicion that the answer lies in factors originating in the period before this play's events. His mother, the Duchess of York, knows him better than most, and in 4.4. presents us with a kind of testimonial:

Tetchy and wayward was thy infancy;
Thy schooldays frightful, desperate, wild, and furious;

Thy prime of manhood, daring, bold, and venturous;
Thy age confirmed, proud, subtle, sly, and bloody ... .

(4.4.169–73)

There is nothing exceptional about the first three stages. People have been variously tetchy, furious, bold even, without resorting to serial murder. She seems to be claiming that it is in the late stage of his life that Richard has become the villain, as his royal opportunities withered away.

We have noted that Richard attributes his attitudes and policy to distortions in his own body, which have become projected into his moral and social psyche. The above passage may give some support to this view: the reality that he is unloved (line 203) has by some malign inversion allowed him the space and the licence to vilify the other courtiers for their 'unlove'. To this end, there is a strong suspicion that, deserting humanity, Richard has signed a pact with some vile preternatural power to avenge his distorted nature. From *3Henry VI*:

Then, since the heavens have shaped my body so,
Let hell make crooked my mind to answer it.

(5.6.7–8)

Richard's attitude in this speech looks forward to the arrival and eventual triumph of the Duke of Richmond, Henry Tudor. An undeniable aura of defeat and doom lingers over Richard's words ('I shall despair ... And if I die'). *Richard III*, like *Henry V*, is the termination of its tetralogy and, as a result, the two plays invite comparison and contrast. Each play is scored around one dominant personality who appears in almost every scene, and each finishes by looking with optimism beyond its own purview to a future generation that each, in its own contrasting way, subtends. Each has its own satisfying feeling of closure, one ending in marriage and the other in annihilation However, Shakespeare makes clear that where the triumph of Henry V delivers only a pause in the sequence of 'horror, fear and mutiny', the crushing of Richard marks its eventual conclusion – in dramatic terms, anyway.

## Henry Tudor, Duke of Richmond

In *Richard III* a major contribution to this feeling of closure is, of course, the arrival from afar of Richmond, who functions less as a realistic individual than as dramatically symbolic device. Although he is long anticipated, Richmond is in effect (and in history) the *deus ex machina* that enters to resolve its problems. While representing the return of the 'sun', he casts a long, threatening shadow over Richard's outlook.

For the purpose of morale-boosting, Richard's pre-battle oratory to his troops rubbishes Richmond's army as a ragbag of mercenaries recruited from the French whom their forebears – including those at Agincourt – had 'beaten, bobbed, and thumped' (5.3.336). In truth, Richard's own enterprise from the very beginning has been singularly venal.

The victory of Richmond marks the founding of the new Tudor dynasty, that will include Elizabeth I. Some critics, notably Tillyard, have interpreted the whole cycle of eight English histories as Shakespeare's obsequious celebration of the Tudor ascendancy and the working-out or atonement of the 'sin' committed by Bullingbrook in originally deposing the rightful king, Richard II.

As a *deus ex machina* of sorts, Richmond's arrival is also messianic. He asks God to 'make us thy ministers of chastisement' (5.3.116). When he delivers his pre-battle pep-talk to his soldiers he makes the orthodox claim that they are fighting with the active support of the Deity:

God and our good cause fight upon our side

(5.3.241)

The mood of the play, from the opening scene to 5.3, has been one of unremitting gloom, sorrow, danger and sinister shadows consuming all signs of virtuous shoots. If there has been any 'glorious summer' then we see nothing of it. By contrast, Richmond the healer is immediately linked with imagery of brightness and warmth. In 5.3 his opening speech includes the glorious imagery of 'sun ... golden ... bright ... fiery'. He has come to cauterise the wounds of England, to restore the 'summer fields' which Richard has dispelled with his murderous shadows and wintry rancour. Richard, by contrast, and as the above extract demonstrates, has turned his back on God (203).

Being thus closely associated with God, light and regeneration, Richmond, for many commentators, has come to symbolise Providence itself ('Now civil wounds are stopped'; 5.5.40). Given Richard's progress towards absolute power and control of the English Court, the most likely possibility of deliverance was always going to be from an outside agency. Richmond fulfils that need, and after his vanquishing of Richard promises unity, symbolised in the Tudor rose (uniting the roses of the divided Lancaster and York houses) and in the prospect of his marriage as a Lancastrian to Elizabeth, granddaughter of the Duchess of York.

## Is *Richard III* a problem play?

In the title of this chapter I raised the question of *Richard III* being a problem play.

Problem plays are so called because while at first each sets up our expectations of one genre of drama, in the end they contain elements which challenge this and could belong to a different genre. What about *Richard III?*

During Shakespeare's life and shortly after, all the printings of *Richard III* label it as '*The Tragedy ...*', yet by the Folio edition of 1623 it has become catalogued as a 'History' play. It is of course usually regarded as fitting into either of these genres. Yet, if *Richard III* really is a tragedy, then whose tragedy is it and who, if anyone, is the tragic hero? These questions point to the heart of the genre problem in the play.

To decide on whether the play is a tragedy we first need to consider what we would expect a tragedy to look like. Furthermore, whether or not the play works as a tragedy will to a great extent depend on how we think of Richard himself.

In my opening chapter, on *Richard II*, I set out some of Aristotle's ideas on tragedy, and these can act as a useful starting point here. Briefly, the features he identified included the following: that the tragic 'hero' is a man of high rank and with humanity, so that his 'tragic fall' should seem significant; he performs actions which express free will, implying that he is responsible for his deeds; at the same time these actions are jeopardised by factors beyond his control – for instance, 'destiny', the ineluctable will of the gods, or a serious flaw in the hero's character; feelings of pity and/or fear are aroused by the purging (*catharsis*) of the 'hero' through death.

Aristotle believed that tragedy is most effective when the plot observes the 'unities' of place and time – that is, the whole of the action taking place in one locality and during 'a single circuit of the sun'. Another important element is that tragedy was likely to be more intense if the 'hero' was to suddenly realise (*anagnorisis*) at a late point in the action that he was the victim of fate or of his own grievous defect – too late to be able to remedy its consequences.

Some of these points are readily identifiable in *Richard III*: a noble setting and an aristocratic pedigree, plus the action being confined by and large to one stiflingly tense location – at least for most of the play. Clearly Richard has a vision, acts freely to impose his will and even boasts of his culpable criminality. Although filling more than one day, the span of the play seems short – Richard's menacing run feels extremely short-lived, and he burns with a fierce intensity while the whole interlocking plot of conspiracy and multiple murder is over almost in a blink.

The passage from 5.3 we have just analysed is important in showing, too, that here are the confused fumblings towards what Aristotle termed *anagnorisis*, the hero's insights on the truth of himself, the horror of his actions and terror of their consequences. He is undoubtedly alienated by this crisis, which focuses on his disaffection with society. But remorse? Does he convincingly show true penitence for his actions? There are words of conscience and there are murders, but no remorse. And are these words of conscience merely 'honey words', as Lady Anne maintains (4.1.81)?

So, do we feel any pity for Richard? Could there be sympathy for such a man? We are more inclined to feel relief at Richmond's purging of this odious tyrant. Any possibility of pity is likely to begin from some diminishment of Richard's responsibility, improbable as this is.

Margaret reviles Richard as the 'slave of nature' (1.3.228). The critic Marie-Hélène Besnault, writing of Richard, says he is the 'physical representation of a monster' whose body is the outward form of evil (Besnault, p. 110). If we try to argue that he is the outcast, victim of nature, of his birthright, of history, of his own body, then this is perhaps a beginning (consider 1.3.46–50 and 293 in this context). Yet, councils for his defence cannot escape the fact that he does consciously set out on a career of iniquity (1.1.30).

Does it matter that most of the murders happen off-stage or that Richard does not actually get his hands dirty by committing them? Or that all of the characters, including Richard's accomplices, barely lift a finger to prevent him, though fully cognisant of his nature?

So, on almost every count *Richard III* does not match Aristotle's characteristics of tragic hero in the same way that *Richard II* may. However, in Renaissance England another classical dramatist had a enormous influence: the Roman tragedian Lucius Annaeus Seneca (4 BC–AD 65), and his theories may help us through.

Dramatist and statesman, Seneca was tutor, speech-writer and, later, victim of emperor Nero, and his writings reflect the terrors and excesses of the emperor's reign. His nine surviving manuscript plays have exerted a powerful influence on the development of Elizabethan drama, starting in 1562 with *Gorboduc*, a highly popular tragedy written by Thomas Norton and Thomas Sackville.

Seneca's dramas are themselves derived from ancient Greek tragedies, but they differ from other Roman and Greek tragedies in that they were not designed primarily for stage acting but for static recitation, in which the speaker takes first one part, then another. His characters have no subtle individuation, no inner life, solely existing to suffer shock and upheaval, the plots delivered through verbal ostentation, especially daring aphoristic conceits.

Typically, Senecan tragedy declaims in a heavy atmosphere of pessimism and terror. Characters are depicted adopting a general posture of stoicism in the face of treachery, brutality, court intrigues, witchcraft and sedition. The victim(s) is/are forced to dig deep for the courage to sustain him/herself in the face of cruelty, alienation and extreme psychological peril.

One apparent influence on Shakespeare's *Richard III* can readily be found in the stolid declamation of Seneca's chorus – clearly evident in the impassive choric style of the women in Act 4, beginning with Margaret's 'I had an Edward, till a Richard killed him ...' (4.4.39ff.).

In terms of dramatic interest, the archetypal Senecan tragedy comprises a world of disastrous misery where order, laws and civil authority are incapable of protecting the innocent from the outrageous excesses of power. Out of this miasma of despair come the stirrings of outrage and prayer to Providence for divine intervention.

Senecan tragedy is tragedy of political forewarning. Literary commentator John Russell Brown sees the play as a timely expression of its author's concerns over gathering political tyrannies in the late sixteenth century:

> Shakespeare might naturally summon Seneca to mind when he wished to alert his audience to outrage, injustice and the pain of estranged families.
>
> (Brown, p. 17)

Unlike Aristotle's theory of tragedy, that of Seneca's paradigm of tragedy inheres in the concept of suffering, together with the stoicism of those who suffer. Their suffering is mitigated by the belief in an external agency that will rally, eventually intervening to rectify the state of injustice and restore proper lawful authority. Also, unlike Aristotle, there is no hero, not inherently so, and as here in *Richard III* the emphasis is on the victims, those who suffer the torment in a hellish world of cruelty and nihilism.

It is through the Senecan emphasis on the *suffering* of the victims and their eventual redemption rather than following Aristotle's model, with its focus on the fall of a heroic individual, that *Richard III* can be construed as a tragedy. On the local scale, the victims here are the people whose ghosts visit Richard's tent at Bosworth. We can to some extent settle the 'problem' of the play by pointing out that while the history is of Richard himself, the tragedy is of his victims. On the national or racial scale, for Shakespeare England is the victim, eventually redeemed, rising into Richmond's golden summer of the incipient Tudor dynasty. *Richard III* challenges and at the same time assimilates the Elizabethan period's clear-cut delineation of tragedy as a fixed genre. Where *Richard II* is presented in the moment of the Tudor revival of chivalric values and ritual, *Richard III* seeks to subvert these, or at least exploit them for its tragicomedy. In *Richard III*, a man who explicitly equates himself with the Vice rises to the surface to bring the cycle to a tragic, yet at the same time, perversely comic finale.

## Conclusions to the Histories

O polished perturbation

(*2Henry IV* 4.2.153[4.5.21])

*Richard III* brings to an end the sequence of the eight history plays that began with *Richard II*. I use the term 'sequence' because the series of eight plays in total is not merely a group of discrete dramas based on a chronology of six successive kings but an identifiable whole, regardless of whether Shakespeare set out with the concept of an inclusive cycle.

The sequence begins and ends with conflict. In *Richard II* the initial battle is exclusively verbal and indecisive, and in a realistic sense this indecisiveness is not finally resolved until 86 years later at the Battle of Bosworth, in artistic terms, anyway. It begins with a future monarch despatched into exile and ends with another future monarch returning from exile. It begins and ends with the death of a Gloucester. The sequence abounds in such symmetries, recurrences, converses and reiterations which help to pull the group into an aesthetic unity. It is through such recurrent and variant patterns of action, themes, decisive moments and formal dramaturgy that characters and actions derive meanings and generate themes that, in turn, generate rise to more comprehensive interpretations of the sequence.

Archetypal personas such as dissidents, rebels, despots and elder statesmen infuse a range of characters, forming the main threads of the tapestry. So characters who are at one time dissident may, via the dynamics of political change, appear later as the new legitimate order. Core themes such as loyalty, family, honour and ambition help to fashion the weft of the discussion.

The major theme that courses throughout is, of course, that of kingship. All of the plays from the English history cycle which we have analysed present a protracted discussion of this issue through its various facets, including the nature of royalty and questions of legal ascendancy.

Dominating the whole dialectic of history in these plays is a familiar Shakespearean challenge of the free will versus destiny, here writ large in the struggle for power. What we may call the English narrative here can be understood as the residual shape emerging from a series of interconnected crises in that struggle.

These moments of the individual are set against a constant struggle with ever-present larger forces of ... what shall we call them? The collective will? Mutability? Death? Plus the overarching paradigm of the new Renaissance humanism. Shakespeare's view of history is a dynamic negotiation between, on the one hand, a series of key decisions made by individuals in the present, and on the other an unremitting legacy of the accumulated folly of the past.

Returning to the theme of kingship, Carlisle's warning in Act 4 of *Richard II* proves most prescient: once a subject gives sentence on a king, 'disorder, horror, fear and mutiny' are let loose. Ascendancy comes to be predicated upon nothing more than force of arms. What Shakespeare offers us in his kings is ultimately not the glorious flower of a nation but a ragbag of warlords who wage bloody internecine war in the clamour for what Richard II identifies as the 'hollow crown'. Presented in this light, kingship is seen as a species of insanity or 'antic':

> sad stories of the death of kings,
> How some have been deposed, some slain in war,
> Some haunted by the ghosts they have deposed,
> Some poisoned by their wives: some sleeping killed,
> All murdered. For within the hollow crown
> That rounds the mortal temples of a king
> Keeps Death his court and there the antic sits ...
>
> (3.2.156–62)

## Suggested Work

In my discussion of *Richard III* I have concentrated on the identity and function of Richard, Duke of Gloucester. To further develop your grasp of the play, I suggest you give some more thought to the important figure of ex-Queen Margaret and, to help this, examine her speech at 4.4.82–115. Try to work out how her specialised use of language there reveals her state of mind and her character as well as her relationship with Queen Elizabeth (compare this speech with that at 1.3.241–78, noting similarities in diction). What do these suggest about Margaret's function in the play, particularly with regard to the theme of time?

# Methods of Analysis

For each of the chapter discussions I have adopted a standard approach to the study of the individual plays. From each play I have chosen four important passages for discussion – but it is important to remember that the whole of a play must be studied in the same or greater detail.

As a first stage of the analysis I have tried to set the selected passage in the context of its play and, where appropriate, in the context of other plays and wider general issues. Then I have analysed passages by looking at them in very close detail. The following outlines the process I have adopted as the preparation to writing up my response to a passage:

(i) **Narrative**. One starting point is to understand exactly what is being said (and to whom), together with descriptions of stage action, making a synopsis if necessary; then to work out what events and choices led to this scene, and how it affects later scenes, and decide why this particular scene is dramatically important to the play as a whole and how it advances the plot.

(ii) **Visuals**. Using clues in the language, try to visualise how a scene might work in a stage performance, including costume, necessary props and setting. To help with this, you could draw a stage plan showing the relative positions and movements of characters.

(iii) **Structure**. Examine the passage as a whole in order to identify where its dramatic interest lies, noting especially conflicts, crises or crucial decisions. Try to work out how the subject matter develops during the extract, then decide what gives the extract its structure and cohesion (for example, common themes running through it, or recurring images) Ask yourself what other developments there are inside this passage, such as mood, emotion, attitudes, release of information.

(iv) **Language 1**. Check how *sentences and phrases* reveal interesting features of character, including their motivation, subjective feelings, tone of voice, relationships, themes, and the characters' attitudes towards these; try to pinpoint *how* sentences and phrases create your impressions.

(v) **Language 2**. *Words and figures.* As you analyse an extract you will need to be aware of a character's use of diction and of figures such as imagery, metaphor and symbol. Check what tensions there are at work in the discourse, such as irony, subtexts, subplots or other factors working to subvert the apparent sense. (You could use the relevant elements of the Glossary below as a checklist.)

(vi) **Verse**. It is highly worthwhile to analyse the verse or prose of each speech in the passage; for verse, note the metre and rhythm and those changes or irregularities which may relate to what is being said explicitly; ask yourself what the metre reveals of a character. If prose is being used, try to think of what effect this creates for readers or an audience.

(vii) **Sound**. The sound of speech is important, too, and this can usually be related to what is happening. On the detailed level, try to relate any recurrent sounds to the mood of a scene, or to a character or theme. On a broader level, think about how a character may deliver a speech in terms of volume, pace and accent – this will help you get a better idea of a character's identity by particularising him/her.

(viii) **Context**. Decide what this extract contributes to the play as a whole and how it connects with other texts. If you imagine that every scene is dramatically essential to the whole, ask yourself what would be lost if any particular scene was omitted from it.

(ix) **Other views**. It is important to read other critics to get a broader grasp of the text and to challenge or extend your responses to the play. Reading critics can be useful in developing your own critical style as well as getting a better grasp of the terminology that Literary Studies employs. (See Further Reading for suggestions.)

**(x)** **Characterisation**. Shakespeare creates character in a number of ways. Naturally, you will have to study an individual's precise language and its nuances. Soliloquies will be highly enlightening here. Examine too what other characters say about him/her. In addition observe how he/she affects the course of the play by decisions and physical actions. An individual's response to others' words and actions is very revealing. Observe how they make alliances – who are their friends and what this tells us about them.

In general terms, it is crucial that you always relate your conclusions about a passage or a text to the exact words there. The above points are offered as just one way of approaching a literary text, and there will be many others. By the same token, my discussions and the points raised in them are not intended as either definitive or final comments on the plays. The analyses are really intended as starting points for stimulating your own discussion and for developing your own methods of analysis and description.

## PART 2

# THE CONTEXT
# AND THE CRITICS

# 5

# Shakespeare and the Writing of History in the Elizabethan Period

In that stirring Western *The Man Who Shot Liberty Valance* (John Ford, 1962), Senator Ranson Stoddard (James Stewart) returns to the town of Shinbone to confess to a fresh-faced news reporter that it was not he who had killed the notorious gunslinger, Liberty Valance (Lee Marvin), so many decades ago when, as a 'tenderfoot' lawyer, he first stepped into the lawless gun-toting frontier town. Although his meteoric political career has been rooted in the popular belief that he had brought justice to the town by gunning down this rowdy out-law, a flashback reveals that it was actually rancher Tom Donifon (John Wayne), firing his rifle simultaneously, who had killed Valance. Returning to the present, just as the cub reporter excitedly begins to hare off with this amazing scoop, his editor rips up his manuscript, telling him that when the legend has turned into truth, he will then publish the legend.

The point I want to discuss in this chapter is one that has sim-mered throughout our discussions: was Shakespeare, like the editor of *The Shinbone Star*, 'printing' the legend, or are his plays the truth? The editor of *The Shinbone Star* privileged the legend, the myth, the lie, because it fitted in with his conception of the hero and with its mythological status in the prevailing political climate. The hero was actually preceded and, in a real sense, created by the requirements of the ideology. No editor ever let the truth get in the way of a good story (although this too may only be a myth!).

I would like to discuss Elizabethan ideas on history writing and Shakespeare's general approach to history plays, along with the issues implicated in it, and we can take this in four sections: history: myth v. fact; the chronicle history plays; Shakespeare's historical sources; and Shakespeare's adaptations.

### History: Myth v. Fact

The Prologue to Shakespeare's *Henry VIII* (alternative title: 'All is True') prays to the audience:

> Such as give
> Their money out of hope they may believe,
> May here find truth too.

(7–9)

However, we do not judge Shakespeare in the court of historical accuracy – whether the events presented were as truly happened or the people as they actually were (even if there were some definitive way of testing these possibilities). But we judge these plays first as plays – call it art, if you like, or call it literature – although we always remain conscious of the discursive agenda working through them.

As the anecdote about the editor of *The Shinbone Star* illustrates, art answers to different laws from documentary writing. Art is legend as well as fact – *mythos* as well as *logos*. As a general rule dramatists do not present a historical reality, but rather the memory of one. They may use real events and characters and write believable dramas based on them, but the facts have been revised for thematic and other effects. Their original sources, too, have submitted the events to the same process of memory, filtration and bias. The performance of the plays tries to distract from this by re-creating a sense of the ever-living present so vivid that we cannot imagine them any other way. Yet this is no more than a psychological presence. King Richard, Falstaff, Buckingham, Bullingbrook and all the others act out extraordinary events in astonishing settings (palaces, bloody battles, robberies, executions), touching us by their ambitions and values, their mortality and suffering humanity, and then are gone.

Returning to Shakespeare's England, the vast majority of the populace of the time did not and could not consult history books to acquire a knowledge of their own history. The accumulated past was living and present all around them in the form of legends, ballads and folk tales, together with the general hearsay and fable of rural and urban myths. None of these were tested against reliable historical documentation, and the discipline of historiography – the study of the writing of history – was yet in its infancy.

In Elizabethan schools the subject of English history was all but unknown on the curriculum, with the focus of attention firmly on Classical Latin and Greek humanistic studies (which had been given an enormous kick-start as a result of the European Renaissance). Classical authors, by dint of their great age and the test of time, were often regarded as the great depository of knowledge and therefore truth. Aristotle, for instance, contrasts history with poetry, that is, with speculative fictions. Plato, too, was also extremely wary of literary history – and yet firmly believed that for cohesion an ideal social would be founded on a necessary lie concerning its history, a noble legend (thus anticipating *The Shinbone Star*). Herodotus (5th century BC) has been lauded as the 'Father of History', yet he has also been decried as the 'father of lies'. As much concerned to entertain as to inform, Herodotus seems happy to conflate the two.

With the rising Tudor curiosity in the culture of Rome and Athens, plus the emergence of the modern Protestant commonwealth, comes the spin-off of a growing interest in the exact origins of the English. Much of the documentation gathered around this interest was in effect merely the chronicling of the country's long-held myths and hearsay until the gradual accretion of genuine archive materials, which thus became privileged over the oral tradition.

For a long age the common people had depended for their more explicit 'education' on the Church: sermons, hymns, Bible readings, books of prayer, together with illustrations of holy stories in painted church murals. The myths and hearsay of their own unregarded lives were contrasted with the stable 'facts' of holy writ.

In terms of their allegorical effect on this relatively uneducated section of his audience, Shakespeare's Histories could have performed a similar educative function as these painted murals in medieval churches. These simple illustrations of Bible scenes were an informal and constant – as well as certified – version of the religious message. Shakespeare himself would have been acutely familiar with this subtle form of religious indoctrination at his own parish church in Stratford (and his father, as a local council member, is documented as having literally whitewashed over the murals when directed to do so by the new Protestant authorities).

In his History plays Shakespeare also follows in the tradition of the medieval miracle plays. These were presented by the craft guilds on wagons hauled around a town centre as a cycle of shows, designed to dramatise religious episodes as though they were history. Equally significantly, Shakespeare taps into the conventions of the highly popular late medieval morality plays. These simple, more secular dramas employed broad stereotypical characterisations (Charity, Folly, Lust, Strength) for allegorical ends, part of the overall ideological mechanism for moral instruction and civil order in the early period (see, for example, *Everyman* or *The Castle of Perseverance*, anonymous both).

Given the paucity of the church experience and the mediocrity of popular entertainments, it is not difficult to appreciate the burgeoning fascination of the new London theatres and of Shakespeare's History plays, depicting illustrious monarchs in fabulously opulent costume (the first of the dedicated Elizabethan theatres was probably The Theatre, built in north London in 1576).

Shakespeare's History plays are, as history, inevitably ideological. Presented in the stunning spectacle of the new stage, they are dangerously provocative and potentially seditious. All history is political. All theatre is political. (Shakespeare is prudent in avoiding explicit portrayal of his own political masters.) Unsurprisingly, the Church, too, becomes increasingly militant towards this new humanistic alternative to its own established eminence.

The censorship of the stage exercised by Henry Carey, Queen Elizabeth's Lord Chamberlain in this period, meant it was exceedingly risky to dramatise contemporary affairs, hence the safest way of writing political drama was to draw figures from the past and leave it to the audience to recognise the parallels in the present. In Shakespeare's cunning hands the historic parallel was a device of enormous power. For instance, it is no surprise that the largely fictive Henry Bullingbrook should become so readily identifiable as the factual Earl of Essex.

Even if the English and Roman history plays concern themselves with political issues of Shakespeare's own day, they very rarely employ direct topical references to contemporary issues. Historical drama works on the parallels between now and then and these correspondences will operate as universal as well as specific analogies.

The model for this practice was the classical Roman historian, Cornelius Tacitus. Tacitus is famed for his capacity to compare past and present times and for his subtle use of historical parallelism to reflect adversely – but safely – on his own political rulers and systems of government. The late Elizabethan writers eagerly exploited the safe cover afforded by parallelism (or 'application' as it was dubbed): satirising contemporary politicians by refashioning the past for the present. In fact the authorities became so irked by this form of dramatic irony that in 1599 a ban on the printing of history books was introduced by Bishops Bancroft and Whitgift (following the publication in the previous year of John Hayward's *The First Part of the Life and Reign of Henry IV*, dedicated to the Earl of Essex).

Perhaps the final words in this section should go to young Prince Edward in *Richard III*. About to be escorted into 'safe' custody at the Tower of London, he enquires if the Tower had been originally constructed by Julius Caesar, and when Buckingham confirms that it has been rebuilt over the intervening period, he muses:

|  | Is it upon record, or else reported |
|  | Successively from age to age, he built it? |
| *Buckingham* | Upon record, my gracious lord. |
| *Edward* | But say my lord, it were not registered, |
|  | Methinks the truth should live from age to age, |
|  | As 'twere retailed to all posterity ... |

(Richard III 3.1.72–7)

Shakespeare, a man for whom myth is a vibrantly plastic medium, sets up in the mouth of this boy a challenge: that history must be somehow fixed 'upon record'. However, he goes on to acknowledge (line 88) that Caesar himself now 'lives in fame', in other words, the legend has replaced the established truth.

History – whether written or spoken – always manages the reality it claims to be showing. Shakespeare is fascinated by the art of mythopoesis – creation of myths out of facts by adapting those facts. His primary interest lies in verisimilitude rather than facsimiles of history – and 'Shakespeare's Historical Sources', below, examines how Shakespeare adapted his source materials to this end. First, though, we should take brief note of the type of history plays that were then available to Tudor audiences.

## The Chronicle History Plays

The first history play as such is usually recognised as Christopher Marlowe's *Edward II*, written in about 1591. Another, earlier, contender is the anonymous *The Famous Victories of Henrie the Fifth* of about 1588. However, there had been plays and tableaux presenting historical events long before these hit the stage, and some of them are discussed below. The most common were the extremely popular English chronicle plays, which were taken around the country on pageant carts. These Tudor chronicle history plays which Shakespeare himself would have witnessed as a boy in Stratford differ from his own history plays in that they invariably limit themselves to simply presenting a parade of famous monarchs, narrating and enacting key moments, usually with a minimum of dialogue. In effect these are close allies of the folk mummer shows, with their stock characters, loosely dramatising the reign of important English kings. There is practically nothing in the way of theme, political debate, character development or the probing of such concepts as kingship. These 'plays' are seldom now read and even more rarely performed.

As early as 1538 John Bale had written his ardently nationalistic drama, *Kynge Johan*, a cross between a morality and a history play (and a platform for Bale's fiercely loyalist politics). Bale, a former priest, was one among many devisers of Protestant interludes which (like the ballad, the sermon and the morality play) were vehicles for the dissemination of anti-papist political dogma.

However, with all of these clunking political tracts and biographical entertainments, Shakespeare appears to have very little sympathy. In essence his Histories, while still dramatising a series of historical events stretching over a number of years, are much more artfully constructed, events being knit artistically together into genuine plots and sub-plots, developing a broad range of characters in addition to the towering eponymous role. And in the variations mediated from those written chronicles which form his starting point arises the possibility of Shakespeare's own unique and partial voice.

All of this attests to the phenomenal leap forward which English history plays enjoyed in the final decades of the sixteenth century. All at once the history play became massive box-office. The factors stimulating the sudden popularity of the history play on the Elizabethan stage in the 1590s are not difficult to find. First, the way forward had been pioneered by Marlowe's highly successful *Edward II*. In addition, they afforded great scope for the drama of sword fights, with whole battles on stage. This had great appeal to audiences – though Ben Jonson later vehemently attacked this vogue. Moreover, Tudor England was a relatively embryonic state, and these tales of a magnificent past provided the foundation myths that rewrote the turbulent past as a prelude to a predestined glorious present, and supplied a unifying sense of nationhood (John of Gaunt's celebrated speech implements the former, while the rousing battle speeches in *Henry V* and of Richmond in *Richard III* speak to the latter).

The critics Jean Howard and Phyllis Rackin add the interesting point that the authorities probably tolerated these history dramas from another, more pragmatic angle: that of military recruitment, in that they present models of heroism and military prowess:

> The theatre makes the dead arise, but it also has the power to refashion the malleable spectator into a person fit for heroic action. It helps, in short, to create subjects defined by a common 'English blood', who identify with the notable deed of their 'forefathers'.
>
> (Howard and Rackin, p. 19)

## Shakespeare's Historical Sources

In the preparation of history plays Shakespeare was singular in his painstaking research. He appears to have steeped himself wholeheartedly in the historical resources available. We have already noted the tradition of historical shows, pageants and interludes out of which his brilliant dramatic sense emerged, but his meticulous research is yet another point of difference from the earlier constructors of populist entertainments. This is not to imply that in handling the historical data he did not freely modify elements such the chronological sequence or impose his own characterisation, increasing emphases here, toning down a troublesome detail there. He was, after all, in the business of entertainment, and this necessitated his own myth-making. For his core information he took what was to hand in the available chronicles and we can briefly consider these and other sources.

### Raphael Holinshed (*c*.1529–*c*.1580)

The crowning achievement of Holinshed was *The Chronicles of England, Scotland and Ireland*, which appeared in 1577 (revised 1587), and this was undoubtedly Shakespeare's first port of call for his basic material. This monumental work, copiously illustrated, spoke with many voices: political, religious and social. Unsurprisingly it met with vigorous official censorship. For example, accounts of Scottish history were removed where they appeared to jeopardise Anglo-Scottish relations; its description of the Babington plot was moderated to suggest that its conspirators received a fair trial; and its account of religious executions was considered too graphic and was toned down to imply a benign regime operating behind them.

The fact that it was from Holinshed that Shakespeare took much of the facts for his history plays suggests how extensively his data were already controlled by the authorities. For example, in *Richard II*, much of Mowbray's speeches in 1.1 and the accusations concerning Gloucester's murder originate in Holinshed's account; likewise the details of the Percys' rebellion in *1Henry IV* and the interview between Prince Hal and the King. For the arrest of

Clarence in *Richard III* (1.1.34–40), Shakespeare discovered the following eloquent passage:

> The death of Clarence rose of a foolish prophesie, which was, that, after K.Edward, one should reigne, whose first letter of his name should be a G. Wherewith the king and queene were sore troubled, and began to conceive a greevous grudge against this duke, and could not be in quiet till they brought him to his end. And as the divell is woont to incumber the minds of men which delite in such divellish fantasies, they said afterward, that that prophesie lost not his effect, when, after king Edward, Gloucester usurped his kingdome.
>
> (Holinshed, ed. Nicoll, p. 138)

While it can readily be argued that Holinshed was Shakespeare's favoured informant, he also mined a great range of his reading in other important historians and was an avid quarrier among the literary works of contemporaries where it suited.

## Edward Hall (*c.*1498–1547)

Edward Hall was the son of a staunchly Protestant family from Shropshire and his chief work was an important source for Shakespeare's early histories. This, *The Union of the two noble and illustre families of Lanacastre and Yorke*, published in 1543, covers the period of English history, 1399 to 1532. It was written to lionise the Tudors and to show that 'as by discord greate thynges decaie and fall to ruine, so the same by concord be revived and erected'. It is to Hall rather than Holinshed that Shakespeare owes the governing idea through the tetralogies: of a moral pattern tracing the discord following the deposition of the divinely ordained order – a discord that is eventually purged by restoration of the true order (the so-called Tudor myth of Tillyard and Campbell – see Chapter 6).

Holinshed himself probably resorted to Hall's chronicle for his own work (the above passage on the death of Clarence is lifted more or less word for word from Hall). While Holinshed tends to focus on the broader movements of political history, Hall has an eye for its personalities. Suddenly, in *The Union*, Richard III lifts off the page of history as a more colourful, energetic character. The role of Margaret in *Richard III* (and in *Henry VI*) barely mentioned in Holinshed is significantly expanded and elevated in importance by Hall and then even further, in turn, by Shakespeare himself. The following extract from Hall's *Union* compares the three Plantagenet brothers, King Edward, George and Richard:

> Richard duke of Gloucester the third sonne was in witte and courage equal with the other, but in beautee and liniamentes of nature far underneeth bothe, for he was litle of stature eivill featured of limnes, croke backed, the left shulder muche higher than the righte, harde favoured of visage, and emonge commen persones a crabbed face. He was malicious, wrothfull and envious ...
>
> (*Hall's Chronicle*, ed. Henry Ellis (London, 1809, n.p.))

This illustrates how Hall was fascinated as much by the human characteristics of historical players as by the events in which they moved.

## Samuel Daniel (*c.*1563–1619)

Samuel Daniel was the son of a music teacher from Taunton, and became tutor to the son of the eminent patron of arts, the Countess of Pembroke. Although disappointed in the dramatic arts, he achieved notable success with two epic verse cycles. In 1592 his brilliant sonnet sequence *To Delia* appeared, helping to accelerate the growing vogue for the imported sonnet form (and it was certainly a spur for Shakespeare's own sonnet collection). The commercial success of *To Delia* was followed by his popular epic, *The Civil Wars betweene the two houses of Lancaster and Yorke* (1595 and 1609), which exerted a strong influence on Shakespeare's histories, especially *Richard II* and *Henry IV*. Constructed in eight-line stanzas (iambic pentameter), the first book relates the period from the Conquest to Bullingbrook's rebellion, the remaining seven books from the Wars of the Roses to the reign of Edward IV. It is a stirringly engaged and dramatic narrative, characterised by unyielding patriotism and also a certain stoical tone.

Like Hall, Daniel sees a providential pattern in the course of English history whose stability is continually undermined by ambitious and selfish nobles and weak or egotistical monarchs. The model for his national teleology is undoubtedly Virgil's *Aeneid*, with its account of the turbulent gestation of a mighty Roman state.

Stanza 67 from Book I gives a good impression of Daniel's style and emotional involvement, focusing here on the reaction of the populace to Bullingbrook's banishment by Richard II:

> At whose departure hence out of the land,
> O how the open multitude reveale
> The wondrous love they bare him underhand,
> Which now in this hote passion of their zeale
> They plainely shewde that all might understand
> How deare he was unto the common weale:
> They feared not to exclaime against the king
> As one that sought all good mens ruining.

Clearly this is the data for Shakespeare's accounts of Bullingbrook's huge popularity among the common people, first by King Richard (who attributes their zeal to Bullingbrook himself):

> How he did seem to dive into their hearts
> With humble and familiar courtesy,
> What reverence did he throw on slaves ...
>
> *(Richard II* 1.4.25–7)

and later by the Archbishop of York (who reassigns this zeal to the 'open multitude'):

> ... he that buildeth on the vulgar heart.
> O thou fond Many, with what loud applause
> Didst thou beat heaven with blessing Bullingbrook ...
> They, that when Richard lived would have him die.
>
> *(2Henry IV* 1.3.90–101)

Although Shakespeare's sources usually purport to be primary accounts, they in fact often feed off each other; for example, Holinshed freely borrowed from his predecessor Hall, who was also retailed by other historians (such as Grafton and Fleming), the effect being not unlike the exponential process described by Rumour in *2Henry IV*, each commentator glossing and embroidering his antecedent.

One source used by both, but chiefly Hall (who lifted great swathes), is Sir Thomas More (1478–1535), the man who is conventionally credited as the source of Richard III's 'rudely stamp'd' and 'bunch-back'd' physique. Traveller, courtier, critic and patron of the arts, More is now better known for his defiance of Henry VIII's authority and subsequent execution for high treason. His brilliantly playful description of an imaginary island-state in *Utopia* published in 1516 had some influence on Shakespeare's *The Tempest* and has rarely been out of print since. For the narrative of Richard of Gloucester Shakespeare fervidly embraced More's own *The History of King Richard III*, written about 1513. Points which in More are freely acknowledged as of doubtful provenance are taken on by Holinshed and Hall almost as testaments of holy writ; for example, regarding details of Clarence's murder in *Richard III*, More confesses:

> But of all this point is there no certainty, and whosoe divineth upon conjectures may as well shoot too far as too short. Howbeit, this have I by credible information learned …
>
> (*The History of King Richard III*, p. 9)

But it turns out that his 'credible information' is third-hand at least. Throughout his *History* More relies heavily on oral testimony of this kind. We may doubt the truth of what he is telling us, but what he does strongly suggest is that this is indeed what people were saying in his time.

To More is usually attributed the particulars of the murder of the Princes in the Tower of London, which Shakespeare eagerly deploys to dramatic effect against Richard via Tyrell:

> For Sir James Tyrell devised that they should be murdered in their beds, to the execution whereof he appointed Miles Forest, one of the four that kept them, a fellow fleshed in murder before time. To him joined one John Dighton and … about midnight (the sely children lying in their beds) came into the chamber and suddenly lapped them up among the clothes – so bewrapped them and entangled them, keeping down by force the featherbed and pillows had unto their mouths, that within a while, smored and stifled, their breath failing.
>
> (More, p. 88)

In his youth More was for a time employed in the household of Cardinal Morton, and it was probably from Morton that he derived his information about Richard's murder of the Princes in the Tower. Shakespeare suppresses the detailed process (see 4.3.27–32) but retains the dark nature of the act.

Many modern historians cry 'Foul' about Shakespeare's portrait of the 'crooked-back king', that he was either simply misinformed or sought to make obeisance to the great Tudor panjandrum. Yet, his uncompromising portrait has a long pedigree. In the early 1500s Henry VII, who as Duke Richmond was the vanquisher of Richard, sought to consolidate his own claim to the throne by commissioning a sympathetic version of his accession. Accordingly in 1534 he hired Polydore Vergil, an Italian humanist, to write an authorised history of England. As if to confirm the maxim that history is written by the victors, Polydore appeased his royal master by lionising the Tudor line, at the same time demonising Richard III. Thomas More, Henry VIII's privy councillor, further vilified him with details of the 'murder' of the Princes in the Tower.

And what of the 'tub of guts'? Where does Shakespeare derive the character of Sir John Falstaff in *Henry IV*? Although Falstaff's name started out as 'Sir John Oldcastle', and this name figures in Holinshed, there is nothing in his description there to suggest that that historical personage – actually a warrior and zealous churchman – was Shakespeare's source. Instead, Falstaff appears to have emerged as a richly imaginative amalgam of stock figures from the casual theatre and roadshows of Shakespeare's own youth, prominent among which (as we have noted already in Chapter 2)was the Vice of the morality plays. We must, however, give sufficient credit to Shakespeare's own brilliant creativity in the concoction of this majestic 'cloak bag'.

For the backgrounds on Glendower, Hotspur and the Percys Shakespeare consulted once again his Holinshed and Hall. As for the madcap antics of Prince Hal, Shakespeare without doubt dipped heavily into a contemporary anonymous drama: *The Famous Victories of Henry the Fifth*. Written in about 1594, its action is startlingly similar to Shakespeare's *Henry IV*, though its language and dramatic wit is a continent removed from Shakespeare's own.

This first passage is taken from the opening scene of *The Famous Victories* in which Oldcastle is nicknamed 'Jockey' and Hal prolepti- cally is 'Henry 5' (cf. *1Henry IV* 2.2 and 2.4)

> Henry 5    But Sirs, I marvell that Sir John Old-castle comes not away.
>                   Sounds! See
>            where he comes.
>                              *Enter Jockey*
>            How now, Jockey? what newes with thee?
> Jockey     Faith, my lord, suche newes as passeth! For the towne of
>                   Detfort is risen
>            with hue and crie after your man, which parted from us the
>                   last night and has
>            set upon and robd a poore carrier
> Henry 5    Sownes! the vilaine that was wont to spie out our booties?
>                              (*Famous Victories*, in Adams, lines 22–30)

The rest of the play continues in the same reported style, wooden and detached. The following equates approximately with *2Henry IV* 4.2 and the King's confrontation with his son over his 'wilde doings':

> *Enter the Prince, with a dagger in his hand*

> Henry 4: Come my sonne; come on, a Gods name! I know wherefore thy comming is. Oh, my sonne, my sonne! what cause hath ever bene that though shouldst forsake me, and follow this vilde and reprobate com- pany which abuseth youth so manifestly? Oh, my sonne, thou knowest that these thy doings will end thy fathers dayes.
>                              [He weepes] (747–55)

The writing substitutes melodrama for genuine feeling, and the writer remains unconscious of the latent dramatic (and commercial) potential of his material.

## Shakespeare's Adaptations

Unlike the majority of the compilers of the chronicle plays, Shakespeare was not concerned with slavishly regurgitating popular myths that exalted the monarchical subject or its kingdom. For one thing, he was acutely conscious that people were complex beings and, moreover, that audiences were interested in the portrayal of this complexity. He recognised above all that monarchs were primarily human and mortal and he knew them with genuine insight; in other words, he guessed they were like real people but draped in the garb and majesty of power.

Nor was Shakespeare motivated by the bland retailing of the two-dimensional stereotypes typical of the chronicle pageant. His plays are far removed from the plodding catalogue of the received facts. Shakespeare adopts the available facts and moulds these into living myths through his own fertile imagination, concocting dynamic interactions of character and situation, probing motives and causes, weaknesses, sins, charms and corruption. Above all he wanted to discuss urgent, intense and often polemical themes that rouse and disturb. Fact becomes myth, and myth fact.

Shakespeare's plays are distinguished by their compression of events and periods, as a kind of metonymy. For instance, in Act 1 of *1 Henry IV* Shakespeare condenses the opening two years of Henry's reign into one, drawing together the rising of Glendower against the English, around 1400, and the Battle of Holmedon which was fought in 1402. And later, at the Battle of Shrewsbury (1403), it is Shakespeare's fanciful invention to have Prince Hal himself slay Hotspur.

In *Richard II* 5.2, Shakespeare compresses the tumultuous welcome of Bullingbrook to occur side by side on the same day as the disgracing of Richard, clearly for pathos and dramatic economy. In *Richard III* the valiant champion of the Lancastrians Queen Margaret stubbornly confronts Richard, but in reality she had already died in exile before the events of the play. In the same play, Buckingham is captured and executed during the preparations for Bosworth (5.1), though he had actually already been dead for nearly two years. *In Richard II*, Shakespeare murders his king for ethical and aesthetic intensity, yet in reality he probably died of starvation, alone and ignored at Pomfret.

Another example of theatrical economy is Shakespeare's synthesising of two characters into one. For instance, in *Richard II*, Richard's single (unnamed) wife is a conflation of his two real wives, first Anne of Bohemia and second Isabella of France, who was only 10 years old at the time of the play's action. Hotspur addresses his wife Lady Percy as 'Kate', though she was actually named Elizabeth (*1 Henry IV* 2.3.30).

Of course, Shakespeare freely invents ballads, songs and speeches. He rehashes his sources and his own works – including John of Gaunt's powerful evocation of England's 'golden' past (*Richard II* 2.1.40ff.), or mines his own imagination as in Henry V's denunciation of Falstaff (*2Henry IV* 5.5.43ff.).

Characterisation also offers Shakespeare fertile opportunities for invention and revision of sources. Vivid individuals like the Gardener in *Richard II*, plus the Hostess and Doll Tearsheet (*Henry IV*), seem to have been drawn from the dramatist's own experiences among the tavern classes. Falstaff shares some traits with Jockey in *The Famous Victories of Henry the Fifth* but he resembles not even remotely his former namesake Sir John Oldcastle, a devout Christian, steadfast gentleman and a 'valiant captain in the French wars' (Holinshed). While Hotspur's legendary valour is carried over from his sources into *1Henry IV*, Shakespeare drastically reduces his age to make 'Fortune's minion' a contemporary moral contrast with Prince Hal (Hotspur being actually three years older than Hal's father, Bullingbrook).

In terms of settings Shakespeare freely relocates action to maximise dramatic effect. Hence in *1Henry IV*, the notorious highway robbery is transferred from neutral Deptford (in *The Famous Victories of Henry the Fifth*) to Gad's Hill on the London–Canterbury road in order to implicate wealthy yet pious pilgrims en route to Canterbury Cathedral.

As a final instance of Shakespeare's modifications, there are his alterations of relationships. In *Richard III* Shakespeare reports that Lady Anne had been married to Edward, Prince of Wales, though she was probably only betrothed. A detail perhaps, but this intensifies the villainous chutzpah and raw sexual appeal of Richard in seducing the reluctant widow of the man he himself has murdered (1.2). And, in truth, Richard and Anne were ardent spouses and lived in connubial bliss at Middleham Castle, Yorkshire, where they had spent their childhoods together and where they also had a son, Edward.

Shakespeare has the eye for coaxing vital and ever-living myth out of the ordinary and mundane, even where the truth militates against it. Even the editor of *The Shinbone Star* could not manage that.

# 6

# A Sample of Critical Views

I, therefore will begin. Soul of the Age!
The Applause! delight! the wonder of our Stage!
    Ben Jonson, 'In memory of Mr William Shakespeare' (*c*.1623)

For there is an upstart crow, beautified with our feathers, that with
his tiger's heart wrapped in a player's hide, supposes he is as well to
bombast out a blank verse as the best of you; and being an absolute
Johannes Fat-totum, is in his own conceit the only Shake-scene in
a country.
    Robert Greene, *A Groats-Worth of Wit* (1592)

During the half-century after his death in 1616 Shakespeare's reputation began to be consolidated as his fellow writers sought to establish
his contribution to English culture as a whole. This early form of adu-
lation spawned a variety of forms, including memorial verses, conspicuously by Ben Jonson, who was Shakespeare's fellow-playwright in the
Lord Chamberlain's and the King's Men theatre companies. But the
most enduring legacy of these efforts is the enormous collection of
Shakespeare's works published in 1623 by his friends John Heminge
and Henry Condell, in the edition now usually referred to as the First
Folio, whose title actually reads:

Mr William Shakespeares
COMEDIES,
HISTORIES, &
TRAGEDIES.
Published according to the True Originall Copies.

233

Throughout the four centuries since the momentous publication of Heminge and Condell's 'Folio', criticism of Shakespeare tends broadly to do two things: to determine what Shakespeare actually wrote, and then to say how good or bad it was. Neither has been definitive or conclusive. The principles of editing the texts have passed through various paradigms, while the grounds on which Shakespeare was assessed remained generally the same. It is not until the twentieth century that there is a thoroughgoing examination of what literary criticism or literary studies were supposed to be actually doing. It is a period of increasing professionalisation of criticism, as the arena of literary discussion centres on the university sector.

Each age of literary criticism has eagerly sought or projected onto Shakespeare the values it hoped would validate its own moral and political attitudes. Until the 1920s in Britain, critics tended to interpret and evaluate texts from their own narrow uninterrogated aesthetic, moral or socio-political culture. Generalising subjective judgements like 'the unalloyed beauty of the verse', 'Richard II's feminine weakness' and 'pure tender spirit of greatness' were not untypical of the sententious intuitions handed down. Critics were almost invariably white, male, protestant and upper-middle-class. Texts (as well as aspiring critics) were generally adjudicated on the basis of whether or not they reinforced the common values of this coterie.

What became known later as the Cambridge School of 1930s critics, notably I.A. Richards, F.R. Leavis and William Empson, embarked on the task of injecting greater academic rigour into the discipline of analysis. Their aim of describing in precise detail the 'imaginative effects of literature' entailed a close linguistic study of individual texts. Practical Criticism, as it became known, exerted an enormous influence on literary criticism, focusing on metaphorical tropes, symbolism, complex patterns of unity and the unearthing of ironies and tensions in these patterns.

Richards was among the first to approach literary criticism via psychoanalytical theory, while Empson advocated highly detailed analysis, even down to individual word-meanings in specific context with the purpose of showing the dazzling complexities of a text. Leavis, developing key influences from Mathew Arnold and T.S. Eliot, talked prescriptively of the significance of cultural tradition to be discovered and celebrated in a text. All three – and others – in their own way came up with a unified theory of art, life, culture and ethics.

## E.M.W. Tillyard

The first critic I have chosen to look at in more detail is E.M.W. Tillyard (1889–1962), and particularly his 1944 study *Shakespeare's History Plays*. A Fellow at the University of Cambridge, Tillyard was one of the most celebrated exponents of the Cambridge 'school' of literature. The groundwork for the above title can be found in his influential study *The Elizabethan World Picture*. Published in 1943, this book set out to show that rather than being a brief, discrete moment of humanism, the English Renaissance is a continuation of the medieval period, epitomising many of its philosophical and cultural tenets. The spine of this thesis is the great Chain of Being, a cosmic system of parallel hierarchies which was believed to govern the whole of creation, and whose links represented preordained niches for each creature within its topical order (so for example, kings, lions and eagles are at the top of their individual chains, of which the human chain is itself the highest). Tillyard argues that this medieval concept pervades and assigns meaning to the references and people of Shakespeare's plays.

Significantly, this brief study attempts (controversially, as it turned out) to locate Shakespeare within his own historical and cultural context. Tillyard's *Shakespeare's History Plays* sets out to do the same, and the first 126 pages – Part I – detail the Elizabethan intellectual period in a series of 'Backgrounds', beginning with a recap of his cosmic order theory plus an account of Shakespeare's 'Access to the Doctrine'. Indeed, among Tillyard's explicit aims is that of establishing how 'steadily aware Shakespeare was of that principle throughout his History Plays from the very beginning' (Tillyard, 1950, p. 319).

The second half of the book is taken up with a detailed analysis of each of the English histories, taking in *King John* and *Macbeth* in addition to the two tetralogies.

Another of Tillyard's expressed aims is to demonstrate the extent to which Shakespeare derived his narratives and perspectives from the English chroniclers, chiefly Hall and Holinshed (see my Chapter 5). He tries to show that each of the histories cannot be truly appreciated in isolation of the other three plays of its tetralogy or of the whole linked sequence of eight plays, running from *Richard II* to *Richard III*. In fact this sequence is a central component of Tillyard's main thesis and it merits quotation in full:

> In the total sequence of his plays dealing with the subject matter of Hall he expressed successfully a universally held and still comprehensible scheme of history: a scheme fundamentally religious, by which events evolve under a law of justice and under the ruling of God's Providence, and of which Elizabeth's England was the acknowledged outcome. The scheme, which in its general outline, consisted of the distortion of nature's course by a crime and its restoration through a long series of disasters and suffering and struggles, may indeed be like Shakespeare's scheme of tragedy.
>
> (Tillyard, 1944, pp. 320–1)

This paragraph has been an enormous stimulus to discussion of the Histories and so deserves our full attention. The 'crime' to which he alludes is, of course, Bullingbrook's deposition and murder of Richard II in the first play of his proposed 'scheme of history'. What Tillyard is submitting here is an analogy between the English Histories and classical Greek tragedy, where a crime such as murdering a king is in fact an offence against the cosmic order, God or Nature. This act of hubris carries with it far-reaching consequences of political or social disaster, until some form of providential action purges the universe of the offending affront and order is once more restored.

A good example of this is Aeschylus's three-part *Oresteia*, whose tragic cycle begins with Clytemnestra's murder of her husband King Agamemnon, which is avenged by their son Orestes, who is eventually pardoned by the gods. Tillyard is trying to say that Bullingbrook's murder and deposition are likewise not simply crimes but sins against God's cosmic order, which cannot be restored until a process of vengeance and catharsis is initiated and finally completed.

He interprets Shakespeare's linked tetralogies as analogous to the Greek revenge-tragedy with England as the victim, undergoing a period of catastrophic tumult, thereby enacting Carlisle's prophecy in *Richard II*:

> The blood of English shall manure the ground
> And future ages groan for this foul act.
>
> (4.1.136–7)

This interpretation is dependent, of course, on the view that regicide is a sin against the universal order.

What follows in the civil wars of *Henry IV* Parts 1 and 2 and through the *Henry VI* trilogy is that 'Disorder, horror, fear and mutiny' previsioned by Carlisle. The curse of Bullingbrook's arrogant offence against God's appointed order is only finally expunged with the vanquishing of Richard III by 'God's Providence' in the figure of the Duke of Richmond, future Tudor King Henry VII.

This final point is itself a key to Tillyard's global conception. In his Chapter 2, 'The Historical Background', he sets out to view the whole sequence with Elizabethan eyes. He concludes that the theme of disorder, as civil war, was one of the great horrors for Elizabethans and that the resolution at the end of the eight plays was intended as a form of reassurance by Shakespeare. The notion of a patriotic pageant of Tudor historiography would undoubtedly have bolstered Shakespeare's own standing by venerating the legitimacy of the victorious Tudor dynasty, in what has become known as the 'Tudor myth'.

On its own terms, *Shakespeare's History Plays* is a magisterial production. The measure of the enduring success of the study is that it has obliged practically all subsequent critics of the history cycle to take cognisance of its argument. Tillyard was arguably the first critic to give a coherent scholarly reading of the history plays as a unified structure, and this approach has shaped the ensuing discussion of them.

A recognition of the book's ground-breaking and controversial status lies in the fact that its thesis was attacked by both conservative and radical critical attitudes. A common objection to Tillyard was that his thesis proposed a strong relationship between the author and cultural ideology and his preface explicitly stressed the view that the plays were political. This proved polemical to critics steeped in a tradition accustomed to regarding the work of art as independent of the period of its genesis. However, Tillyard's thesis that the history plays could be conceived as an extended narrative cycle in an inclusive natural order became a strongly persuasive position dominating discussion of the plays to this day. Comparable contextual approaches followed, for example in Lily B. Campbell's *Shakespeare's 'Histories'* (1947), Derek Traversi's *Shakespeare from Richard II to Henry V* (1957) and J. Dover Wilson's *The Fortunes of Falstaff* (1964).

Tillyard's vision is typical of an old-style kind of generalising critical stance that has invited the iconoclasm of modern critics. Since, in essence, Tillyard's historical thesis relies heavily on his Elizabethan sources, subsequent critical questioning began by examining the historical basis on which his overarching model of Elizabethan culture was constructed.

Critics have claimed that Tillyard was selective in his gleanings from Holinshed for setting up his 'Tudor myth'. His Chapter 2 casts doubt on the idea that Shakespeare was familiar with Machiavelli's theories, but later research traces the plays' striking correspondences with the Italian's political philosophy (see Sanders, 1968). Moreover, beginning with Irving Ribner (1957) and later Robert Ornstein (1972), critics began to show that Elizabethan attitudes to history and the 'Tudor Myth' were far more diverse than Tillyard maintained and even that Shakespeare may not have believed in a hierarchical world order.

*Shakespeare's History Plays*, in essence, also regards Shakespeare's 'history' as teleological, that history has a purpose or design, and that it works towards a particular end point, namely the 'Tudor myth'. This is a symbolic, literary account of history, one that stresses the theme of destiny, and so legitimates retrospectively any causes (wars, power play, skulduggery) working towards this end. Very few critics or philosophers would support this position today.

Because Tillyard's interpretation is a synthesis of both literary, political and historical theorising, it is susceptible to the radical shifts in both literary and historical paradigms that have occurred in the years since his ground-breaking study first appeared. Hence cultural changes in the strategies of postmodern criticism have tended to distance Tillyard from late twentieth-century approaches.

Nevertheless, Tillyard's work has anticipated some of the methodology of the new-historicist critical school. Prior to *Shakespeare's History Plays* critics tended to interpret texts in isolation from the ideologies that helped to produce them. New Criticism, like Practical Criticism before it, for instance, encouraged the interpretation of plays as autonomous works of art. Tillyard's approach is historicist in the sense that his work sets out to understand a text in the broader totality of political and cultural currents. In this method, literary works become the product of their time and inevitably express the ideologies in which they were produced.

## Graham Holderness

One of the most prolific and original of critics of Shakespeare's history plays, Graham Holderness has written, edited and refereed numerous books and essays. He is also himself a published dramatist, poet and novelist. The book I have chosen to review is his *Shakespeare: The Histories* (2000), published as one in a series of studies devoted to each of the Shakespeare genres.

In one important way Holderness's approach is the antithesis of Tillyard's, since at the very outset he questions the so-called unity of the Histories. He argues that the apparent sequential linearity of the group is a contrived one, tracing this back to the editors of the 1623 Folio who 'reordered' the plays into a chronological and linear sequence, chronological in the sense of their correspondent factual sequence of kings and events. This enabled or compelled them to be read as a monarchical history of England.

To support this challenge to the received sequence, he points out that the plays themselves were not composed in the order of the royal lineage. Moreover, in compiling the Folio contents the editors changed some of the names of the individual plays: 'The act of compiliation satisfied the contemporary conditions of printing, particularly those required for the relatively new form of a single author's "collected works"' (p. 3). This, Holderness believes, was part of a process of transforming the vital spoken and performed word into a 'permanently pinned-down' form for reading, changing a freely interpretative form into a fixed literal one.

The Folio editors were aided and abetted by the more recent labours of Tillyard and Campbell. These critics worked to establish that the History Plays were an integrated 'octology', but further, that as such they expressed a distinctive historical interpretation of that period, that of the 'Tudor Myth', beginning with the deposition of Richard II as a kind of original sin. The printed page gave authority to this interpretation of the 'sequence' as a unified national epic.

This process of visualising a 'fallacious' unity was reinforced by the post-war phenomenon of sequential productions in the theatre with the RSC's *The Plantagenets* in 1986, on television with the BBC's *An Age of Kings* (1960) and in film through Orson Welles's *Chimes at Midnight* (1966).

Holderness goes on to question even the stability of the term 'history' as a discrete but homogenous genre of dramatic text. This categorisation can again be traced back to the tripartite division imposed by the Folio editors. While 'comedy' and 'tragedy' are ancient classifications, 'history' is of relatively recent origin for the Elizabethans, and the classification may itself be emblematic of a political semantics. The Folio includes in its list only those 'histories' from the nearer present that deal with English historical figures, while *Macbeth* and *King Lear*, hailing from a more distant epoch, together with the Roman plays are not acknowledged as 'histories'.

The counter-argument for seeing the pays as a sequence is that there is good evidence to suppose they were composed in chronological order of monarchs. Also, as we noted in Part I, the individual plays themselves are interrelated by prophecies, flashbacks and cross-referencing.

Holderness ends this section of his argument with the conclusion that

the history plays were from the outset a diversified, discontinuous, fragmentary series of historico-dramatic explorations, each individually and independently shaped by contemporary cultural pressures (though the plays have often been integrated, in criticism and theatrical practice, for general ideological reasons)   (p. 8)

One alternative to the 'integrated sequence' approach is to encounter the plays as discontinuous, discretely independent texts to be seen from the perspective of the cultural conditions that produced them. But Holderness decides to transcend these contrasting attitudes in his analysis of the plays by way of focusing on the word 'history' rather than the concept, and his critical language, structured through verbal opposites as past and present, absence and presence, male and female, 'will also be found preoccupied with polarities such as nothing and something, language and silence, substance and shadow, image and reflection, womb and tomb' (p. 13).

After a discussion of the problematics of historiography, Holderness launches into a discussion of individual plays. He begins with *Hamlet*, which he accepts is not conventionally designated as a 'history play' at all, but which is demonstrably historical in character and within the 'heroic tradition' from which the historical drama of the 1590s derived.

The main cast of this study is taken up with these historical dramas, but Holderness reverses the conventional order to deconstruct the received sense of sequence. So kicking off with *Richard III*, and closing with *Richard II*, each of his treatments is in the form of a highly penetrative running commentary. He demonstrates that each eponymous king has an acute awareness of history and of their own location in that history, and that each of them ruthlessly struggles to force the present to conform to the exigencies of their individual will.

In *Richard III* Holderness discovers no sense of a 'Tudor myth' of providential retribution or determining curse, while Richard himself is a victim of his own will. In the *Henry IV* plays (taken together as a unity here) he detects a challenge to the causal assumption in history, that arguments extricated from the past prove inconclusive since they are based on myth and legend. The course of Prince Hal's career is the figuration of the unstable and confounding nature of interpretation. '*Richard II* is a historical drama in a self-conscious and metadramatic sense, as well as history play that purports to re-enact the past' (p. 175). The play's main character dramatises his failed attempt to redefine his own elusive shape – an outcome which, incidentally, he shares with Richard III.

He concludes that in the late sixteenth century the competing patterns for a writer of histories were manifold and that Shakespeare's
Histories do not conform to the 'providentialism of Tillyard' but
instead approximate to a classical tradition of 'heroic achievement
and masculine supremacy' (p. 215).

Holderness rises brilliantly to the challenge of revitalising the
Histories as independent but connected units. This is a beautifully
inspired exercise in anachronism, to confront and dismantle our pre-
conceptions, exciting the imagination to reorientate our interpretations of this group of plays and the genre itself.

It is a truly refreshing experience to encounter the plays without
that received sense of one preluding another (though the denial of
the sequence has the inevitable effect of drawing attention to traditional order of the plays). Even so, Holderness recognises that while
we may not wish to regard the History Plays as an integrated aggre-
gate (in the form of Tillyard's 'Tudor myth'), he does acknowledge
the cross-textual nature of their referencing and that they cannot be
seen absolutely as fragmentary isolates. The definition of *history plays
as a succession* thus becomes one of degree.

In spite of all this, Holderness engages in longish discussions of
the connections between the plays, and far from obviating the need
to do this, his reversal of the conventional sequence actually exacer-
bates it (since much of a play's context effectively derives from the
'preceding' play). Holderness notes on King Richard II's history: 'It
can certainly be rewritten; but it cannot be effaced' (p. 208), and the
same may be said about Tillyard's legacy. Which is, of course, testament to the force of Tillyard's model, casting such a long and almost
indelible shadow (or indeed light) over all subsequent discussion of
the plays as a progressive sequence.

## Tom McAlindon

Tom McAlindon is, like Holderness, a veteran of Shakespearean
scholarship – though their approaches are quite dissimilar. The
book I have chosen to discuss is *Shakespeare's Tudor History: A Study*

*of Henry IV, Parts 1 and 2*, published in 2001, in which the author treats the Henry IV plays as a single continuous text. In his Preface McAlindon clearly sets out his procedure and direction: 'an overall comprehensiveness of approach appropriate to an essentially historicist study'. However, what he means by 'historicist' is not identifiable with the New Historicism of say, Stephen Greenblatt or Stephen Orgel, nor the customary philosophical historicist concept of determinism.

McAlindon's 'historicism' is manifest in the strategy he adopts in Part One of this study: in Chapter 1 an account of 'the plays' critical history from 1700 until the 1980's' is followed up in Chapter 2 by a concise survey of Tudor history 'relevant to an understanding of *Henry IV*'. This pattern is the model for his line of attack throughout the book.

McAlindon's motive in making a survey of over two and half centuries of *Henry IV* criticism is to draw attention to the rich variety of what he regards as neglected criticism prior to Tillyard's *Shakespeare's History Plays*. The opening chapter insists that with the advent of postmodernist analytics much of this has been disparaged or simply ignored as 'uniformly monologic'. McAlindon is primarily interested in the reception history of *Henry IV*. He seeks to return to the complex humanistic kind of literary criticism widespread before the 1970s, maintaining that a knowledge of history is just as important for the reader's own critical standpoint as for his/her understanding of the environment of the plays.

McAlindon even traces Tillyard's thesis – of a grand design behind the Histories – to the 'pioneer' German critic and philosopher A.W. Schlegel in 1811 (and even as far back as Dr Johnson's introduction to his 1765 edition). Schlegel's conception was further developed by his compatriot Herman Ulrici, who in 1839 maintained that the essential unity of the two parts of *Henry IV* derives less from common plot and character than from shared theme and analogy (happily, McAlindon sidesteps Harold Jenkins's quagmire of whether or not Shakespeare set out to write a single play; Hunter, 1970, p. 169).

McAlindon lays much of what he sees as the faults of recent criticism (the blanket rejection of the liberal-humanist tradition especially) at the door of Michel Foucault, whose model of history is characterised as a 'series of ruptures' in the continuum.

Chapter 2 – 'A Tudor History'– has as its primary aim the job of outlining 'those aspects of sixteenth-century history which allow me to show that Shakespeare interpreted the great conflicts of late medieval England through the lens of Tudor experience'. What McAlindon is hoping to do here is to recover what he believes is the religious and political context that underpins *Henry IV.*

He attempts to achieve this aim by examining those rebellions, divisions and uncertainties caused by the Reformation, and the shift from late medieval feudalism towards a new model of nobility and social value. More particularly he focuses on the rebellions of 1536, 1547 and 1569, which haunted the government in the closing decades of the century when the state was threatened by an alliance of Catholic forces both internally and from western Europe. McAlindon discovers echoes of these rebellions in *Henry IV*, which appears to 'endorse the prevailing Tudor conception of history as repetitive and cyclical'. His investigations into the political, religious, social and intellectual history lead him to an admiration for Shakespeare's intricate patterning, the 'finely spun lines with which the dramatist articulates Bullingbrook's England' and its relation to the past.

Chapters 3–5 consist of close readings respectively of the play's 'three dominant concepts': time, truth and grace. Chapter 3 details the pervasiveness of time in Renaissance culture, where it is manifested in a diversity of forms both quotidian and symbolic. In particular, time is very much linked to the notion of control: men and women are time's subjects:

> and as such must respond to its signs and requirements with due promptness or patience if they are to fructify within their allotted span. It follows too that although time dictates incessant change or 'mutability' ... and although perceiving and understanding its signs may require preternatural sagacity, it represents none the less a stable order, reconciling in its cyclical and dynamic structure the opposites of change and permanence.  (p. 54)

McAlindon superbly draws out the paradoxical nature of time: being both change and constancy as a means of stability. For the

Elizabethans time also means timeliness, the occasion, judging and taking the moment at its ripest, in the political as well as personal spheres. Time was also indissolubly wedded to principles and practice of religion, its rhetoric, and rites as well as its scriptures.

Applying his research to *Henry IV*, McAlindon presents a detailed analysis of the impact of time as a theme and a structuring principle. These are expressed in the play's myriad allusions to age, health, death, decay, ascendancy, memory and prediction, and together with the historical perspectives of the play ('the presence of the past'), work to configure its form.

McAlindon next turns to the concept of truth as second of the key concepts behind Shakespeare's delineation of the social and ideological map in *Henry IV*. Drawing on a wealth of research, the author delves into the themes of the 'royal duplicity' of Bullingbrook and Prince John and the honour and honesty of the rebels. The concept of truth in *Henry IV* is marked chiefly by its negotiation. A discussion of Falstaff's chicanery is the cue to draw in a (fleeting) consideration of the 'lesser mortals', and Chapter 4 concludes with a defence of Prince Hal against charges of hypocrisy:

> In his characterisation of Hal, Shakespeare recognises that a ruler must have a capacity for cool detachment, an awareness of his public image, and an ability to curtail some of the more attractive and humane aspects of his character in the interests of justice and law. (p. 140)

The theme of truth is closely bound up with other ethical notions, among which 'grace' becomes the chief focus of attention in Chapter 5:

> Due to a combination of social, political and ideological changes associated mainly with the Renaissance and the Reformation, grace and honour were to become notions of exceptional consequence in the Tudor period. (p. 141)

Grace is identifiable with peace, amiability and unity. It is closely allied with ideas of gratitude, plus selfless and disinterested bounty towards others. It is also bound in with notions of chivalric decorum, which in turn is consonant with self-discipline, modesty and loyalty. Then, once more applying his historical researches to the business of *Henry IV*, McAlindon discovers them as manifested in an implicit measure of conduct that all the royal characters are at least conscious of. King Henry is distressed at Hal's shameless and dishonourable way of life, while the King himself seeks absolution (for past discredit) via a 'pilgrimage of grace' to the Holy Land; Falstaff's social ambitioning is a satire on the machinations of others; and, surprisingly, Hotspur is to be considered an 'untaught and unmannerly soldier' (p. 159).

McAlindon's study is a work of exemplary scholarship, of meticulous research and its eminently cogent application. It is written in a brilliantly lucid style that make difficult ideas readily accessible and is an engaging read, even for novices. In fact his lucidity is all one with his reaction against the opaque stylisation of much modern criticism, whose modish diction he eschews.

His Preface flags up his recoil from recent theoretical models of literary study in favour of a return to older critical paradigms. However, he does not sufficiently make clear his quarrel with the current 'materialist view' in literary criticism, with the result that his discourse sometimes reads like nostalgia for the old liberal humanist myth of unmediated interpretation.

McAlindon's painstaking analysis seeks to re-situate Shakespeare's play within the context of a post-Reformation world, to interpret the dramatist as the embodiment of a diverse but consistent system of humanist values. His emphasis is on Shakespeare as a touchstone of the prevailing cultural *Zeitgeist* (if this can be said to exist at all) and less on him as the simulacrum of its ideologies.

## General currents in late twentieth-century critical theory

The late twentieth century witnessed a dynamic succession of literary theories largely inspired by French philosophical theorists, in which existing assumptions and literary attitudes were challenged and radically reshaped. Predominant among these have been

Structuralism and Deconstructionism, along with psychoanalytical, feminist and Marxist theories that have fundamentally altered the perspective by which readers may approach and respond to a text. There is not space here to discuss in detail the philosophical bases or their implications, but as a result of this gravitational shift there have been at least two far-reaching revolutions in the techniques of literary criticism (often in tension with each other). (For a lucid and highly accessible study of currents and cross-currents in literary theory, see Eagleton).

First, there has evolved a stress on the *reception* of a text, that is, viewing a text from the individual reader's position. This transfers emphasis away from authorial intentionalism and onto the experiences of the reader (acknowledging his or her gender, social group, ethnicity, and so on). The other major consequence has been an emphasis on understanding a text as the product of its own time.

This latter strand is more commonly associated with theories of New Historicism. This recognises, say, a Shakespeare text as a political system, both a construct of and an accomplice in the ideology of the period of its composition. Thus all texts are political and in this context cannot be said to be autonomous. But where a critic such as Tillyard recognises the context of a literary work, he differs essentially from many contemporary theorists in regarding its constructs such as 'mankind', 'nature', and so on as given and fixed.

New Historicist and Cultural Materialist readers are also more likely to be alert to the multiplicity of voices and ideologies at work in a text, including the politics of gender, social class, religion, ethnicity and sexual orientation.

Stephen Greenblatt's writings have been a seminal influence in this field (see Further Reading for key titles). Of specific interest to Shakespeare's Histories is his essay 'Invisible Bullets: Renaissance Authority and its Subversion, *Henry IV* and *Henry V*' (in Dollimore and Sinfield). In this essay he begins by examining early colonial reports to posit the 'Machiavellian hypothesis' of religion: that since biblical times, religions have been concocted with a view to underpinning the power of civil authority in order to ensure social cohesion.

The 'invisible bullets' of the title refer to the use of illusion and fraud to impose alternative or contrary ideology. With regard to the colonial reports, Greenblatt applies his thesis to Shakespeare's plays, claiming that they too are concerned with 'the production and containment of subversion and disorder' (p. 29). As for *Henry IV*, Greenblatt claims that the power hierarchy that has Henry IV at the top and Robin Ostler near the bottom is unstable, precariously in danger of radical subversion. In order for Hal to succeed as his ideal of king he must constantly be both reappraising his own position as ruler and ensuring that his subjects are subdued by the illusion of stability.

The next critic for discussion writes in the spirit of Greenblatt's historicist approach but takes it into a new and inspiring direction.

## Alison Thorne

There is a history in all men's lives: reinventing history in *2Henry IV*.

Alison Thorne

Thorne's essay can be found in *Shakespeare's Histories and Counter Histories* (2006), edited by Dermot Cavanagh and others, a lively and stimulating collection of essays. This project sets out with the stated aim of reassessing Shakespeare's history plays from new critical perspectives by 'exploring official and unofficial version of the past, histories and counter histories, in the plays of Shakespeare and his contemporaries'.

Thorne's essay, which appears in the opening section of this collection, 'Memory and mourning', focuses on the antipathy between historiographic or written accounts of history and oral versions – word of mouth, such as storytelling, hearsay and rumour. Her work extends some of the methodologies of New Historicism and develops them in new and exciting avenues.

The quotation that heads Thorne's essay evokes Warwick's speech in *2Henry IV*, 3.1.79, where the insomniac king in his nightshirt has been tormented by memories of King Richard II whom he had deposed and had murdered. It suggests two things: that each ordinary life has its own rich and informal history, and also that history is made not just by the rich and powerful but by ordinary men and women.

Thorne's starting point is the view that until relatively recently historians have accorded primacy to written and factual chronicles as sources of history to the detriment of oral versions and the fiction, myth and legend 'of the collective imagination' (p. 49). She finds evidence of this discrimination at work in *2Henry IV* where the 'age-old struggle' between written and oral history is played out:

> For most of the play's duration the 'high' political history, centred on issues of dynastic succession, affairs of State and military conflict, that had formed the staple of the Tudor chronicles and of Shakespeare's previous English history plays is displaced by the meanderings of the oral tradition in which the past is typically reconstituted in the anecdotal form through the informal medium of rumour, hearsay, gossip and personal reminiscence.   (p. 49)

She finds that for most of the play these so-called 'unauthorised constructions of the past' are the dominant mode for transmitting the truths of the play's progress and that they cede this status only after Hal's accession to the throne when the new political rigour becomes pre-eminent. Thorne's thesis, or part of it, is that Shakespeare sets up these contending models –oral storytelling and written chronicle – in *2Henry IV* in order to pose the question of what exactly constitutes 'history'.

Detailed analysis begins, of course, with Rumour's speech, the prologue to *2Henry IV*, which announces a redefinition of history as essentially oral in content and practice, heteroglossic, and radically unstable in nature. Oral versions of history are associated with the 'still-discordant wavr'ing multitude' who are accused of spreading sedition by way of volatile half-truths. This observation is confirmed by Elizabeth I herself, in a letter noting how the vulgar people are readily exploited by those wishing to utilise them for dissemination of seditious rumours. The 'vulgar people' were also the group most likely to be prosecuted under Tudor statutes for defamatory talk deemed to threaten the stability of the regime. Although gossip and rumour were rife throughout all levels of society, it was that of the lower orders which was most likely to make the authorities nervous of plebeian unrest (a point illustrated in the Archbishop of York's deprecation of the 'fond many' in 1.3.

Critics have on the whole tended to accept the 'paranoid images' of Rumour's speech, regarding these as a signal anticipation from Shakespeare of the riotous or dystopian unrest and moral decay which could be traced back ultimately to Bullingbrook's act of regicide. Critics have supported this reading via the shared iconography in Falstaff's 'a whole school of tongues in this belly of mine' (*2Henry IV*, 4.1.367–72 [4.3.16–21]).

Thorne urges caution here, that we should not be eager to see Falstaff as Rumour's avatar, and thereby read the play as an endorsement of a link between false reporting and lawlessness. By the same token Falstaff cannot be regarded as either the sole or even the most important proponent of oral history. On the other hand it is undeniable that Falstaff has a multiplicity of associations with popular culture.

Although recent commentators have foregrounded the time-honoured bias against spoken word as history in favour of written records, in *2Henry IV* traditional history is conspicuously absent. Documented events such as Glendower's guerrilla marauding are absent or pushed to the periphery. In fact Thorne suggests that 'Rumour [supplants] Bolingbroke ... as the symbolic source and focus of historical report' (p. 53). This swing towards more popular forms of historical transmission is likely to have had a 'strong topical resonance' for the play's contemporary audiences.

If the characteristics of the oral tradition can be described as 'elusive', 'transient', 'inventive' and 'voluble', its effects in the play are 'nervous', 'unsettling' and 'usurping'.

In the central section of her essay Thorne reminds us that the world of *2Henry IV* is one dominated by an older generation, led by Falstaff, while younger characters such as Hal must bide their time. This leads to the play's climate of 'incessant retrospection' and is the source of some satire in the play against these ageing and declining power figures. While the written histories are often associated with these figures, Thorne cites research by Keith Thomas to demonstrate that older figures such as Shallow are in fact the repository of 'history and custom, pedigree and descent' (54).

As we might expect, the wealth of social heritage stored up in the common folk-memory frequently diverges from the written sources. Moreover their versions of history diverge from historiographical conventions in their protocols, being narrowly parochial, evolving archetypal characterisations, omitting temporal markers and having a propensity for embellishing, condensing and partial selection (though many of these practices can also be applied to the printed chronicles).

An extract from Shallow's speech (3.2. 11–15) is analysed to apply and substantiate these observations in the play. Thorne construes that Shallow typifies the oral tradition in his repetitions, erratic recall and highly localised recollections – the latter being instances of a play teeming with precise topographical allusions such as the names of taverns, brothels and the law colleges. Shallow's recollections are typified by vividness, immediacy and a predisposition for creativity. Behind many of his memories is a belief in the immanence of the past in the present.

The female equivalent in the play of these old tattlers is Mistress Quickly, with her penchant for copious, expansive and dilatory narrative. Her speech shares many of the same linguistic characteristics as Shallow's but is remarkable for the astonishing elasticity of syntactical forms, expanding by clausal accretion to embrace more and wider digressions of reference. And it should not be forgotten how much Shallow's and Quickly's narrational histories, with their partialities, hiatuses and non-sequiturs, contribute to the rich vein of comic irony in the play.

In her concluding section 'Reforming historical consciousness', Thorne considers the possibility that Hal's coronation is the sign for the abrupt end of the play's 'memory-history'. Hal's rhetoric of majesty in 5.2, declaring a reformation of himself and the kingdom, heralds a new dominating strain of discourse and one more closely aligned with the chronicle history. In short, a reinvention of the past (p. 63).

Thorne traces a parallel movement of reform in the Elizabethan recording of history – newly limited to factual statements about political history or that of the lives of eminent people.

She concludes by convincingly arguing that *2Henry IV* enacts the processes of the oral tradition in its redeployment of 'images, speeches and whole scenes' from the two previous plays of the tetralogy. In its reworking of popular legends concerning Hal's dissolute life, the play itself becomes one version of that life in the chronicles (and, we could add, that to the extent that we have multiple versions of the play, this too subverts any sense of a definitive or authorised historiography).

# Glossary of Literary Terms

**alliteration** The recurrence of consonant sounds close together within a phrase or lines; for example, the /l/ sounds in 'full-grown lambs loud bleat'

**anaphora** The repetition of a word or words at the beginning of successive lines or sentences

**assonance** The recurrence of vowel sounds close together within a phrase or lines; for example, the /o/ sounds in 'down some profound and hollow of the ground'

**caesura** A slight pause within a line of verse (indicated in the discussion by an oblique: /)

**catalectic** (*see also* **metre**) A line verse which is less than ten syllables

**the chain of being** This phrase is used by the critic E.M.W. Tillyard in his book *The Elizabethan World Picture* to explain Elizabethan beliefs of hierarchy in the cosmos: the constituents of the Earth (animal, vegetable, and mineral) existed in interrelated parallel hierarchies; so, for instance, at the head of each chain of beings in the natural world were kings, lions, eagles, and so on

**deus ex machina** A narrative device in which a sudden unexpected event or an intervention by a force from outside the main action resolves a problematic situation

**the elements** Elizabethans understood the whole of earthly matter to be constituted of four irreducible elements: earth, water, air and fire (human beings were thought to possess a fifth, the quintessence, or soul); *see also* **the humours**

**euphuism** An exaggeratedly ornate style of writing named after John Lyly's 1578 novel, *Euphues: The Anatomy of Wit*

**hendiadys** A phrase connecting two separate nouns, verbs, etc., to spell out a more complex idea, as in 'she was confident and cheerful' (instead of saying, 'cheerfully confident'); for an example in Shakespeare, see *Richard II* 3.4.40–1

**Henriad** the sequence of eight English history plays running from *Richard II* to *Richard III*

**the humours** Consistent with Elizabethan theories of order, humans were believed to be composed of four humours produced in varying quantities by the liver: melancholy, phlegm, blood and choler. The predominance of any one humour was understood to be the determinant of one's psychology (so, for example, an excess of blood leads to a sanguine – optimistic, cheerful – temperament); *see also* **the elements**

**in medias res** A method of beginning a narrative in the midst of events which had already started before the opening of the play, novel, etc.

**kenning** A compound expression which strikingly describes, say, a thing or an action by combining its mundane components; so, a fight may be 'a game of blades'; for an example from Shakespeare, see *2 Henry IV* 3.1.31

**logocentrism** Literally this means 'centred on the word', and it refers to the traditional method of seeking truth through the printed word rather than through experience. It involves an uncritical trust that words conventionally reflect reality. As an evaluative term it implies fixed ways of thinking, accepting received ideas uncritically

**metonymy** A figure in which the name or attribute of something is used to represent it; for example, in the clause 'The ring is a tough career', the 'ring' stands for boxing in general

**metre** The rhythmic pattern of beats in a line of verse. Shakespeare's dramatic verse typically contains ten syllables in his regular lines, using a rhythm of one stressed syllable followed by an unstressed one. This produces the familiar 'di-dah di-dah' rhythm of his poetry. Technically this unit of rhythm is called *iambic*, and there are thus five (Greek, *penta*) iambic units in a line of this verse, or *pentameter*. Another name for *unrhymed* iambic pentameter is *blank verse*

**oxymoron** The combination in one expression of terms that are apparently contradictory; for example, 'a cheerful pessimist', 'a loving hate'

**psychomachy** A dramatic device in which two conflicting figures (usually representing abstract forces or principles) wrangle for domination; for example *1Henry IV* 5.1.127–38)

**Quarto and Folio** 'Quarto' refers to the printing of an individual play, usually during Shakespeare's own lifetime; the 'first Folio' describes the first collected edition of Shakespeare's plays in 1625 (the two words originally referred to sizes of printed books)

**soliloquy** A speech given by a single character alone on the stage; the convention is that the character is presenting true thoughts, as a projection of conscience or consciousness

**solipsism** This is a view of the world that regards the self as the only object in real existence, a self-centred position which may claim that the rest of the world is simply a projection of my mind

**stichomythia** A highly formal arrangement in which (usually) single lines of verse are delivered by each character speaking alternate lines (as in *Richard III* 4.4.347–71)

**synecdoche** A poetic figure in which a part of something stands for the whole thing; for example, in the phrase 'Wiser heads advised against it' the word 'heads' stands for 'people'

**tetralogy** A group of four plays; Shakespeare's first tetralogy of history plays comprises the plays *Henry VI Parts 1, 2* and *3*, with *Richard III*. The second tetralogy consists of *Richard II, Henry IV Part 1, Henry IV Part 2* and *Henry V.*

**zeugma** A clause in which a single adjective or verb applies to two nouns; for example, 'he polished his shoes with wax and a smile'

# Further Reading

## Shakespeare Criticism

Adams, John Quincy, *Chief Pre-Shakespearean Dramas* (London: Harrap & Co., n.d.).

Besnault, Marie-Hélène and Michel Bitot, 'Historical Legacy and Fiction: The Poetical Reinvention of King Richard III' (in Hattaway).

Bloom, Harold (ed.), *Sir John Falstaff* (Broomall, PA: Chelsea House, 2004).

Brooke, Nicholas (ed.), *Richard II: A Casebook* (Basingstoke: Macmillan, 1973).

Brown, John Russell, *Shakespeare: The Tragedies* (Basingstoke: Palgrave Macmillan, 2001).

Campbell, Lily B., *Shakespeare's 'Histories': Mirrors of Elizabethan Policy* (San Marino, CA: Huntington Library, 1947).

Cartelli, Richard (ed.), *Richard III* (New York: W.W. Norton, 2009).

Cavanagh, Dermot et al. (eds), *Shakespeare's Histories and Counter Histories* (Manchester: Manchester University Press, 2006).

Chernaik, Warren, *The Cambridge Introduction to Shakespeare's History Plays* (Cambridge: Cambridge University Press, 2007).

Clemen, W.H., *A Commentary on Shakespeare's Richard III* (London: Methuen, 1968).

Coleridge, Samuel Taylor, *Shakespearean Criticism* (2 vols, London: Dent, 1960).

Dollimore, Jonathan and Alan Sinfield (eds), *Political Shakespeare: Essays in Cultural Materialism* (2nd edn, Manchester: Manchester University Press, 1994).

Dowden, Edward, *Shakespeare: A Critical Study of His Mind and Art* (1875; extracted in Cartelli).

Dutton, Richard and Jean E. Howard (eds), *A Companion to Shakespeare's Works: The Histories* (Oxford: Blackwell, 2003).

Eagleton, Terry, *Literary Theory* (Oxford: John Wiley, 2008).

Greenblatt, Stephen, *Representing the English Renaissance* (Berkeley: University of California Press, 1988).

Greenblatt, Stephen, *Learning to Curse* (London: Routledge, 1990).

Greenblatt, Stephen, 'Invisible Bullets: Renaissance Authority and its Subversion, *Henry IV* and *Henry V*' (in Dollimore and Sinfield).

Gurr, Andrew, *The Shakespearean Stage 1574–1642* (Cambridge: Cambridge University Press, 2009).

Hattaway, Michael (ed.), *The Cambridge Companion to Shakespeare's History Plays* (Cambridge: Cambridge University Press, 2002).

Hazlitt, William, *The Fight and Other Writings* (Harmondsworth: Penguin, 2000).

Holderness, Graham, *William Shakespeare: Richard II* (Harmondsworth: Penguin, 1989).

Holderness, Graham, *Shakespeare Recycled: The Making of Historical Drama* (Hemel Hempstead: Harvester Wheatsheaf, 1992).

Holderness, Graham, *Shakespeare: The Histories* (Basingstoke: Palgrave Macmillan, 2000).

Howard, Jean E. and Phyllis Rackin, *Engendering a Nation: A Feminist Account of Shakespeare's English Histories* (London: Routledge, 1997).

Hunter, G.K. (ed.), *Shakespeare Henry IV Parts I and II* (Basingstoke: Macmillan, 1970).

Knights, L.C., *Some Shakespearean Themes* (Harmondsworth: Penguin, 1966).

Laroque, François, *Shakespeare and Carnival: After Bakhtin* (Basingstoke: Macmillan, 1999).

Loehlin, James N., *Henry IV: Parts I and II* (Basingstoke: Palgrave Macmillan, 2008).

Lopez, Jeremy, *Shakespeare Handbooks: Richard II* (Basingstoke: Palgrave Macmillan, 2009).

McAlindon, Tom, *Shakespeare's Tudor History: A Study of Henry IV, Parts 1 and 2* (Aldershot, UK: Ashgate, 2001).

McNeir, Waldo, 'The Masks of Richard III', *Studies in English Literature 1500–1900* 11(2) (Spring 1971), 167–86.

Nuttall, A.D., *Shakespeare The Thinker* (New Haven, CT: Yale University Press, 2007).

Orgel, Stephen, *The Illusion of Power: Political Theatre in the English Renaissance* (Berkeley: University of California Press, 1975).

Ornstein, Robert, *A Kingdom for a Stage: the Achievement of Shakespeare's History Plays* (Cambridge, MA: Harvard University Press, 1972).

Rackin, Phyllis, *Stages of History: Shakespeare's English Chronicles* (London: Routledge, 1990).

Rackin, Phyllis, *Shakespeare and Women* (Oxford: Oxford University Press, 2005).

Ribner, Irving, *The English History Play in the Age of Shakespeare* (Princeton, NJ: Princeton University Press, 1957).

Sanders, Wilbur, *The Dramatist and the Received Idea* (Cambridge: Cambridge University Press, 1968)

Thorne, Alison, 'There Is a History in All Men's Lives: Reinventing History in *2Henry IV*' (in Cavanagh et al.).

Tillyard, E.M.W., *Shakespeare's History Plays* (London: Chatto & Windus, 1944).

Tucker Brooke, C.F. (ed.), *The Shakespeare Apocrypha* (Oxford: Oxford University Press, 1918).

Vickers, Brian, *Shakespeare: The Critical Heritage* (3 vols, London: Routledge, 2008–09)

## Shakespeare's Sources

Daniel, Samuel, *The Civil Wars*, ed Laurence Michael (New Haven, CT: Yale University Press, 1958 [1595]).

Hall, Edward, *The Union of the Two Noble and Illustre Families of Lancaster & Yorke* (London: AMS Press, 1965 [1548]).

Kewes, Paulina et al. (eds), *The Oxford Handbook of Holinshed's Chronicles* (Oxford: Oxford University Press, 2012).

More, St Thomas, *The History of King Richard III and Selections from the English and Latin Poems*, ed. Richard S. Sylvester (New Haven, CT: Yale University Press, 1976).

Nicoll, Josephine and Allardyce Nicoll (eds), *Holinshed's Chronicle as Used in Shakespeare's Plays* (London: Dent, 1927).

## Biographies of Shakespeare

Bate, Jonathan, *Soul of the Age: The Life, Mind and World of William Shakespeare* (London: Viking, 2008).

Greenblatt, Stephen, *Will in the World: How Shakespeare Became Shakespeare* (London: Jonathan Cape, 2004).

Greer, Germaine, *Shakespeare's Wife* (London: Bloomsbury, 2007).

Honan, Park, *Shakespeare: A Life* (Oxford: Oxford University Press, 1998).

Potter, Lois, *The Life of William Shakespeare: A Critical Biography* (Oxford: Wiley-Blackwell, 2012).

Shapiro, James, *1599: A Year in the Life of William Shakespeare* (London: Faber & Faber, 2005).

## General and Background Reading

Aristotle, *The Poetics*, trans Malcolm Heath (Harmondsworth: Penguin, 1996).

Bacon, Francis, *Essays*, ed. Michael Kiernan (Oxford: Oxford University Press, 2000).

Castiglione, Baldesar, *The Book of the Courtier*, trans George Bull (London: Penguin, 1967 [1528]).

Clark, Peter, *British Clubs and Societies 1580–1800* (Oxford: Oxford University Press, 2000).

Cuddon, J.A., *A Dictionary of Literary Terms and Literary Theory* (5th edn, Oxford: Wiley-Blackwell, 2012).

Grady, Hugh, *Shakespeare, Machiavelli and Montaigne* (Oxford: Oxford University Press, 2004).

Hollingdale, R.J., *Nietzsche: the Man and his Philosophy* (2nd edn, Cambridge: Cambridge University Press, 2001).

Lucas, F.L., *Seneca and Elizabethan Tragedy* (Cambridge: Cambridge University Press, 2009).

Machiavelli, Niccolò, *The Prince*, trans Quentin Skinner and Russell Price (Cambridge: Cambridge University Press, 1988).

Montaigne, Michel de, *Essays*, trans. John Florio (3 vols, London: Everyman Dent, 1965).

Nietzsche, Friedrich, *Beyond Good and Evil*, trans. Judith Norman (Cambridge: Cambridge University Press, 2001).

Ridolfi, Roberto, *The Life of Niccolò Machiavelli* (London: Routledge, 2009).

Tillyard, E.M.W., *The Elizabethan World Picture* (London: Chatto & Windus, 1950).

Wheen, Francis, *How Mumbo-Jumbo Conquered the World* (London: Harper, 2004).

# Index